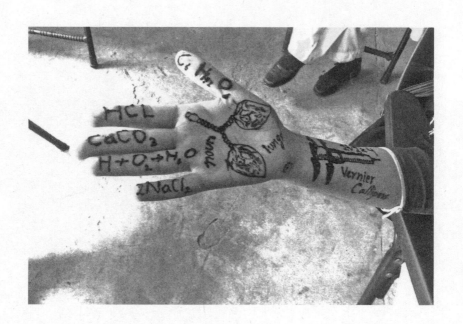

I Am Malala

THE GIRL WHO STOOD UP
FOR EDUCATION AND WAS
SHOT BY THE TALIBAN

MALALA
YOUSAFZAI

with CHRISTINA LAMB

LITTLE, BROWN AND COMPANY

LARGE PRINT EDITION

Little, Brown and Company
Hachette Book Group
237 Park Avenue, New York, NY 10017
littlebrown.com

First Edition: October 2013

Little, Brown and Company is a division of Hachette Book Group, Inc. The Little, Brown name and logo are trademarks of Hachette Book Group, Inc.

Map by John Gilkes

Grateful thanks to the Jinnah Archive (jinnaharchive.com) for the use of selections from the work of Quaid-i-Azam M. A. Jinnah, and to Rahmat Shah Sayel for use of his poems. For the help with the translations of *tapae* from Pashto, thanks to my father's friends Mr. Hamayun Masaud, Mr. Muhammad Amjad, Mr. Ataurrahman, and Mr. Usman Ulasyar.

Excerpt from Jinnah's speech at Jinnah Islamia College for Women, 25 March 1940, is taken from *Mohammah Ali Jinnah: The Nation's Voice*, Vol. I, edited by W. Ahmad, Quaid-i-Azam Academy, 1992.

ISBN 978-0-316-32240-9 (hc) / 978-0-316-40346-7 (international) / 978-0-316-28663-3 (lp)
LCCN 2013941811

10 9 8 7 6 5 4

RRD-C

Book designed by Marie Mundaca

Printed in the United States of America

*To all the girls who have faced injustice
and been silenced.
Together we will be heard.*

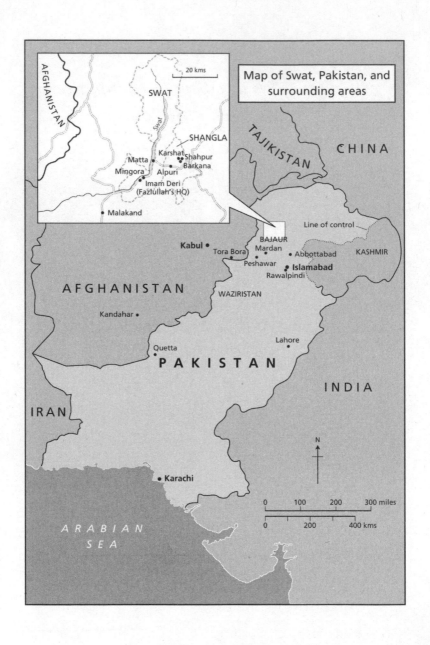

20 kms

AFGHANISTAN

SWAT

Swat

SHANGLA

Karshat
Matta • •• Shahpur
Mingora • Alpuri • • Barkana
• Imam Deri
(Fazlullah's HQ)

• Malakand

Map of Swat, Pakistan, and
surrounding areas

TAJIKISTAN   CHINA

Line of control

BAJAUR
Kabul •   Mardan
Tora Bora •   • Abbottabad   KASHMIR
Peshawar   • Islamabad
Rawalpindi

AFGHANISTAN   WAZIRISTAN

Kandahar •

Lahore •

Quetta •

P A K I S T A N

INDIA

IRAN

N

• Karachi

0   100   200   300 miles
0   200   400 kms

*A R A B I A N
S E A*

Contents

Contents

I Am Malala

Prologue

The Day My World Changed

I come from a country that was created at midnight. When I almost died it was just after midday.

One year ago I left my home for school and never returned. I was shot by a Taliban bullet and was flown out of Pakistan unconscious. Some people say I will never return home, but I believe firmly in my heart that I will. To be torn from the country that you love is not something to wish on anyone.

Now, every morning when I open my eyes, I long to see my old room full of my things, my clothes all over the floor, and my school prizes on the shelves. Instead I am in a country which is five hours behind my beloved homeland Pakistan and my home in the Swat Valley. But my country is centuries behind this one. Here there is any convenience you can imagine. Water running from every tap, hot or cold as you wish; lights at the flick of a switch, day and night, no need for oil lamps; ovens to cook on that don't need anyone to go and fetch gas cylinders from the bazaar. Here everything is so modern one can even find food ready cooked in packets.

When I stand in front of my window and look out, I see tall buildings, long roads full of vehicles moving in orderly lines, neat green hedges and lawns, and tidy pavements to walk on. I close my eyes and for a moment I am back in my valley—the high snow-topped mountains, green waving fields and fresh blue rivers—and my heart smiles when it looks at the people of Swat. My mind transports me back to my school and there I am reunited with my friends and teachers. I meet my best friend Moniba and we sit together, talking and joking as if I had never left.

Then I remember I am in Birmingham, England.

The day when everything changed was Tuesday, 9 October 2012. It wasn't the best of days to start with, as it was the middle of school exams, though as a bookish girl I didn't mind them as much as some of my classmates.

That morning we arrived in the narrow mud lane off Haji Baba Road in our usual procession of brightly painted rickshaws sputtering diesel fumes, each one crammed with five or six girls. Since the time of the Taliban our school has had no sign and the ornamented brass door in a white wall across from the woodcutter's yard gives no hint of what lies beyond.

For us girls that doorway was like a magical entrance to our own special world. As we skipped through, we cast off our headscarves like winds puffing away clouds to make way for the sun then ran helter-skelter up the steps. At the top of the steps was an open courtyard with doors to all the classrooms. We dumped our backpacks in our rooms then gathered for morning assembly under the sky, our backs to the mountains as we stood to attention. One girl commanded, *"Assaan bash!"* or "Stand at ease!" and we clicked our heels and responded, *"Allah."* Then she said, *"Hoo she yar!"* or "Attention!" and we clicked our heels again. *"Allah."*

The school was founded by my father before I was born, and on the wall above us KHUSHAL SCHOOL was painted proudly in red and white letters. We went to school six mornings a week, and as I was a fifteen-year-old in Year 9, my classes were spent chanting chemical equations or studying Urdu grammar; writing stories in English with morals like "Haste makes waste" or drawing diagrams of blood circulation—most of my classmates wanted to be doctors. It's hard to imagine that anyone would see that as a threat. Yet, outside the door to the school lay not only the noise and craziness of Mingora, the main city of Swat, but also those like the Taliban who think girls should not go to school.

That morning had begun like any other, though a little later than usual. It was exam time, so school started at nine instead of eight, which was good, as I don't like getting up and can sleep through the crows of the cocks and the prayer calls of the muezzin. First my father would try to rouse me. "Time to get up, *Jani Mun*," he would say. This means "soulmate" in Persian, and he always called me that at the start of the day. "A few more minutes, *Aba*, please," I'd beg, then burrow deeper under the quilt. Then my mother would come. *"Pisho,"* she would call. This means "cat" and is her name for me. At this point I'd realize the time and shout, *"Bhabi*, I'm late!" In our culture, every man is your "brother" and every woman your "sister." That's how we think of each other. When my father first brought his wife to school, all the teachers referred to her as "my brother's wife," or *bhabi*. That's how it stayed from then on. We all call her *bhabi* now.

I slept in the long room at the front of our house, and the only furniture was a bed and a cabinet which I had bought with some of the money I had been given as an award for campaigning for peace in our valley and the right for girls to go to school. On some shelves were all the gold-colored plastic cups and trophies I had won for coming first in my class. Only twice had I not come top—both times when I was beaten by my class rival Malka-e-Noor. I was determined it would not happen again.

The school was not far from my home and I used to walk, but since the start of last year I had been going with other girls by bus. It was a journey of just five minutes along the stinky stream, past the giant billboard for Dr. Humayun's Hair Transplant Institute where we joked that one of our bald male teachers must have gone when he suddenly started to sprout hair. I liked the bus because I didn't get as sweaty as when I walked, and I could chat with my friends and gossip with Usman Ali, the driver, who we called *Bhai Jan,* or "Brother." He made us all laugh with his crazy stories.

I had started taking the bus because my mother

was scared of me walking on my own. We had been getting threats all year. Some were in the newspapers, some were notes or messages passed on by people. My mother was worried about me, but the Taliban had never come for a girl and I was more concerned they would target my father, as he was always speaking out against them. His close friend and fellow campaigner Zahid Khan had been shot in the face in August on his way to prayers and I knew everyone was telling my father, "Take care, you'll be next."

Our street could not be reached by car, so coming home I would get off the bus on the road below by the stream and go through a barred iron gate and up a flight of steps. I thought if anyone attacked me it would be on those steps. Like my father I've always been a daydreamer, and sometimes in lessons my mind would drift and I'd imagine that on the way home a terrorist might jump out and shoot me on those steps. I wondered what I would do. Maybe I'd take off my shoes and hit him, but then I'd think if I did that there would be no difference between me and a terrorist. It would be better to plead, "OK, shoot me, but first listen to me. What you are doing is wrong. I'm not against you personally, I just want every girl to go to school."

I wasn't scared, but I had started making sure the gate was locked at night and asking God what happens when you die. I told my best friend Moniba everything. We'd lived on the same street when we were little and been friends since primary school and we shared everything, Justin Bieber songs and Twilight movies, the best face-lightening creams. Her dream was to be a fashion designer although she knew her family would never agree to it, so she told everyone she wanted to be a doctor. It's hard for girls in our society to be anything other than teachers or doctors if they can work at all. I was different—I never hid my desire when I changed from wanting to be a doctor to wanting to be an inventor or a politician. Moniba always knew if something was wrong. "Don't worry," I told her. "The Taliban have never come for a small girl."

When our bus was called, we ran down the steps. The other girls all covered their heads before emerging from the door and climbing up into the back. The bus was actually what we call a *dyna,* a white Toyota TownAce truck with three parallel benches, one along either side and one in the middle. It was cramped with twenty girls and three teachers. I was sitting on the left between Moniba and a girl from the year below called

Shazia Ramzan, holding our exam folders to our chests and our school bags under our feet.

After that it is all a bit hazy. I remember that inside the *dyna* was hot and sticky. The cooler days were late coming and only the faraway mountains of the Hindu Kush had a frosting of snow. The back where we sat had no windows, just thick plastic sheeting at the sides which flapped and was too yellowed and dusty to see through. All we could see was a little stamp of open sky out of the back and glimpses of the sun, at that time of day a yellow orb floating in the dust that streamed over everything.

I remember that the bus turned right off the main road at the army checkpoint as always and rounded the corner past the deserted cricket ground. I don't remember any more.

In my dreams about the shooting my father is also in the bus and he is shot with me, and then there are men everywhere and I am searching for my father.

In reality what happened was we suddenly stopped. On our left was the tomb of Sher Mohammad Khan, the finance minister of the first ruler of Swat, all overgrown with grass, and on our right the snack factory. We must have been less than 200 meters from the checkpoint.

We couldn't see in front, but a young bearded man in light-colored clothes had stepped into the road and waved the van down.

"Is this the Khushal School bus?" he asked our driver. Usman Bhai Jan thought this was a stupid question, as the name was painted on the side. "Yes," he said.

"I need information about some children," said the man.

"You should go to the office," said Usman Bhai Jan.

As he was speaking another young man in white approached the back of the van. "Look, it's one of those journalists coming to ask for an interview," said Moniba. Since I'd started speaking at events with my father to campaign for girls' education and against those like the Taliban who want to hide us away, journalists often came, even foreigners, though not like this in the road.

The man was wearing a peaked cap and looked like a college student. He swung himself onto the tailboard at the back and leaned in right over us.

"Who is Malala?" he demanded.

No one said anything, but several of the girls looked at me. I was the only girl with my face not covered.

That's when he lifted up a black pistol. I later learned it was a Colt .45. Some of the girls screamed. Moniba tells me I squeezed her hand.

My friends say he fired three shots, one after another. The first went through my left eye socket and out under my left shoulder. I slumped forward onto Moniba, blood coming from my left ear, so the other two bullets hit the girls next to me. One bullet went into Shazia's left hand. The third went through her left shoulder and into the upper right arm of Kainat Riaz.

My friends later told me the gunman's hand was shaking as he fired.

By the time we got to the hospital my long hair and Moniba's lap were full of blood.

Who is Malala? I am Malala and this is my story.

Part One

Before the Taliban

سوري سوري په ګولو راشي   د بي ننګئ آواز د رامه شه مئينه

Sorey sorey pa golo rashey
Da be nangai awaz de ra ma sha mayena

Rather I receive your bullet-riddled body
with honor
Than news of your cowardice on the battlefield
Traditional Pashto couplet

1

A Daughter Is Born

When I was born, people in our village commiserated with my mother and nobody congratulated my father. I arrived at dawn as the last star blinked out. We Pashtuns see this as an auspicious sign. My father didn't have any money for the hospital or for a midwife, so a neighbor helped at my birth. My parents' first child was stillborn, but I popped out kicking and screaming. I was a girl in a land where rifles are fired in celebration of a son, while daughters are hidden away behind a curtain, their role in life simply to prepare food and give birth to children.

For most Pashtuns it's a gloomy day when a daughter is born. My father's cousin Jehan Sher Khan Yousafzai was one of the few who came to celebrate my birth and even gave a handsome gift of money. Yet, he brought with him a vast family tree of our clan, the Dalokhel Yousafzai, going right back to my great-great-grandfather and showing only the male line. My father, Ziauddin, is different from most Pashtun men. He took the tree, drew a line like a lollipop from his name and at the end of it he wrote, "Malala." His cousin laughed in astonishment. My father didn't care. He says he looked into my eyes after I was born and fell in love. He told people, "I know there is something different about this child." He even asked friends to throw dried fruits, sweets and coins into my cradle, something we usually only do for boys.

I was named after Malalai of Maiwand, the greatest heroine of Afghanistan. Pashtuns are a proud people of many tribes split between Pakistan and Afghanistan. We live as we have for centuries by a code called *Pashtunwali,* which obliges us to give hospitality to all guests and in which the most important value is *nang,* or honor. The worst thing that can happen to a Pashtun is loss of face. Shame is a very terrible thing for a Pashtun man. We have a saying, "Without honor, the world counts for nothing." We fight and feud among ourselves so much that our word for cousin—*tarbur*—is the same as our word for enemy. But we always come together against outsiders who try to conquer our lands. All Pashtun children grow up with the story of how Malalai inspired the Afghan army to defeat the British in 1880 in one of the biggest battles of the Second Anglo-Afghan War.

Malalai was the daughter of a shepherd in Maiwand, a small town on the dusty plains west of Kandahar. When she was a teenager, both her father and the man she was supposed to marry were among thousands of Afghans fighting against the British occupation of their country. Malalai went to the battlefield with other women from the village to tend the wounded and take them water. She saw their men were losing, and when the flag bearer fell she lifted her white veil up high and marched onto the battlefield in front of the troops.

"Young love!" she shouted. "If you do not fall in the battle of Maiwand then, by God, someone is saving you as a symbol of shame."

Malalai was killed under fire, but her words and bravery inspired the men to turn the battle around. They destroyed an entire brigade, one of the worst defeats in the history of the British army. The Afghans were so proud that the last Afghan king built a Maiwand victory monument in the center of Kabul. In high school I read some

Sherlock Holmes and laughed to see that this was the same battle where Dr. Watson was wounded before becoming partner to the great detective. In Malalai we Pashtuns have our very own Joan of Arc. Many girls' schools in Afghanistan are named after her. But my grandfather, who was a religious scholar and village cleric, didn't like my father giving me that name. "It's a sad name," he said. "It means grief-stricken."

When I was a baby my father used to sing me a song written by the famous poet Rahmat Shah Sayel of Peshawar. The last verse ends,

O Malalai of Maiwand,
Rise once more to make Pashtuns understand
* the song of honor,*
Your poetic words turn worlds around,
I beg you, rise again

My father told the story of Malalai to anyone who came to our house. I loved hearing the story and the songs my father sang to me, and the way my name floated on the wind when people called it.

We lived in the most beautiful place in all the world. My valley, the Swat Valley, is a heavenly kingdom of mountains, gushing waterfalls and crystal-clear lakes. WELCOME TO PARADISE, it says on a sign as you enter the valley. In olden times Swat was called Uddyana, which means "garden." We have fields of wildflowers, orchards of delicious fruit, emerald mines and rivers full of trout. People often call Swat the Switzerland of the East—we even had Pakistan's first ski resort. The rich people of Pakistan came on holiday to enjoy our clean air and scenery and our Sufi festivals of music and dancing. And so did many foreigners, all of whom we called *angrezan*—"English"—wherever they came from. Even the queen of England came, and stayed in the White Palace that was built from the same marble as the Taj Mahal by our king, the first *wali,* or ruler, of Swat.

We have a special history too. Today Swat is part of the province of Khyber Pakhtunkhwa, or KPK, as many Pakistanis call it, but Swat used to be separate from the rest of Pakistan. We were once a princely state, one of three with the neighboring lands of Chitral and Dir. In colonial times our kings owed allegiance to the British but ruled their own land. When the British gave India independence in 1947 and divided it, we went with the newly created Pakistan but stayed autonomous. We used the Pakistani rupee, but the government of Pakistan could only intervene on foreign policy. The *wali* administered justice, kept the peace between warring tribes, and collected *ushur*—a tax of 10 percent of income—with which he built roads, hospitals and schools.

We were only a hundred miles from Pakistan's capital Islamabad as the crow flies, but it felt as if it were in another country. The journey took at least five hours by road over the Malakand Pass, a vast bowl of mountains where long ago our ancestors led by a preacher called Mullah Saidullah (known by the British as the Mad Fakir) battled British forces among the craggy peaks. Among them was Winston Churchill, who wrote a book about it, and we still call one of the peaks Churchill's Picket even though he was not very complimentary about our people. At the end of the pass is a green-domed shrine where people throw coins to give thanks for their safe arrival.

No one I knew had been to Islamabad. Before the troubles came, most people, like my mother, had never been outside Swat.

We lived in Mingora, the biggest town in the valley, in fact the only city. It used to be a small place, but many people had moved in from surrounding villages, making it dirty and crowded. It has hotels, colleges, a golf course and a famous bazaar for buying our traditional embroidery, gemstones and anything you can think of. The Marghazar stream loops through it, milky brown from the plastic bags and rubbish thrown into it. It is not clear like the streams in the hilly areas or like the wide River Swat just outside town, where people fished for trout and which we visited on holidays. Our house was in Gulkada, which means "place of flowers," but it used to be called Butkara, or "place of the Buddhist statues." Near our home was a field scattered with mysterious ruins—statues of lions on their haunches, broken columns, headless figures and, oddest of all, hundreds of stone umbrellas.

Islam came to our valley in the eleventh century when Sultan Mahmud of Ghazni invaded from Afghanistan and became our ruler, but in ancient times Swat was a Buddhist kingdom. The Buddhists had arrived here in the second century and their kings ruled the valley for more than 500 years. Chinese explorers wrote stories of how there were 1,400 Buddhist monasteries along the banks of the River Swat, and the magical sound of temple bells would ring out across the valley. The temples are long gone, but almost anywhere you go in Swat, amid all the primroses and other wildflowers, you find their remains. We would often picnic among rock carvings of a smiling fat Buddha sitting cross-legged on a lotus flower. There are many stories that Lord Buddha himself came here because it is a place of such peace, and some of his ashes are said to be buried in the valley in a giant stupa.

Our Butkara ruins were a magical place to play hide-and-seek. Once some foreign archaeologists arrived to do some work there and told us that in times gone by it was a place of pilgrimage, full of beautiful temples domed with gold where Buddhist kings lay buried. My father wrote a poem, "The Relics of Butkara," which summed up perfectly how temple and mosque could exist side by side: "When the voice of truth rises from the minarets, / The Buddha smiles, / And the broken chain of history reconnects."

We lived in the shadow of the Hindu Kush mountains, where the men went to shoot ibex and golden cockerels. Our house was one story and proper concrete. On the left were steps up to a flat roof big enough for us children to play cricket on. It was our playground. At dusk my father and his friends often gathered to sit and drink tea there. Sometimes I sat on the roof too, watching the smoke rise from the cooking fires all around and listening to the nightly racket of the crickets.

Our valley is full of fruit trees on which grow the sweetest figs and pomegranates and peaches, and in our garden we had grapes, guavas and persimmons. There was a plum tree in our front yard which gave the most delicious fruit. It was always a race between us and the birds to get to them. The birds loved that tree. Even the woodpeckers.

For as long as I can remember my mother has talked to birds. At the back of the house was a veranda where the women gathered. We knew what it was like to be hungry, so my mother always cooked extra and gave food to poor families. If there was any left she fed it to the birds. In Pashto we love to sing *tapae,* two-line poems, and as she scattered the rice she would sing one: "Don't kill doves in the garden. / You kill one and the others won't come."

I liked to sit on the roof and watch the mountains and dream. The highest mountain of all is the pyramid-shaped Mount Elum. To us it's a sacred mountain and so high that it always wears a necklace of fleecy clouds. Even in summer it's frosted with snow. At school we learned that in 327 BC, even before the Buddhists came to Swat, Alexander the Great swept into the valley with thousands of elephants and soldiers on his way from Afghanistan to the Indus. The Swati people fled up the mountain, believing they would be protected by their gods because it was so high. But Alexander was a determined and patient leader. He built a wooden ramp from which his catapults and arrows could reach the top of the mountain. Then he climbed up so he could catch hold of the star of Jupiter as a symbol of his power.

From the rooftop I watched the mountains change with the seasons. In the autumn chill winds would come. In the winter everything was white snow, long icicles hanging from the roof like daggers, which we loved to snap off. We raced around, building snowmen and snow bears and trying to catch snowflakes. Spring was when Swat was at its greenest. Eucalyptus blossom blew into the house, coating everything white, and the wind carried the pungent smell of the rice fields. I was born in summer, which was perhaps why it was my favorite time of year, even though in Mingora summer was hot and dry and the stream stank where people dumped their garbage.

When I was born we were very poor. My father and a friend had founded their first school and we lived in a shabby shack of two rooms opposite the school. I slept with my mother and father in one room and the other was for guests. We had no bathroom or kitchen, and my mother cooked on a wood fire on the ground and washed our clothes at a tap in the school. Our home was always full of people visiting from the village. Hospitality is an important part of Pashtun culture.

Two years after I was born my brother Khushal arrived. Like me he was born at home, as we still could not afford the hospital, and he was named Khushal like my father's school, after the Pashtun hero Khushal Khan Khattak, a warrior and poet. My mother had been waiting for a son and could not hide her joy when he was born. To me he seemed very thin and small, like a reed that could snap in the wind, but he was the apple of her eye, her *ladla*. It seemed to me that his every wish was her command. He wanted tea all the time, our traditional tea with milk and sugar and cardamom, but even my mother tired of this and eventually made some so bitter that he lost the taste for it. She wanted to buy a new cradle for him—when I was born my father couldn't afford one, so they used an old wooden one from the neighbors which was already third or fourth hand—but my father refused. "Malala swung in that cradle," he said. "So can he." Then, nearly five years later, another boy was born—Atal, bright-eyed and inquisitive like a squirrel. After that, said my father, we were complete. Three children is a small family by Swati standards, where most people have seven or eight.

I played mostly with Khushal because he was just two years younger than me, but we fought all the time. He would go crying to my mother and I would go to my father. "What's wrong, *Jani?*" he would ask. Like him I was born double-jointed and can bend my fingers right back on themselves. And my ankles click when I walk, which makes adults squirm.

My mother is very beautiful and my father adored her as if she were a fragile china vase, never laying a hand on her, unlike many of our men. Her name Tor Pekai means "raven tresses" even though her hair is chestnut brown. My grandfather, Janser Khan, had been listening to Radio Afghanistan just before she was born and heard the name. I wished I had her white-lily skin, fine features and green eyes, but instead had inherited the sallow complexion, wide nose and brown eyes of my father. In our culture we all have nicknames—aside from *Pisho,* which my mother had called me since I was a baby, some of my cousins called me *Lachi,* which is Pashto for "cardamom." Black-skinned people are often called white and short people tall. We have a funny sense of humor. My father was known in the family as *Khaista Dada,* which means "beautiful."

When I was around four years old I asked my father, "*Aba,* what color are you?" He replied, "I don't know, a bit white, a bit black."

"It's like when one mixes milk with tea," I said.

He laughed a lot, but as a boy he had been so self-conscious about being dark-skinned that he went to the fields to get buffalo milk to spread on his face, thinking it would make him lighter. It was only when he met my mother that he became comfortable in his own skin. Being loved by such a beautiful girl gave him confidence.

In our society marriages are usually arranged by families, but theirs was a love match. I could listen endlessly to the story of how they met. They came from neighboring villages in a remote valley in the upper Swat called Shangla and would see each other when my father went to his uncle's house to study, which was next door to that of my aunt. They glimpsed enough of each other to know they liked one another, but for us it is taboo to express such things. Instead he sent her poems she could not read.

"I admired his mind," she says.

"And me, her beauty," he laughs.

There was one big problem. My two grand-fathers did not get on. So when my father announced his desire to ask for the hand of my mother, Tor Pekai, it was clear neither side would welcome the marriage. His own father said it was up to him and agreed to send a barber as a messenger, which is the traditional way we Pashtuns do this. Malik Janser Khan refused the proposal, but my father is a stubborn man and persuaded my grandfather to send the barber again. Janser Khan's *hujra* was a gathering place for people to talk politics, and my father was often there, so they had got to know each other. He made him wait nine months but finally agreed.

My mother comes from a family of strong women as well as influential men. Her grand-mother — my great-grandmother — was widowed when her children were young, and her eldest son, Janser Khan, was locked up because of a tribal feud with another family when he was only nine. To get him released she walked forty miles alone over mountains to appeal to a powerful cousin. I think my mother would do the same for us. Though she cannot read or write, my father shares everything with her, telling her about his day, the good and the bad. She teases him a lot and gives him advice about who she thinks is a genuine friend and who is not, and my father says she is always right. Most Pashtun men never do this, as sharing problems with women is seen as weak. "He even asks his wife!" they say as an insult. I see my parents happy and laughing a lot. People would see us and say we are a sweet family.

My mother is very pious and prays five times a day, though not in the mosque, as that is only for the men. She disapproves of dancing because she says God would not like it, but she loves to decorate herself with pretty things, embroidered clothes and golden necklaces and bangles. I think I am a bit of a disappointment to her, as I am so like my father and don't bother with clothes and jewels. I get bored going to the bazaar, but I love to dance behind closed doors with my school friends.

Growing up we children spent most of our time with our mother. My father was out a lot, as he was busy, not just with his school, but also with literary societies and *jirgas,* as well as trying to save the environment, trying to save our valley. My father came from a backward village, yet through education and force of personality he made a good living for us and a name for himself.

People liked to hear him talk, and I loved the

evenings when guests visited. We would sit on the floor around a long plastic sheet which my mother laid with food, and eat with our right hands, as is our custom, balling together rice and meat. As darkness fell we sat by the light of oil lamps, batting away the flies as our silhouettes made dancing shadows on the walls. In the summer months there would often be thunder and lightning crashing outside and I would crawl closer to my father's knee.

I would listen, rapt, as he told stories of warring tribes, Pashtun leaders and saints, often through poems that he read in a melodious voice, crying sometimes as he read. Like most people in Swat we are from the Yousafzai tribe. We Yousafzai (which some people spell Yusufzai or Yousufzai) are originally from Kandahar and are one of the biggest Pashtun tribes, spread across Pakistan and Afghanistan.

Our ancestors came to Swat in the sixteenth century from Kabul, where they had helped a Timurid emperor win back his throne after his own tribe removed him. The emperor rewarded them with important positions in the court and army, but his friends and relatives warned him that the Yousafzai were becoming so powerful they would overthrow him. So one night he invited all the chiefs to a banquet and set his men on them while they were eating. Around 600 chiefs were massacred. Only two escaped, and they fled to Peshawar along with their tribesmen. After some time they went to visit some tribes in Swat to win their support so they could return to Afghanistan. But they were so captivated by the beauty of Swat they instead decided to stay there and forced the other tribes out.

The Yousafzai divided up all the land among the male members of the tribe. It was a peculiar system called *wesh* under which every five or ten years all the families would swap villages and redistribute the land of the new village among the men so that everyone had the chance to work on good as well as bad land. It was thought this would then keep rival clans from fighting. Villages were ruled by khans, and the common people, craftsmen and laborers, were their tenants. They had to pay them rent in kind, usually a share of their crop. They also had to help the khans form a militia by providing an armed man for every small plot of land. Each khan kept hundreds of armed men both for feuds and to raid and loot other villages.

As the Yousafzai in Swat had no ruler, there were constant feuds between the khans and even within their own families. Our men all have rifles though these days don't walk around with them like they do in other Pashtun areas, and my great-grandfather used to tell stories of gun battles when he was a boy. In the early part of the last century they became worried about being taken over by the British, who by then controlled most of the surrounding lands. They were also tired of the endless bloodshed. So they decided to try and find an impartial man to rule the whole area and resolve their disputes.

After a couple of rulers who did not work out, in 1917 the chiefs settled on a man called Mian-gul Abdul Wadood as their king. We know him affectionately as Badshah Sahib, and though he was completely illiterate, he managed to bring peace to the valley. Taking a rifle away from a Pashtun is like taking away his life, so he could not disarm the tribes. Instead he built forts on mountains all across Swat and created an army. He was recognized by the British as the head of state in 1926 and installed as *wali*. He set up the first telephone system and built the first primary school and ended the *wesh* system because the constant moving between villages meant no one could sell land or had any incentive to build bet-ter houses or plant fruit trees.

In 1949, two years after the creation of Pakistan, he abdicated in favor of his elder son, Miangul Abdul Haq Jehanzeb. My father always says, "While Badshah Sahib brought peace, his son brought prosperity." We think of Jehanzeb's reign as a golden period in our history. He had studied in a British school in Peshawar, and perhaps because his own father was illiterate he was passionate about schools and built many, as well as hospitals and roads. In the 1950s he ended the system where people paid taxes to the khans. But there was no freedom of expression, and if anyone criticized the *wali,* they could be expelled from the valley. In 1969, the year my father was born, the *wali* gave up power and we became part of Pakistan's North West Frontier Province, which a few years ago changed its name to Khyber Pakhtunkhwa.

So I was born a proud daughter of Pakistan, though like all Swatis I thought of myself first as Swati and then Pashtun, before Pakistani.

Near us on our street there was a family with a girl my age called Safina and two boys similar in age to my brothers, Babar and Basit. We all played cricket on the street or rooftops together, but I knew as we got older the girls would be expected to stay inside. We'd be expected to cook and serve our brothers and fathers. While boys and men could roam freely about town, my mother and I could not go out without a male relative to accompany us, even if it was a five-year-old boy! This was the tradition.

I had decided very early I would not be like that. My father always said, "Malala will be free as a bird." I dreamed of going to the top of Mount Elum like Alexander the Great to touch Jupiter and even beyond the valley. But, as I watched my brothers running across the roof, flying their kites and skillfully flicking the strings back and forth to cut each other's down, I wondered how free a daughter could ever be.

2

My Father the Falcon

I always knew my father had trouble with words. Sometimes they would get stuck and he would repeat the same syllable over and over like a record caught in a groove as we all waited for the next syllable to suddenly pop out. He said it felt like a wall came down in his throat. M's, p's and k's were all enemies lying in wait. I teased him that one of the reasons he called me *Jani* was because he found it easier to say than Malala. A stutter was a terrible thing for a man who so loved words and poetry. On each side of the family he had an uncle with the same affliction. But it was almost certainly made worse by his father, whose own voice was a soaring instrument that could make words thunder and dance.

"Spit it out, son!" he'd roar whenever my father got stuck in the middle of a sentence. My grandfather's name was Rohul Amin, which means "honest spirit" and is the holy name of the Angel Gabriel. He was so proud of the name that he would introduce himself to people with a famous verse in which his name appears. He was an impatient man at the best of times and would fly into a rage over the smallest thing—like a hen going astray or a cup getting broken. His face would redden and he would throw kettles and pots around. I never knew my grandmother, but my father says she used to joke with my grandfather, "By God, just as you greet us only with a frown, when I die may God give you a wife who never smiles."

My grandmother was so worried about my father's stutter that when he was still a young boy she took him to see a holy man. It was a long journey by bus, then an hour's walk up the hill to where he lived. Her nephew Fazli Hakim had to carry my father on his shoulders. The holy man was called Lewano Pir, Saint of the Mad, because he was said to be able to calm lunatics. When they were taken in to see the *pir*, he instructed my father to open his mouth and then spat into it. Then he took some *gur*, dark molasses made from sugar cane, and rolled it around his mouth to moisten it with spit. He then took out the lump and presented it to my grandmother to give to my father, a little each day. The treatment did not cure the stutter. Actually, some people thought it got worse. So when my father was thirteen and told my grandfather he was entering a public speaking competition he was stunned. "How can you?" Rohul Amin asked, laughing. "You take one or two minutes to utter just one sentence."

"Don't worry," replied my father. "You write the speech and I will learn it."

My grandfather was famous for his speeches. He taught theology in the government high school in the village of Shahpur. He was also an imam at the local mosque. He was a mesmerizing speaker. His sermons at Friday prayers were so popular that people would come down from the mountains by donkey or on foot to hear him.

My father comes from a large family. He had one much older brother, Saeed Ramzan, who I call Uncle *Khan dada,* and five sisters. Their village of Barkana was very primitive and they lived crammed together in a one-story ramshackle house with a mud roof which leaked whenever it rained or snowed. As in most families, the girls stayed at home while the boys went to school. "They were just waiting to be married," says my father.

School wasn't the only thing my aunts missed out on. In the morning when my father was given cream or milk, his sisters were given tea with no milk. If there were eggs, they would only be for the boys. When a chicken was slaughtered for dinner, the girls would get the wings and the neck while the luscious breast meat was enjoyed by my father, his brother and my grandfather. "From early on I could feel I was different from my sisters," my father says.

There was little to do in my father's village. It was too narrow even for a cricket pitch and only one family had a television. On Fridays the brothers would creep into the mosque and watch in wonder as my grandfather stood in the pulpit and preached to the congregation for an hour or so, waiting for the moment when his voice would rise and practically shake the rafters.

My grandfather had studied in India, where he had seen great speakers and leaders including Mohammad Ali Jinnah (the founder of Pakistan), Jawaharlal Nehru, Mahatma Gandhi and Khan Abdul Ghaffar Khan, our great Pashtun leader who campaigned for independence. *Baba,* as I called him, had even witnessed the moment of freedom from the British colonialists at midnight on 14 August 1947. He had an old radio set my uncle still has, on which he loved to listen to the news. His sermons were often illustrated by world events or historical happenings as well as stories from the Quran and the Hadith, the sayings of the Prophet, *Peace Be Upon Him.* He also liked to talk about politics. Swat became part of Pakistan in 1969, the year my father was born. Many Swatis were unhappy about this, complaining about the Pakistani justice system, which they said was much slower and less effective than their old tribal ways. My grandfather would rail against the class system, the continuing power of the khans, and the gap between the haves and have-nots.

My country may not be very old, but unfortunately it already has a history of military coups, and when my father was eight a general called Zia ul-Haq seized power. There are still many pictures of him around. He was a scary man with dark panda shadows around his eyes, large teeth that seemed to stand to attention and hair pomaded flat on his head. He arrested our elected prime minister, Zulfikar Ali Bhutto, and had him tried for treason then hanged from a scaffold in Rawalpindi jail. Even today people talk of Mr. Bhutto as a man of great charisma. They say he was the first Pakistani leader to stand up for the common people, though he himself was a feudal lord with vast estates of mango fields. His execution shocked everybody and made Pakistan look bad all around the world. The Americans cut off aid.

To try to get people at home to support him, General Zia launched a campaign of Islamization to make us a proper Muslim country with the army as the defenders of our country's ideological as well as geographical frontiers. He told our people it was their duty to obey his government because it was pursuing Islamic principles. Zia even wanted to dictate how we should pray, and set up *salat,* or prayer committees, in every district, even in our remote village, and appointed 100,000 prayer inspectors. Before then mullahs had almost been figures of fun — my father said at wedding parties they would just hang around in a corner and leave early — but under Zia they became influential and were called to Islamabad for guidance on sermons. Even my grandfather went.

Under Zia's regime life for women in Pakistan became much more restricted. Jinnah said, "No struggle can ever succeed without women participating side by side with men. There are two powers in the world; one is the sword and the other is the pen. There is a third power stronger than both, that of women." But General Zia brought in Islamic laws which reduced a woman's evidence in court to count for only half that of a man's. Soon our prisons were full of cases like that of a thirteen-year-old girl who was raped and became pregnant and was then sent to prison for adultery because she couldn't produce four male witnesses to prove it was a crime. A woman couldn't even open a bank account without a man's permission. As a nation we have always been good at hockey, but Zia made our female hockey players wear baggy trousers instead of shorts, and stopped women playing some sports altogether.

Many of our madrasas, or religious schools, were opened at that time, and in all schools religious studies, what we call *deeniyat,* was replaced by *Islamiyat,* or Islamic studies, which children in Pakistan still have to do today. Our history textbooks were rewritten to describe Pakistan as a "fortress of Islam," which made it seem as if we had existed far longer than since 1947, and denounced Hindus and Jews. Anyone reading them might think we won the three wars we have fought and lost against our great enemy, India.

Everything changed when my father was ten. Just after Christmas 1979 the Russians invaded our neighbor Afghanistan. Millions of Afghans fled across the border and General Zia gave them refuge. Vast camps of white tents sprang up mostly around Peshawar, some of which are still there today. Our biggest intelligence service belongs to the military and is called the ISI. It started a massive program to train Afghan refugees recruited from the camps as resistance fighters, or mujahideen. Though Afghans are renowned fighters, Colonel Imam, the officer heading the program, complained that trying to organize them was "like weighing frogs."

The Russian invasion transformed Zia from an international pariah to the great defender of freedom in the Cold War. The Americans became friends with us once again, as in those days Russia was their main enemy. Next door to us the Shah of Iran had been overthrown in a revolution a few months earlier, so the CIA had lost their main base in the region. Pakistan took its place. Billions of dollars flowed into our exchequer from the United States and other Western countries, as well as weapons to help the ISI train the Afghans to fight the communist Red Army. General Zia was invited to meet President Ronald Reagan at the White House and Prime Minister Margaret Thatcher at 10 Downing Street. They lavished praise on him.

Prime Minister Zulfikar Bhutto had appointed

Zia as his army chief because he thought he was not very intelligent and would not be a threat. He called him his "monkey." But Zia turned out to be a very wily man. He made Afghanistan a rallying point not only for the West, which wanted to stop the spread of communism from the Soviet Union, but also for Muslims from Sudan to Tajikistan, who saw it as a fellow Islamic country under attack from infidels. Money poured in from all over the Arab world, particularly Saudi Arabia, which matched whatever the US sent, and volunteer fighters too, including a Saudi millionaire called Osama bin Laden.

We Pashtuns are split between Pakistan and Afghanistan and don't really recognize the border that the British drew more than 100 years ago. So our blood boiled over the Soviet invasion for both religious and nationalist reasons. The clerics of the mosques would often talk about the Soviet occupation of Afghanistan in their sermons, condemning the Russians as infidels and urging people to join the jihad, saying it was their duty as good Muslims. It was as if under Zia jihad had become the sixth pillar of our religion on top of the five we grow up to learn—the belief in one God; *namaz,* or prayers five times a day; giving *zakat,* or alms; *roza,* fasting from dawn till sunset during the month of Ramadan; and Haj, the pilgrimage to Mecca, which every able-bodied Muslim should do once in their lifetime. My father says that in our part of the world this idea of jihad was very much encouraged by the CIA. Children in the refugee camps were even given school textbooks produced by an American university which taught basic arithmetic through fighting. They had examples like "If out of 10 Russian infidels, 5 are killed by one Muslim, 5 would be left" or "15 bullets – 10 bullets = 5 bullets."

Some boys from my father's district went off to fight in Afghanistan. My father remembers that one day a *maulana* called Sufi Mohammad came to the village and asked young men to join him to fight the Russians in the name of Islam. Many did, and they set off, armed with old rifles or just axes and bazookas. Little did we know that years later the same *maulana*'s organization would become the Swat Taliban. At that time my father was only twelve years old and too young to fight. But the Russians ended up stuck in Afghanistan for ten years, through most of the 1980s, and when he became a teenager my father decided he too wanted to be a jihadi. Though later he became less regular in his prayers, in those days he used to leave home at dawn every morning to walk to a mosque in another village, where he studied the Quran with a senior *talib*. At that time *talib* simply meant "religious student." Together they studied all the 30 chapters of the Quran, not just recitation but also interpretation, something few boys do.

The *talib* talked of jihad in such glorious terms that my father was captivated. He would endlessly point out to my father that life on earth was short and that there were few opportunities for young men in the village. Our family owned little land, and my father did not want to end up going south to work in the coal mines like many of his classmates. That was tough and dangerous work, and the coffins of those killed in accidents would come back several times a year. The best that most village boys could hope for was to go to Saudi Arabia or Dubai and work in construction. So heaven with its seventy-two virgins sounded attractive. Every night my father would pray to God, "O Allah, please make war between Muslims and infidels so I can die in your service and be a martyr."

For a while his Muslim identity seemed more important than anything else in his life. He began to sign himself "Ziauddin Panchpiri" (the Panchpiri are a religious sect) and sprouted the first signs of a beard. It was, he says, a kind of brain-washing. He believes he might even have thought of becoming a suicide bomber had there been such a thing in those days. But from an early age he had been a questioning kind of boy who rarely took anything at face value, even though our education at government schools meant learning by rote and pupils were not supposed to question teachers.

It was around the time he was praying to go to heaven as a martyr that he met my mother's brother, Faiz Mohammad, and started mixing with her family and going to her father's *hujra*. They were very involved in local politics, belonged to secular nationalist parties and were against involvement in the war. A famous poem was written at that time by Rahmat Shah Sayel, the same Peshawar poet who wrote the poem about my namesake. He described what was happening in Afghanistan as a "war between two elephants"—the US and the Soviet Union—not our war, and said that we Pashtuns were "like the grass crushed by the hooves of two fierce beasts." My father often used to recite the poem to me when I was a child, but I didn't know then what it meant.

My father was very impressed by Faiz Mohammad and thought he talked a lot of sense, particularly about wanting to end the feudal and
capitalist systems in our country, where the same
big families had controlled things for years while
the poor got poorer. He found himself torn between the two extremes, secularism and socialism
on one side and militant Islam on the other. I
guess he ended up somewhere in the middle.

My father was in awe of my grandfather and
told me wonderful stories about him, but he also
told me that he was a man who could not meet
the high standards he set for others. *Baba* was
such a popular and passionate speaker that he
could have been a great leader if he had been
more diplomatic and less consumed by rivalries
with cousins and others who were better off. In
Pashtun society it is very hard to stomach a cousin
being more popular, wealthier or more influential
than you are. My grandfather had a cousin who
also joined his school as a teacher. When he got
the job he gave his age as much younger than
my grandfather. Our people don't know their exact dates of birth — my mother, for example, does
not know when she was born. We tend to remember years by events, like an earthquake. But
my grandfather knew that his cousin was actually

much older than him. He was so angry that he made the daylong bus journey to Mingora to see the Swat minister of education. "Sahib," he told him, "I have a cousin who is ten years older than me and you have certified him ten years younger." So the minister said, "OK, *Maulana,* what shall I write down for you? Would you like to have been born in the year of the earthquake of Quetta?" My grandfather agreed, so his new date of birth became 1935, making him much younger than his cousin.

This family rivalry meant that my father was bullied a lot by his cousins. They knew he was insecure about his looks because at school the teachers always favored the handsome boys for their fair skin. His cousins would stop my father on his way home from school and tease him about being short and dark skinned. In our society you have to take revenge for such slights, but my father was much smaller than his cousins.

He also felt he could never do enough to please my grandfather. *Baba* had beautiful handwriting and my father would spend hours painstakingly drawing letters, but *Baba* never once praised him.

My grandmother kept his spirits up—he was her favorite and she believed great things lay in store for him. She loved him so much that she would slip him extra meat and the cream off the milk while she went without. But it wasn't easy to study, as there was no electricity in the village in those days. He used to read by the light of the oil lamp in the *hujra,* and one evening he went to sleep and the oil lamp fell over. Fortunately my grandmother found him before a fire started. It was my grandmother's faith in my father that gave him the courage to find his own proud path he could travel along. This is the path that he would later show me.

Yet she too got angry with him once. Holy men from a spiritual place called Derai Saydan used to travel the villages in those days begging for flour. One day while his parents were out, some of them came to the house. My father broke the seal on the wooden storage box of maize and filled their bowls. When my grandparents came home they were furious and beat him.

Pashtuns are famously frugal (though generous with guests), and *Baba* was particularly careful with money. If any of his children accidentally spilled their food he would fly into a rage. He was an extremely disciplined man and could not understand why they were not the same. As a teacher he was eligible for a discount on his sons' school fees for sports and joining the Boy Scouts.

It was such a small discount that most teachers did not bother, but he forced my father to apply for the rebate. Of course my father detested doing this. As he waited outside the headmaster's office, he broke out into a sweat, and once inside his stutter was worse than ever. "It felt as if my honor was at stake for five rupees," he told me. My grandfather never bought him new books. Instead he would tell his best students to keep their old books for my father at the end of the year and then he would be sent to their homes to get them. He felt ashamed but had no choice if he didn't want to end up illiterate. All his books were inscribed with other boy's names, never his own.

"It's not that passing books on is a bad practice," he says. "It's just I so wanted a new book, unmarked by another student and bought with my father's money."

My father's dislike of *Baba*'s frugality has made him a very generous man both materially and in spirit. He became determined to end the traditional rivalry between him and his cousins. When his headmaster's wife fell ill, my father donated blood to help save her. The man was astonished and apologized for having tormented him. When my father tells me stories of his childhood, he always says that though *Baba* was a difficult man he gave him the most important gift—the gift of education. He sent my father to the government high school to learn English and receive a modern education rather than to a madrasa, even though as an imam people criticized him for this. *Baba* also gave him a deep love of learning and knowledge as well as a keen awareness of people's rights, which my father has passed on to me. In my grandfather's Friday addresses he would talk about the poor and the landowners and how true Islam is against feudalism. He also spoke Persian and Arabic and cared deeply for words. He read the great poems of Saadi, Allama Iqbal and Rumi to my father with such passion and fire it was as if he were teaching the whole mosque.

My father longed to be eloquent with a voice that boomed out with no stammer, and he knew my grandfather desperately wanted him to be a doctor, but though he was a very bright student and a gifted poet, he was poor at math and science and felt he was a disappointment. That's why he decided he would make his father proud by entering the district's annual public speaking competition. Everyone thought he was mad. His teachers and friends tried to dissuade him, and his father was reluctant to write the speech for him. But eventually *Baba* gave him a fine speech, which my father practiced and practiced. He committed every word to memory while walking in the hills, reciting it to the skies and birds, as there was no privacy in their home.

There was not much to do in the area where they lived, so when the day arrived there was a huge gathering. Other boys, some known as good speakers, gave their speeches. Finally my father was called forward. "I stood at the lectern," he told me, "hands shaking and knees knocking, so short I could barely see over the top and so terrified the faces were a blur. My palms were sweating and my mouth was as dry as paper." He tried desperately not to think about the treacherous consonants lying ahead of him, just waiting to trip him up and stick in his throat, but when he spoke, the words came out fluently like beautiful butterflies taking flight. His voice did not boom like his father's, but his passion shone through and as he went on he gained confidence.

At the end of the speech there were cheers and applause. Best of all, as he went up to collect the cup for first prize, he saw his father clapping and enjoying being patted on the back by those standing around him. "It was," he says, "the first thing I'd done that made him smile."

After that my father entered every competition

in the district. My grandfather wrote his speeches and he almost always came first, gaining a reputation locally as an impressive speaker. My father had turned his weakness into strength. For the first time *Baba* started praising him in front of others. He'd boast, "Ziauddin is a *shaheen*"—a falcon—because this is a creature that flies high above other birds. "Write your name as 'Ziauddin Shaheen,'" he told him. For a while my father did this but stopped when he realized that although a falcon flies high it is a cruel bird. Instead he just called himself Ziauddin Yousafzai, our clan name.

3

Growing Up in a School

My mother started school when she was six and stopped the same term. She was unusual in the village, as she had a father and brothers who encouraged her to go to school. She was the only girl in a class of boys. She carried her bag of books proudly into school and claims she was brighter than the boys. But every day she would leave behind her girl cousins playing at home and she envied them. There seemed no point in going to school to just end up cooking, cleaning and bringing up children, so one day she sold her books for nine annas, spent the money on boiled sweets and never went back. Her father said nothing. She says he didn't even notice, as he would set off early every morning after a breakfast of cornbread and cream, his German pistol strapped under his arm, and spend his days busy with local politics or resolving feuds. Besides he had seven other children to think about.

It was only when she met my father that she felt regret. Here was a man who had read so many books, who wrote her poems she could not read, and whose ambition was to have his own school. As his wife, she wanted to help him achieve that. For as long as my father could remember it had been his dream to open a school, but with no family contacts or money it was extremely hard for him to realize this dream. He thought there was nothing more important than knowledge. He remembered how mystified he had been by the river in his village, wondering where the water came from and went to, until he learned about the water cycle from the rain to the sea.

His own village school had been just a small building. Many of his classes were taught under a tree on the bare ground. There were no toilets, and the pupils went to the fields to answer the call of nature. Yet he says he was actually lucky. His sisters—my aunts—did not go to school at all, just like millions of girls in my country. Education had been a great gift for him. He believed that lack of education was the root of all of Pakistan's problems. Ignorance allowed politicians to fool people and bad administrators to be re-elected. He believed schooling should be available for all, rich and poor, boys and girls. The school that my father dreamed of would have desks and a library, computers, bright posters on the walls and, most important, washrooms.

My grandfather had a different dream for his youngest son—he longed for him to be a doctor—and as one of just two sons, he expected him to contribute to the household budget. My father's elder brother Saeed Ramzan had worked for years as a teacher at a local school. He and his family lived with my grandfather, and whenever he saved up enough of his salary, they built a small concrete *hujra* at the side of the house for guests. He brought logs back from the mountains for firewood, and after teaching he would work in the fields where our family had a few buffaloes. He also helped *Baba* with heavy tasks like clearing snow from the roof.

When my father was offered a place for his A Levels at Jehanzeb College, which is the best further education institution in Swat, my grandfather refused to pay for his living expenses. His own education in Delhi had been free—he had lived like a *talib* in the mosques, and local people had provided the students with food and clothes. Tuition at Jehanzeb was free, but my father needed money to live on. Pakistan doesn't have student loans and he had never even set foot in a bank. The college was in Saidu Sharif, the twin town of Mingora, and he had no family there with whom he could stay. There was no other college in Shangla, and if he didn't go to college, he would never be able to move out of the village and realize his dream.

My father was at his wits' end and wept with frustration. His beloved mother had died just before he graduated from school. He knew if she had been alive, she would have been on his side. He pleaded with his father but to no avail. His only hope was his brother-in-law in Karachi. My grandfather suggested that he might take my father in so he could go to college there. The couple would soon be arriving in the village, as they were coming to offer condolences after my grandmother's death.

My father prayed they would agree, but my grandfather asked them as soon as they arrived, exhausted after the three-day bus journey, and his son-in-law refused outright. My grandfather was so furious he would not speak to them for their entire stay. My father felt he had lost his chance and would end up like his brother teaching in a local school. The school where Uncle *Khan dada* taught was in the mountain village of

Sewoor, about an hour and a half's climb from their house. It didn't even have its own building. They used the big hall in the mosque, where they taught more than a hundred children ranging from five to fifteen years old.

The people in Sewoor were Gujars, Kohistanis and Mians. We regard Mians as noble or landed people, but Gujars and Kohistanis are what we call hilly people, peasants who look after buffaloes. Their children are usually dirty and they are looked down upon by Pashtuns, even if they are poor themselves. "They are dirty, black and stupid," people would say. "Let them be illiterate." It is often said that teachers don't like to be posted to such remote schools and generally make a deal with their colleagues so that only one of them has to go to work each day. If the school has two teachers, each goes in for three days and signs the other in. If it has three teachers, each goes in for just two days. Once there, all they do is to keep the children quiet with a long stick, as they cannot imagine education will be any use to them.

My uncle was more dutiful. He liked the hilly people and respected their tough lives. So he went to the school most days and actually tried to teach the children. After my father had graduated from school he had nothing to do, so he volunteered to help his brother. There his luck changed. Another of my aunts had married a man in that village and they had a relative visiting called Nasir Pacha, who saw my father at work. Nasir Pacha had spent years in Saudi Arabia working in construction, making money to send back to his family. My father told him he had just finished school and had won a college place at Jehanzeb. He did not mention he could not afford to take it, as he did not want to embarrass his father.

"Why don't you come and live with us?" asked Nasir Pacha.

"Oof, I was so happy, by God," says my father. Pacha and his wife Jajai became his second family. Their home was in Spal Bandi, a beautiful mountain village on the way to the White Palace, and my father describes it as a romantic and inspirational place. My father went there by bus and it seemed so big to him compared to his home village that he thought he'd arrived in a city. As a guest, he was treated exceptionally well. Jajai replaced his late mother as the most important woman in my father's life. When a villager complained to her that he was flirting with a girl living across the road, she defended him. "Ziauddin is as clean as an egg with no hair," she said. "Look instead to your own daughter."

It was in Spal Bandi that my father came across women who had great freedom and were not hidden away as in his own village. The women of Spal Bandi had a beautiful spot on top of the mountain where only they could congregate to chat about their everyday lives. It was unusual for women to have a special place to meet outside the home. It was also there that my father met his mentor Akbar Khan, who although he had not gone to college himself lent my father money so he could. Like my mother, Akbar Khan may not have had much of a formal education, but he had another kind of wisdom. My father often spoke of the kindness of Akbar Khan and Nasir Pacha to illustrate that if you help someone in need you might also receive unexpected aid.

My father arrived at college at an important moment in Pakistan's history. That summer, while he was walking in the mountains, our dictator General Zia was killed in a mysterious plane crash, which many people said was caused by a bomb hidden in a crate of mangoes. During my father's first term at college national elections were held, which were won by Benazir Bhutto, daughter of the prime minister who had been executed when my father was a boy. Benazir was our first female prime minister and the first in the Islamic world. Suddenly there was a lot of optimism about the future.

Student organizations which had been banned under Zia became very active. My father quickly got involved in student politics and became known as a talented speaker and debater. He was made general secretary of the Pakhtoon Students Federation (PSF), which wanted equal rights for Pashtuns. The most important jobs in the army, bureaucracy and government are all taken by Punjabis because they come from the biggest and most powerful province.

The other main students' organization was Islami Jamaat-e-Talaba, the student wing of the religious party Jamaat-e-Islami, which was powerful in many universities in Pakistan. They provided free textbooks and grants to students but held deeply intolerant views and their favorite pastime was to patrol universities and sabotage music concerts. The party had been close to General Zia and done badly in the elections. The president of the students' group in Jehanzeb College was Ihsan ul-Haq Haqqani. Though he and my father were great rivals, they admired each other and later became friends. Haqqani says he is sure my father would have been president of the PSF and become a politician if he had been from a rich khan family. Student politics was all about debating and charisma, but party politics required money.

One of their most heated debates in that first year was over a novel. The book was called *The Satanic Verses* by Salman Rushdie, and it was a parody of the life of the Prophet, PBUH, set in Bombay. Muslims widely considered it blasphemous and it provoked so much outrage that it seemed people were talking of little else. The odd thing was no one had even noticed the publication of the book to start with — it wasn't actually on sale in Pakistan — but then a series of articles appeared in Urdu newspapers by a mullah close to our intelligence service, berating the book as offensive to the Prophet, PBUH, and saying it was the duty of good Muslims to protest. Soon mullahs all over Pakistan were denouncing the book, calling for it to be banned, and angry demonstrations were held. The most violent took place in Islamabad on 12 February 1989, when American flags were set alight in front of the American Center — even though Rushdie and his publishers were British. Police fired into the crowd, and five people were killed. The anger wasn't just in Pakistan. Two days later Ayatollah Khomeini, the supreme leader of Iran, issued a fatwa calling for Rushdie's assassination.

My father's college held a heated debate in a packed room. Many students argued that the book should be banned and burned and the fatwa upheld. My father also saw the book as offensive to Islam but suggested: "First, let's read the book and then why not respond with our own book." He ended by asking in a thundering voice my grandfather would have been proud of, "Is Islam such a weak religion that it cannot tolerate a book written against it? Not *my* Islam!"

For the first few years after graduating from Jehanzeb my father worked as an English teacher in a well-known private college. But the salary was low, just 1,600 rupees a month (around $19), and my grandfather complained he was not contributing to the household. It was also not enough for him to save for the wedding he hoped for to his beloved Tor Pekai.

One of my father's colleagues at the school was his friend Mohammad Naeem Khan. He and my father had studied for their bachelor's and master's degrees in English together and were both passionate about education. They were also both frustrated, as the school was very strict and unimaginative. Neither the students nor the teachers were supposed to have their own opinions, and the owners' control was so tight they even frowned upon friendship between teachers. My father longed for the freedom that would come with running his own school. He wanted to encourage independent thought and hated the way the school he was in rewarded obedience above open-mindedness and creativity. So when Naeem lost his job after a dispute with the college administration, they decided to start their own school.

Their original plan was to open a school in my father's village of Shahpur, where there was a desperate need: "Like a shop in a community where there are no shops," he said. But when they went there to look for a building, there were banners everywhere advertising a school opening—someone had beaten them to it. So they decided to set up an English-language school in Mingora, thinking that since Swat was a tourist destination there would be a demand for learning in English.

As my father was still teaching, Naeem wandered the streets looking for somewhere to rent.

One day he called my father excitedly to say he'd found the ideal place. It was the ground floor of a two-story building in a well-off area called Landikas with a walled courtyard where students could gather. The previous tenants had also run a school—the Ramada School. The owner had called it that because he had once been to Turkey and seen a Ramada Hotel! But the school had gone bankrupt, which perhaps should have made them think twice. Also the building was on the banks of a river where people threw their rubbish, and it smelled foul in hot weather.

My father went to see the building after work. It was a perfect night with stars and a full moon just above the trees, which he took to be a sign. "I felt so happy," he recalls. "My dream was coming true."

Naeem and my father invested their entire savings of 60,000 rupees. They borrowed 30,000 rupees more to repaint the building, rented a shack across the road to live in and went from door to door trying to find students. Unfortunately the demand for English tuition turned out to be low, and there were unexpected drains on their income. My father's involvement in political discussions continued after college. Every day his fellow activists came to the shack or the school for lunch. "We can't afford all this entertaining!" Naeem would complain. It was also becoming clear that while they were best friends, they found it hard to work as business partners.

On top of that there was a stream of guests from Shangla now that my father had a place for them to stay. We Pashtuns cannot turn away relatives or friends, however inconvenient. We don't respect privacy and there is no such thing as making an appointment to see someone. Visitors can turn up whenever *they* wish and can stay as long as *they* want. It was a nightmare for someone trying to start a business and it drove Naeem to distraction. He joked to my father that if either of them had relatives to stay, they should pay a fine. My father kept trying to persuade Naeem's friends and family to stay so he could be fined too!

After three months Naeem had had enough. "We are supposed to be collecting money in enrollment fees. Instead the only people knocking on our doors are beggars! This is a Herculean task," he added. "I can't take any more!"

By this time the two former friends were hardly speaking to each other and had to call in local elders to mediate. My father was desperate not to give up the school so agreed to pay Naeem a return on his share of the investment. He had no idea how. Fortunately another old college friend called Hidayatullah stepped in and agreed to put up the money and take Naeem's place. The new partners again went from door to door, telling people they had started a new kind of school. My father is so charismatic that Hidayatullah says he is the kind of person who, if invited to your house, will make friends with your friends. But while people were happy to talk to him, they preferred to send their children to established schools.

They named it the Khushal School after one of my father's great heroes, Khushal Khan Khattak, the warrior poet from Akora just south of Swat, who tried to unify all Pashtun tribes against the Moghuls in the seventeenth century. Near the entrance they painted a motto: WE ARE COMMITTED TO BUILD FOR YOU THE CALL OF THE NEW ERA. My father also designed a shield with a famous quote from Khattak in Pashto: "I girt my sword in the name of Afghan honor." My father wanted us to be inspired by our great hero, but in a manner fit for our times—with pens, not swords. Just as Khattak had wanted the Pashtuns to unite against a foreign enemy, so we needed to unite against ignorance.

Unfortunately not many people were convinced. When the school opened they had just three students. Even so my father insisted on starting the day in style by singing the national anthem. Then his nephew Aziz, who had come to help, raised the Pakistan flag.

With so few students, they had little money to equip the school and soon ran out of credit. Neither man could get any money from their families, and Hidayatullah was not pleased to discover that my father was still in debt to lots of people from college, so they were always receiving letters demanding money.

There was worse in store when my father went to register the school. After being made to wait for hours, he was finally ushered into the office of the official of schools, who sat behind towering piles of files surrounded by hangers-on drinking tea. "What kind of school is this?" asked the official, laughing at his application. "How many teachers do you have? Three! Your teachers are not trained. Everyone thinks they can open a school just like that!"

The other people in the office laughed along, ridiculing him. My father was angry. It was clear the official wanted money. Pashtuns cannot stand anyone belittling them, nor was he about to pay a bribe for something he was entitled to. He and

Hidayatullah hardly had money to pay for food, let alone bribes. The going rate for registration was about 13,000 rupees, more if they thought you were rich. And schools were expected to treat officials regularly to a good lunch of chicken or trout from the river. The education officer would call to arrange an inspection then give a detailed order for his lunch. My father used to grumble, "We're a school not a poultry farm."

So when the official angled for a bribe, my father turned on him with all the force of his years of debating. "Why are you asking all these questions?" he demanded. "Am I in an office or am I in a police station or a court? Am I a criminal?" He decided to challenge the officials to protect other school owners from such bullying and corruption. He knew that to do this he needed some power of his own, so he joined an organization called the Swat Association of Private Schools. It was small in those days, just fifteen members, and my father quickly became vice president.

The other principals took paying bribes for granted, but my father argued that if all the schools joined together they could resist. "Running a school is not a crime," he told them. "Why should you be paying bribes? You are not running brothels; you are educating children! Government officials are not your bosses," he reminded them; "they are your servants. They are taking salaries and have to serve you. You are the ones educating *their* children."

He soon became president of the organization and expanded it until it included 400 principals. Suddenly the school owners were in a position of power. But my father has always been a romantic rather than a businessman and in the meantime he and Hidayatullah were in such desperate straits that they ran out of credit with the local shopkeeper and could not even buy tea or sugar. To try and boost their income they ran a sweet shop at school, going off in the mornings and buying snacks to sell to the children. My father would buy maize and stay up late at night making and bagging popcorn.

"I would get very depressed and sometimes collapse seeing the problems all around us," said Hidayatullah, "but when Ziauddin is in a crisis he becomes strong and his spirits high."

My father insisted that they needed to think big. One day Hidayatullah came back from trying to enroll pupils to find my father sitting in the office talking about advertising with the local head of Pakistan TV. As soon as the man had gone, Hidayatullah burst into laughter. "Ziauddin, we don't even have a TV," he pointed out. "If we advertise we won't be able to watch it." But my father is an optimistic man and never deterred by practicalities.

One day my father told Hidayatullah he was going back to his village for a few days. He was actually getting married, but he didn't tell any of his friends in Mingora, as he could not afford to entertain them. Our weddings go on for several days of feasting. In fact, as my mother often reminds my father, he was not present for the actual ceremony. He was only there for the last day, when family members held a Quran and a shawl over their heads and held a mirror for them to look into. For many couples in arranged marriages this is the first time they see each other's faces. A small boy was brought to sit on their laps to encourage the birth of a son.

It is our tradition for the bride to receive furniture or perhaps a fridge from her family and some gold from the groom's family. My grandfather would not buy enough gold, so my father had to borrow more money to buy bangles. After the wedding my mother moved in with my grandfather and my uncle. My father returned to the village every two or three weeks to see her. The plan was to get his school going then, once it was successful, send for his wife. But *Baba* kept complaining about the drain on his income and made my mother's life miserable. She had a little money of her own, so they used it to hire a van and she moved to Mingora. They had no idea how they would manage. "We just knew my father didn't want us there," said my father. "At that time I was unhappy with my family, but later I was grateful, as it made me more independent."

He had however neglected to tell his partner. Hidayatullah was horrified when my father returned to Mingora with a wife. "We're not in a position to support a family," he told my father. "Where will she live?"

"It's OK," replied my father. "She will cook and wash for us."

My mother was excited to be in Mingora. To her it was a modern town. When she and her friends had discussed their dreams as young girls by the river, most had just said they wanted to marry and have children and cook for their husbands. When it was my mother's turn she said, "I want to live in the city and be able to send out for kebabs and naan instead of cooking it myself." However, life wasn't quite what she expected. The shack had just two rooms, one where Hidayatullah and my father slept and one which was a small office. There was no kitchen, no plumbing. When my mother arrived, Hidayatullah had to move into the office and sleep on a hard wooden chair.

My father consulted my mother on everything. "Pekai, help me resolve my confusion on this," he would say. She even helped whitewash the school walls, holding up the lanterns so they could paint when the light went off in power cuts.

"Ziauddin was a family man and they were unusually close," said Hidayatullah. "While most of us can't live with our wives, he couldn't be without his."

Within a few months my mother was expecting. Their first child, born in 1995, was a girl and stillborn. "I think there was some problem with hygiene in that muddy place," says my father. "I assumed women could give birth without going to hospital, as my mother and my sisters had in the village. My mother gave birth to ten children in this way."

The school continued to lose money. Months would pass and they could not pay the teachers' wages or the school rent. The goldsmith kept coming and demanding his money for my mother's wedding bangles. My father would make him good tea and offer him biscuits in the hope that would keep him satisfied. Hidayatullah laughed. "You think he will be happy with tea? He wants his money."

The situation became so dire that my father was forced to sell the gold bangles. In our culture wedding jewelry is a bond between the couple. Often women sell their jewelry to help set up their husbands in business or to pay their fares to go abroad. My mother had already offered her bangles to pay for my father's nephew to go to college, which my father had rashly promised to fund—fortunately, my father's cousin Jehan Sher had stepped in—and she did not realize the bangles were only partly paid for. She was then furious when she learned that my father did not get a good price for them.

Just when it seemed matters could not get worse, the area was hit by flash floods. There was a day when it did not stop raining, and in the late afternoon there was a warning of flooding. Everyone had to leave the district. My mother was away and Hidayatullah needed my father to help him move everything up to the first floor, safe from the fast-rising waters, but he couldn't find him anywhere. He went outside, shouting "Ziauddin, Ziauddin!" The search almost cost Hidayatullah his life. The narrow street outside the school was totally flooded and he was soon up to his neck in water. There were live electric cables hanging loose and swaying in the wind. He watched paralyzed with fear as they almost touched the water. Had they done so, he would have been electrocuted.

When he finally found my father, he learned that he had heard a woman crying that her husband was trapped in their house and he had rushed in to save him. Then he helped them save their fridge. Hidayatullah was furious. "You saved this woman's husband but not your own house!" he said. "Was it because of the cry of a woman?"

When the waters receded, they found their home and school destroyed: their furniture, carpets, books, clothes and the audio system entirely caked in thick foul-smelling mud. They had nowhere to sleep and no clean clothes to change into. Luckily, a neighbor called Mr. Aman-ud-din took them in for the night. It took them a week to clear the debris. They were both away when, ten days later, there was a second flood and the building again filled with mud. Shortly afterward they had a visit from an official of WAPDA, the water and power company, who claimed their meter was rigged and demanded a bribe. When my father refused, a bill arrived with a large fine. There was no way they could pay this, so my father asked one of his political friends to use his influence.

It started to feel as though the school was not meant to be, but my father would not give up on his dream so easily. Besides, he had a family to provide for. I was born on 12 July 1997. My mother was helped by a neighbor who had delivered babies before. My father was in the school waiting and when he heard the news he came running. My mother was worried about telling him he had a daughter not a son, but he says he looked into my eyes and was delighted.

"Malala was a lucky girl," says Hidayatullah. "When she was born our luck changed."

But not immediately. On Pakistan's fiftieth anniversary on 14 August 1997 there were parades and commemorations throughout the country. However, my father and his friends said there was nothing to celebrate, as Swat had only suffered since it had merged with Pakistan. They wore black armbands to protest, saying the celebrations were for nothing, and were arrested. They had to pay a fine they could not afford.

A few months after I was born the three rooms above the school became vacant and we all moved in. The walls were concrete and there was running water, so it was an improvement on our muddy shack, but we were still very cramped, as we were sharing it with Hidayatullah and we almost always had guests. That first school was a mixed primary school and very small. By the time I was born it had five or six teachers and around a hundred pupils paying a hundred rupees a month. My father was teacher, accountant and principal. He also swept the floors, whitewashed the walls and cleaned the bathrooms. He used to climb up electricity poles to hang banners advertising the school, even though he was so afraid of heights that when he got to the top of the ladder his feet shook. If the water pump stopped working, he would go down the well to repair it himself. When I saw him disappear down there, I would cry, thinking he wouldn't come back. After paying the rent and salaries, there was little money left for food. We drank green tea, as we could not afford milk for regular tea. But after a while the school started to break even and my father began to plan a second school, which he wanted to call the Malala Education Academy.

I had the run of the school as my playground. My father tells me even before I could talk I would toddle into classes and talk as if I were a teacher.

Some of the female staff like Miss Ulfat would pick me up and put me on their laps as if I were their pet or even take me home with them for a while. When I was three or four I was placed in classes for much older children. I used to sit in wonder, listening to everything they were being taught. Sometimes I would mimic the teachers. You could say I grew up in a school.

As my father had found with Naeem, it is not easy to mix business and friendship. Eventually Hidayatullah left to start his own school and they divided the students, each taking two of the four years. They did not tell their pupils, as they wanted people to think the school was expanding and had two buildings. Though Hidayatullah and my father were not speaking at that time, Hidayatullah missed me so much he used to visit me.

It was while he was visiting one afternoon in September 2001 that there was a great commotion and other people started arriving. They said there had been a big attack on a building in New York. Two planes had flown into it. I was only four and too young to understand. Even for the adults it was hard to imagine—the biggest buildings in Swat are the hospital and a hotel, which are two or three stories. It seemed very far away.

I had no idea what New York and America were. The school was my world and my world was the school. We did not realize then that 9/11 would change our world too, and would bring war into our valley.

4

The Village

In our tradition on the seventh day of a child's life we have a celebration called *Woma* (which means "seventh") for family, friends and neighbors to come and admire the newborn. My parents had not held one for me because they could not afford the goat and rice needed to feed the guests, and my grandfather would not help them out because I was not a boy. When my brothers came along and *Baba* wanted to pay, my father refused, as he hadn't done this for me. But *Baba* was the only grandfather I had as my mother's father had died before I was born and we became close. My parents say I have qualities of both grandfathers—humorous and wise like my mother's father and vocal like my father's father! *Baba* had grown soft and white-bearded in his old age and I loved going to visit him in the village.

Whenever he saw me he would greet me with a song, as he was still concerned about the sad meaning of my name and wanted to lend some happiness to it: *"Malala Maiwand wala da. Pa tool jehan ke da khushala da,"* he sang. "Malala is of Maiwand and she's the happiest person in the whole world."

We always went to the village for the Eid holidays. We would dress in our finest clothes and pile into the Flying Coach, a minibus with brightly painted panels and jangling chains, and drive north to Barkana, our family village in Shangla. Eid happens twice a year—Eid ul-Fitr or "Small Eid" marks the end of the Ramadan fasting month, and Eid ul-Azha or "Big Eid" commemorates the Prophet Abraham's readiness to sacrifice his son Ismail to God. The dates of the feasts are announced by a special panel of clerics who watch for the appearance of the crescent moon. As soon as we heard the broadcast on the radio, we set off.

The night before we hardly slept because we were so excited. The journey usually took about five hours, as long as the road had not been washed away by rains or landslides, and the Flying Coach left early in the morning. We struggled to Mingora bus station, our bags laden with gifts for our family—embroidered shawls and boxes of rose and pistachio sweets as well as medicine they could not get in the village. Some people took sacks of sugar and flour, and most of the baggage was tied to the top of the bus in a towering pile. Then we crammed in, fighting over the window seats even though the panes were so encrusted with dirt it was hard to see out of them. The sides of Swat buses are painted with scenes of bright pink and yellow flowers, neon-orange tigers and snowy mountains. My brothers liked it if we got one with F-16 fighter jets or nuclear missiles, though my father said if our politicians hadn't spent so much money on building an atomic bomb we might have had enough for schools.

We drove out of the bazaar, past the grinning red mouth signs for dentists, the carts stacked with wooden cages crammed with beady-eyed white chickens with scarlet beaks, and jewelry stores with windows full of gold wedding bangles. The last few shops as we headed north out of Mingora were wooden shacks that seemed to lean on each other, in front of which were piles of reconditioned tires for the bad roads ahead. Then we were on the main road built by the last *wali*, which follows the wide Swat River on the left and hugs the cliffs to the right with their emerald mines. Overlooking the river were tourist restaurants with big glass windows we had never been to. On the road we passed dusty-faced children bent double with huge bundles of grass on their backs and men leading flocks of shaggy goats that wandered hither and thither.

As we drove on, the landscape changed to paddy fields of deep lush green that smelled so fresh and orchards of apricot and fig trees. Occasionally we passed small marble works over streams which ran milky white with the discharge of chemicals. This made my father cross. "Look at what these criminals are doing to pollute our beautiful valley," he always said. The road left the river and wound up through narrow passes over steep fir-clad heights, higher and higher, until our ears popped. On top of some of the peaks were ruins where vultures circled, the remains of forts built by the first *wali*. The bus strained and labored, the driver cursing as trucks overtook us on blind bends with steep drops below. My brothers loved this, and they would taunt me and my mother by pointing out the wreckage of vehicles on the mountainside.

Finally we made it up onto Sky Turn, the gateway to Shangla Top, a mountain pass which feels as if it's on top of the world. Up there we were higher than the rocky peaks all around us. In the far distance we could see the snows of Malam Jabba, our ski resort. By the roadside were fresh springs and waterfalls, and when we stopped for a break and to drink some tea, the air was clean and fragrant with cedar and pine. We breathed it into our lungs greedily. Shangla is all mountain, mountain, mountain, and just a small sky. After this the road winds back down for a while then follows the Ghwurban River and peters out into a rocky track. The only way to cross the river is by rope bridges or on a pulley system by which people swing themselves across in a metal box. The foreigners call them suicide bridges, but we loved them.

If you look at a map of Swat you'll see it is one long valley with little valleys we call *darae* off to the sides like the branches of a tree. Our village lies about halfway along on the east. It's in the Kana *dara,* which is enclosed by craggy mountain walls and so narrow there is not even room for a cricket ground. We call our village Shahpur, but really there is a necklace of three villages along the bottom of the valley—Shahpur, the biggest; Barkana, where my father grew up; and Karshat, which is where my mother lived. At either end is a huge mountain—Tor Ghar, the Black Mountain to the south, and Spin Ghar, the White Mountain to the north.

We usually stayed in Barkana at my grandfather's house, where my father grew up. Like almost all the houses in the area, it was flat-roofed and made of stone and mud. I preferred staying in Karshat with my cousins on my maternal side because they had a concrete house with a bathroom and there were lots of children to play with. My mother and I stayed in the women's quarters downstairs. The women spent their days looking after the children and preparing food to serve to the men in their *hujra* upstairs. I slept with my cousins Aneesa and Sumbul in a room which had a clock in the shape of a mosque and a cabinet on the wall containing a rifle and some packets of hair dye.

In the village the day started early and even I, who liked to sleep late, woke with the sound of cocks crowing and the clatter of dishes as the women prepared breakfast for the men. In the morning the sun reflected off the top of Tor Ghar; when we got up for the *fajr* prayers, the first of our five daily prayers, we would look left and see the golden peak of Spin Ghar lit with the first rays of the sun like a white lady wearing a *jumar tika*—a gold chain on her forehead.

Often rain would then come to wash everything clean, and the clouds would linger on the green terraces of the hills where people grew radishes and walnut trees. Dotted around were hives of bees. I loved the gloopy honey, which we ate with walnuts. Down on the river at the Karshat end were water buffaloes. There was also a shed with a wooden waterwheel providing power to turn huge millstones to grind wheat and maize into flour, which young boys would then pour into sacks. Next to that was a smaller shed containing a panel with a confusion of wires sprouting from it. The village received no electricity from the government, so many villagers got their power from these makeshift hydroelectric projects.

As the day went on and the sun climbed higher in the sky, more and more of the White Mountain would be bathed in golden sun. Then as evening came it fell in shadow as the sun moved up the Black Mountain. We timed our prayers by the shadow on the mountains. When the sun hit a certain rock, we used to say our *asr* or afternoon prayers. Then in the evening, when the white peak of Spin Ghar was even more beautiful than in the morning, we said the *makkam* or evening prayers. You could see the White Mountain from everywhere, and my father told me he used to think of it as a symbol of peace for our land, a white flag at the end of our valley. When he was a child he thought this small valley was the entire world and that if anyone went beyond the point where either mountain kissed the sky, they would fall off.

Though I had been born in a city, I shared my father's love of nature. I loved the rich soil, the greenness of the plants, the crops, the buffaloes and the yellow butterflies that fluttered about me as I walked. The village was very poor, but when we arrived our extended family would lay on a big feast. There would be bowls of chicken, rice, local spinach and spicy mutton, all cooked over the fire by the women, followed by plates of crunchy apples, slices of yellow cake and a big kettle of milky tea. None of the children had toys or books. The boys played cricket in a gully and even the ball was made from plastic bags tied together with elastic bands.

The village was a forgotten place. Water was carried from the spring. The few concrete houses had been built by families whose sons or fathers had gone south to work in the mines or to the

Gulf, from where they sent money home. There are forty million of us Pashtuns, of which ten million live outside our homeland. My father said it was sad that they could never return, as they needed to keep working to maintain their families' new lifestyle. There were many families with no men. They would visit only once a year, and usually a new baby would arrive nine months later.

Scattered up and down the hills there were houses made of wattle and daub, like my grandfather's, and these often collapsed when there were floods. Children sometimes froze to death in winter. There was no hospital. Only Shahpur had a clinic, and if anyone fell ill in the other villages they had to be carried there by their relatives on a wooden frame, which we jokingly called the Shangla Ambulance. If it was anything serious they would have to make the long bus journey to Mingora unless they were lucky enough to know someone with a car.

Usually politicians only visited during election time, promising roads, electricity, clean water and schools and giving money and generators to influential local people we called stakeholders, who would instruct their communities on how to vote. Of course this only applied to the men;

women in our area don't vote. Then they disappeared off to Islamabad if they were elected to the
National Assembly, or Peshawar for the Provincial
Assembly, and we'd hear no more of them or their
promises.

My cousins made fun of me for my city ways.
I did not like going barefoot. I read books and I
had a different accent and used slang expressions
from Mingora. My clothes were often from shops
and not homemade like theirs. My relatives
would ask me, "Would you like to cook chicken
for us?" and I'd say, "No, the chicken is innocent.
We should not kill her." They thought I was modern because I came from town. They did not
realize people from Islamabad or even Peshawar
would think me very backward.

Sometimes we went up to the mountains and
sometimes down to the river on family trips. It
was a big stream, too deep and fast to cross when
the snows melted in summer. The boys would
fish using earthworms threaded like beads on a
string hanging from a long stick. Some of them
whistled, believing this would attract the fish.
They weren't particularly tasty fish. Their mouths
were very rough and horny. We called them
chaqwartee. Sometimes a group of girls would go
down to the river for a picnic with pots of rice

and sherbet. Our favorite game was "weddings." We would get into two groups, each supposed to be a family, then each family would have to betroth a girl so we could perform a marriage ceremony. Everyone wanted me in their family, as I was from Mingora and modern. The most beautiful girl was Tanzela, and we often gave her to the other group so we could then have her as our bride.

The most important part of the mock wedding was jewelry. We took earrings, bangles and necklaces to decorate the bride, singing Bollywood songs as we worked. Then we would put makeup on her face that we'd taken from our mothers, dip her hands in hot limestone and soda to make them white, and paint her nails red with henna. Once she was ready, the bride would start crying and we would stroke her hair and try to convince her not to worry. "Marriage is part of life," we said. "Be kind to your mother-in-law and father-in-law so they treat you well. Take care of your husband and be happy."

Occasionally there would be real weddings with big feasts which went on for days and left the family bankrupt or in debt. The brides would wear exquisite clothes and be draped in gold, necklaces and bangles given by both sides of the family. I read that Benazir Bhutto insisted on wearing glass bangles at her wedding to set an example but the tradition of adorning the bride still continued. Sometimes a plywood coffin would be brought back from one of the mines. The women would gather at the house of the dead man's wife or mother and a terrible wailing would start and echo around the valley, which made my skin crawl.

At night the village was very dark with just oil lamps twinkling in houses on the hills. None of the older women had any education, but they all told stories and recited what we call *tapa*, Pashto couplets. My grandmother was particularly good at them. They were usually about love or being a Pashtun. "No Pashtun leaves his land of his own sweet will," she would say. "Either he leaves from poverty or he leaves for love." Our aunts scared us with ghost stories, like the one about Shalgwatay, the twenty-fingered man, who they warned would sleep in our beds. We would cry in terror, though in fact as "toe" and "finger" in Pashto are the same, we were all twenty-fingered, but we didn't realize. To make us wash, our aunts told stories about a scary woman called Shashaka, who would come after you with her muddy hands and stinking breath if you didn't take a bath or wash your hair, and turn you into a dirty woman with hair like rats' tails filled with insects. She might even kill you. In the winter when parents didn't want their children to stay outside in the snow they would tell the story about the lion or tiger which must always make the first step in the snow. Only when the lion or tiger has left their footprint were we allowed to go outside.

As we got older the village began to seem boring. The only television was in the *hujra* of one of the wealthier families, and no one had a computer.

Women in the village hid their faces whenever they left their purdah quarters and could not meet or speak to men who were not their close relatives. I wore more fashionable clothes and didn't cover my face even when I became a teenager. One of my male cousins was angry and asked my father, "Why isn't she covered?" He replied, "She's my daughter. Look after your own affairs." But some of the family thought people would gossip about us and say we were not properly following *Pashtunwali*.

I am very proud to be a Pashtun, but sometimes I think our code of conduct has a lot to answer for, particularly where the treatment of women is concerned. A woman named Shahida who worked for us and had three small daughters told me that when she was only ten years old her father had sold her to an old man who already had a wife but wanted a younger one. When girls disappeared it was not always because they had been married off. There was a beautiful fifteen-year-old girl called Seema. Everyone knew she was in love with a boy, and sometimes he would pass by and she would look at him from under her long dark lashes, which all the girls envied. In our society for a girl to flirt with any man brings shame on the family, though it's all right for the man. We were told she had committed suicide, but we later discovered her own family had poisoned her.

We have a custom called *swara* by which a girl can be given to another tribe to resolve a feud. It is officially banned but still continues. In our village there was a widow called Soraya who married a widower from another clan which had a feud with her family. Nobody can marry a widow without the permission of her family. When Soraya's family found out about the union they were furious. They threatened the widower's family until a *jirga* of village elders was called to resolve the dispute. The *jirga* decided that the widower's family should be punished by handing over their most beautiful girl to be married to the least eligible man of the rival clan. The boy was a good-for-nothing, so poor that the girl's father had to pay all their expenses. Why should a girl's life be ruined to settle a dispute she had nothing to do with?

When I complained about these things to my father he told me that life was harder for women in Afghanistan. The year before I was born a group called the Taliban led by a one-eyed mullah had taken over the country and was burning girls' schools. They were forcing men to grow beards as long as a lantern and women to wear burqas. Wearing a burqa is like walking inside big fabric shuttlecock with only a grille to see through and on hot days it's like an oven. At least I didn't have to wear one. He said that the Taliban had even banned women from laughing out loud or wearing white shoes, as white was "a color that belonged to men." Women were being locked up and beaten just for wearing nail varnish. I shivered when he told me such things.

I read my books like *Anna Karenina* and the novels of Jane Austen and trusted in my father's words: "Malala is free as a bird." When I heard stories of the atrocities in Afghanistan I felt proud to be in Swat. "Here a girl can go to school," I used to say. But the Taliban were right around the corner and were Pashtuns like us. For me the valley was a sunny place and I couldn't see the clouds gathering behind the mountains. My father used to say, "I will protect your freedom, Malala. Carry on with your dreams."

5

Why I Don't Wear Earrings and Pashtuns Don't Say Thank You

By the age of seven I was used to being top of my class. I was the one who would help other pupils who had difficulties. "Malala is a genius girl," my class fellows would say. I was also known for participating in everything—badminton, drama, cricket, art, even singing, though I wasn't much good. So when a new girl named Malka-e-Noor joined our class, I didn't think anything of it. Her name means "Queen of Light" and she said she wanted to be Pakistan's first female army chief. Her mother was a teacher at a different school, which was unusual, as none of our mothers worked. To begin with she didn't say much in class. The competition was always between me and my best friend Moniba, who had beautiful writing and presentation, which the examiners liked, but I knew I could beat her on content. So when we did the end-of-year exams and Malka-e-Noor came first, I was shocked. At home I cried and cried and had to be comforted by my mother.

Around that time we moved away from where we had been living on the same street as Moniba to an area where I didn't have any friends. On our new road there was a girl called Safina, who was a bit younger than me, and we started to play together. She was a pampered girl who had lots of dolls and a shoebox full of jewelry. But she kept eyeing up the pink plastic pretend mobile phone my father had bought me, which was one of the only toys I had. My father was always talking on his mobile so I loved to copy him and pretend to make calls on mine. One day it disappeared.

A few days later I saw Safina playing with a phone exactly the same as mine. "Where did you get that?" I asked. "I bought it in the bazaar," she said.

I realize now she could have been telling the truth but back then I thought, *She is doing this to me and I will do the same to her*. I used to go to her house to study, so whenever I was there I would pocket her things, mostly toy jewelry like earrings and necklaces. It was easy. At first stealing gave me a thrill, but that did not last long. Soon it became a compulsion. I did not know how to stop.

One afternoon I came home from school and rushed into the kitchen as usual for a snack. "Hello, *Bhabi!*" I called. "I'm starving!" There was silence. My mother was sitting on the floor pounding spices, brightly colored turmeric and cumin, filling the air with their aroma. Over and over she pounded. Her eyes would not meet mine. What had I done? I was very sad and went to my room. When I opened my cupboard, I saw that all the things I had taken were gone. I had been caught.

My cousin Reena came into my room. "They knew you were stealing," she said. "They were waiting for you to come clean, but you just kept on."

I felt a terrible sinking feeling in my stomach. I walked back to my mother with my head bowed. "What you did was wrong, Malala," she said. "Are you trying to bring shame on us that we can't afford to buy such things?"

"It's not true!" I lied. "I didn't take them."

But she knew I had. "Safina started it," I protested. "She took the pink phone that *Aba* bought me."

My mother was unmoved. "Safina is younger than you and you should have taught her better," she said. "You should have set an example."

I started crying and apologized over and over again. "Don't tell *Aba*," I begged. I couldn't bear for him to be disappointed in me. It's horrible to feel unworthy in the eyes of your parents.

It wasn't the first time. When I was little I went to the bazaar with my mother and spotted a pile of almonds on a cart. They looked so tasty that I couldn't resist grabbing a handful. My mother told me off and apologized to the cart owner. He was furious and would not be placated. We still had little money and my mother checked her purse to see what she had. "Can you sell them to me for ten rupees?" she asked. "No," he replied. "Almonds are very costly."

My mother was very upset and told my father. He immediately went and bought the whole lot from the man and put them in a glass dish.

"Almonds are good," he said. "If you eat them with milk just before bed it makes you brainy." But I knew he didn't have much money and the almonds in the dish were a reminder of my guilt. I promised myself I'd never do such a thing again. And now I had. My mother took me to say sorry to Safina and her parents. It was very hard. Safina said nothing about my phone, which didn't seem fair, but I didn't mention it either.

Though I felt bad, I was also relieved it was over.

Since that day I have never lied or stolen. Not a single lie nor a single penny, not even the coins my father leaves around the house, which we're allowed to buy snacks with. I also stopped wearing jewelry because I asked myself, *What are these baubles which tempt me? Why should I lose my character for a few metal trinkets?* But I still feel guilty, and to this day I say sorry to God in my prayers.

My mother and father tell each other everything, so *Aba* soon found out why I was so sad. I could see in his eyes that I had failed him. I wanted him to be proud of me, like he was when I was presented with the first-in-year trophies at school. Or the day our kindergarten teacher Miss Ulfat told him I had written "Only Speak in Urdu" on the blackboard for my classmates at the start of an Urdu lesson so we would learn the language faster.

My father consoled me by telling me about the mistakes great heroes made when they were children. He told me that Mahatma Gandhi said, "Freedom is not worth having if it does not include the freedom to make mistakes." At school we had read stories about Mohammad Ali Jinnah. As a boy in Karachi he would study by the glow of street lights because there was no light at home. He told other boys to stop playing marbles in the dust and to play cricket instead so their clothes and hands wouldn't get dirty. Outside his office my father had a framed copy of a letter written by Abraham Lincoln to his son's teacher, translated into Pashto. It is a very beautiful letter, full of good advice. "Teach him, if you can, the wonder of books...But also give him quiet time to ponder the eternal mystery of birds in the sky, bees in the sun, and the flowers on a green hillside," it says. "Teach him it is far more honorable to fail than to cheat."

I think everyone makes a mistake at least once in their life. The important thing is what you learn from it. That's why I have problems with our *Pashtunwali* code. We are supposed to take revenge for wrongs done to us, but where does that end? If a man in one family is killed or hurt by another man, revenge must be exacted to restore *nang*. It can be taken by killing any male member of the attacker's family. Then that family in turn must take revenge. And on and on it goes. There is no time limit. We have a saying: "The Pashtun took revenge after twenty years and another said it was taken too soon."

We are a people of many sayings. One is "The stone of Pashto does not rust in water," which means we neither forget nor forgive. That's also why we rarely say thank you, *manana*, because we believe a Pashtun will never forget a good deed and is bound to reciprocate at some point, just as he will a bad one. Kindness can only be repaid with kindness. It can't be repaid with expressions like "thank you."

Many families live in walled compounds with watchtowers so they can keep an eye out for their enemies. We knew many victims of feuds. One was Sher Zaman, a man who had been in my father's class and always got better grades than him. My grandfather and uncle used to drive my father mad, teasing him, "You're not as good as Sher Zaman," so much he once wished that rocks would come down the mountain and flatten him. But Sher Zaman did not go to college and ended up becoming a dispenser in the village pharmacy. His family became embroiled in a dispute with their cousins over a small plot of forest. One day, as Sher Zaman and two of his brothers were on their way to the land, they were ambushed by his uncle and some of his men. All three brothers were killed.

As a respected man in the community, my father was often called on to mediate feuds. He did not believe in *badal*—revenge—and would try to make people see that neither side had anything to gain from continuing the violence, and it would be better for them to get on with their lives. There were two families in our village he could not convince. They had been locked in a feud for so long no one even seemed to remember how it had started—probably some small slight, as we are a hot-headed people. First a brother on one side would attack an uncle on the other. Then vice versa. It consumed their lives.

Our people say it is a good system, and our crime rate is much lower than in non-Pashtun areas. But I think that if someone kills your brother, you shouldn't kill them or their brother, you should teach them instead. I am inspired by Khan Abdul Ghaffar Khan, the man who some call the Frontier Gandhi, who introduced a non-violent philosophy to our culture.

It's the same with stealing. Some people, like me, get caught and vow they will never do it again. Others say, "Oh it's no big deal—it was just a little thing." But the second time they will steal something bigger and the third something bigger still. In my country too many politicians think nothing of stealing. They are rich and we are a poor country yet they loot and loot. Most of them don't pay tax, but that's the least of it. They take out loans from state banks, but they don't pay them back. They get kickbacks on government contracts from friends or the companies they award them to. Many of them own expensive flats in London.

I don't know how they can live with their consciences when they see our people going hungry or sitting in the darkness of endless power cuts, or children unable to go to school, as their parents need them to work. My father says that Pakistan has been cursed with more than its fair share of politicians who only think about money. They don't care if the army is actually flying the plane, they are happy to stay out of the cockpit and sit in business class, close the curtains and enjoy the fine food and service while the rest of us are squashed in economy.

I had been born into a sort of democracy in which for ten years Benazir Bhutto and Nawaz Sharif kept replacing each other, none of their governments ever completing a term and always accusing each other of corruption. But two years after I was born the generals again took over. It happened in a manner so dramatic that it sounds like something out of a movie. Nawaz Sharif was prime minister at the time and had fallen out with his army chief General Pervez Musharraf and sacked him. At the time General Musharraf was on a plane of our national airline PIA coming back from Sri Lanka. Nawaz Sharif was so worried about his reaction that he tried to stop the plane from landing in Pakistan. He ordered Karachi airport to switch off its landing lights and to park fire engines on the runway to block the plane even though it had 200 other passengers on board and not enough fuel to get to another country. Within an hour of the announcement on television of Musharraf's sacking, tanks were on the streets and troops had taken over the newsrooms and the airports. The local commander, General Iftikhar, stormed the control tower at Karachi so that Musharraf's plane could land. Musharraf then seized power and threw Sharif into a dungeon in Attock Fort. Some people celebrated by handing out sweets as Sharif was unpopular, but my father cried when he heard the news. He had thought we were done with military dictatorships. Sharif was accused of treason and only saved by his friends in the Saudi royal family, who arranged his exile.

Musharraf was our fourth military ruler. Like all our dictators, he started by addressing the nation on TV, beginning, *Mere aziz hamwatano*— "My dear countrymen"—then went into a long tirade against Sharif, saying under him Pakistan had "lost our honor, dignity and respect." He vowed to end corruption and go after those "guilty of plundering and looting the national wealth." He promised he would make his own assets and tax return public. He said he would only run the country for a short time, but no one believed him. General Zia had promised to be in power for ninety days and had stayed more than eleven years until he was killed in an air crash.

It's the same old story, my father said, and he was right. Musharraf promised to end the old feudal system by which the same few dozen families controlled our entire country, and bring fresh young clean faces into politics. Instead his cabinet was made up of the very same old faces. Once again our country was expelled from the Commonwealth and became an international black sheep. The Americans had already suspended most aid the year before when we conducted nuclear tests, but now almost everyone boycotted us.

With such a history, you can see why the people of Swat did not always think it was a good idea to be part of Pakistan. Every few years Pakistan sent us a new deputy commissioner, or DC, to govern Swat, just as the British had done in colonial days. It seemed to us that these bureaucrats came to our province simply to get rich, then went back home. They had no interest in developing Swat. Our people are used to being subservient because under the *wali* no criticism was tolerated. If anyone offended him, their entire family could be expelled from Swat. So when the DCs came from Pakistan, they were the new kings and no one questioned them. Older people often looked back nostalgically to the days of the last *wali*. Back then, they said, the mountains were all still covered in trees, there were schools every five kilometers and the *wali* sahib would visit them in person to resolve problems.

After what happened with Safina, I vowed that I would never treat a friend badly again. My father always says it's important to treat friends well. When he was at college and had no money for food or books many of his friends helped him out and he never forgot that. I have three good friends—Safina from my area, Sumbul from the village and Moniba from school. Moniba had become my best friend in primary school when we lived near each other, and I persuaded her to come to our school. She is a wise girl, though we often fall out, particularly when we go on school trips. She comes from a large family with three sisters and four brothers. I think of her as my big sister even though I am six months older than her. Moniba sets down rules which I try to follow. We don't have secrets from each other and we don't share our secrets with anyone else. She doesn't like me talking to other girls and says we must be careful of associating with people who are badly behaved or have a reputation for trouble. She always says, "I have four brothers, and if I do even the slightest thing wrong they can stop me going to school."

I was so eager not to disappoint my parents that I ran errands for anyone. One day our neighbors asked me to buy some maize for them from the bazaar. On the way a boy on a bicycle crashed into me and my left shoulder hurt so much that my eyes watered. But I still went and bought the maize, took it to my neighbors and then went home. Only then did I cry. Shortly after that I found the perfect way to try to win back the respect of my father. Notices had gone up at school for a public speaking competition and Moniba and I both decided to enter. I remembered the story of my father surprising my grandfather and longed to do the same.

When we got the topic, I couldn't believe my eyes. It was "Honesty is the best policy."

The only practice we'd had was reading out poems at morning assembly, but there was an older girl at school called Fatima who was a very good speaker. She was beautiful and spoke in an animated way. She could speak confidently in front of hundreds of people and they would hang on her every word. Moniba and I longed to be like her and studied her carefully.

In our culture speeches are usually written by our fathers, uncles or teachers. They tend to be in English or Urdu, not in our native Pashto. We thought speaking in English meant you were more intelligent. We were wrong of course. It does not matter what language you choose, the important thing is the words you use to express yourself. Moniba's speech was written by one of her older brothers. She quoted beautiful poems by Allama Iqbal, our national poet. My father wrote my speech. In it he argued that if you want to do good, but do it in a bad way, that's still bad. In the same way, if you choose a good method to do something bad it's still bad. He ended it with Lincoln's words: "It is far more honorable to fail than to cheat."

On the day only eight or nine boys and girls turned up. Moniba spoke well—she was very composed and her speech was more emotional and poetic than mine, though mine might have had the better message. I was so nervous before the speech, I was trembling with fear. My grandfather had come to watch and I knew he really wanted me to win the competition, which made me even more nervous. I remembered what my father had said about taking a deep breath before starting, but then I saw that all eyes were on me and I rushed through. I kept losing my place as the pages danced in my shaking hands, but as I ended with Lincoln's words, I looked up at my father. He was smiling.

When the judges announced the results at the end, Moniba had won. I came second.

It didn't matter. Lincoln also wrote in the letter to his son's teacher, "Teach him how to gracefully lose." I was used to coming top of my class. But I realized that even if you win three or four times, the next victory will not necessarily be yours without trying—and also that sometimes it's better to tell your own story. I started writing my own speeches and changing the way I delivered them, from my heart rather than from a sheet of paper.

6

Children of the Rubbish Mountain

As the Khushal School started to attract more pupils, we moved again and finally had a television. My favorite program was *Shaka Laka Boom Boom,* an Indian children's series about a boy called Sanju who has a magic pencil. Everything he drew became real. If he drew a vegetable or a policeman, the vegetable or policeman would magically appear. If he accidentally drew a snake he could erase it and the snake would disappear. He used his pencil to help people—he even saved his parents from gangsters—and I wanted that magic pencil more than anything else in the world.

At night I would pray, "God, give me Sanju's pencil. I won't tell anyone. Just leave it in my cupboard. I will use it to make everyone happy." As soon as I finished praying, I would check the

111

drawer. The pencil was never there, but I knew who I would help first. Just along the street from our new house was an abandoned strip of land that people used as a rubbish dump—there is no rubbish collection in Swat. Quickly, it became a rubbish mountain. I didn't like walking near it, as it smelled so bad. Sometimes we would spot rats running through it and crows would circle over-head.

One day my brothers were not home and my mother had asked me to throw away some potato peel and eggshells. I wrinkled my nose as I approached, swatting away flies and making sure I didn't step on anything in my nice shoes. As I threw the rubbish on the mountain of rotting food, I saw something move and I jumped. It was a girl about my age. Her hair was matted and her skin was covered in sores. She looked like I imagined Shashaka, the dirty woman they told us about in tales in the village to make us wash. The girl had a big sack and was sorting rubbish into piles, one for cans, one for bottle tops, another for glass and another for paper. Nearby there were boys fishing in the pile for metal using magnets on strings. I wanted to talk to the children, but I was too scared.

That afternoon, when my father came home

from school, I told him about the scavenger children and begged him to go with me to look. He tried to talk to them, but they ran away. He explained that the children would sell what they had sorted to a garbage shop for a few rupees. The shop would then sell it on at a profit. On the way back home I noticed that he was in tears.

"*Aba,* you must give them free places at your school," I begged. He laughed. My mother and I had already persuaded him to give free places to a number of girls.

Though my mother was not educated, she was the practical one in the family, the doer while my father was the talker. She was always out helping people. My father would get angry sometimes— he would arrive home at lunchtime and call out, "Tor Pekai, I'm home!" only to find she was out and there was no lunch for him. Then he would find she was at the hospital visiting someone who was ill, or had gone to help a family, so he could not stay cross. Sometimes though she would be out because she was shopping for clothes in the Cheena Bazaar, and that would be a different matter.

Wherever we lived my mother filled our house with people. I shared my room with my cousin Aneesa from the village, who had come to live with us so she could go to school, and a girl called Shehnaz whose mother Sultana had once worked in our house. Shehnaz and her sister had also been sent out to collect garbage after their father had died leaving them very poor. One of her brothers was mentally ill and was always doing strange things like setting fire to their clothes or selling the electric fan we gave them to keep cool. Sultana was very short-tempered and my mother did not like having her in the house, but my father arranged a small allowance for her and a place for Shehnaz and her other brother at his school. Shehnaz had never been to school, so even though she was two years older than me she was put two classes below, and she came to live with us so that I could help her.

There was also Nooria, whose mother Kharoo did some of our washing and cleaning, and Alishpa, one of the daughters of Khalida, the woman who helped my mother with the cooking. Khalida had been sold into marriage to an old man who used to beat her, and eventually she ran away with her three daughters. Her own family would not take her back because it is believed that a woman who has left her husband has brought shame on her family. For a while her daughters also had to collect rubbish to survive. Her story was like something out of the novels I had started reading.

The school had expanded a lot by then and had three buildings—the original one in Landikas was a primary school, and then there was a high school for girls on Yahya Street and one for boys with a big garden of roses near the remains of the Buddhist temple. We had about 800 students in total, and although the school was not really making money, my father gave away more than a hundred free places. One of them was to a boy whose father, Sharafat Ali, had helped my father when he was a penniless college student. They were friends from the village. Sharafat Ali worked at the electricity company and he would give my father a few hundred rupees whenever he could spare them. My father was happy to be able to repay his kindness. Another was a girl in my class called Kausar, whose father embroidered clothes and shawls—a trade our region is famous for. When we went on school trips to visit the mountains, I knew she couldn't afford them, so I would pay for her with my pocket money.

Giving places to poor children didn't just mean my father lost their fees. Some of the richer parents took their children out of the school when they realized they were sharing classrooms with the sons and daughters of people who cleaned their houses or stitched their clothes. They thought it was shameful for their children to mix with those from poor families. My mother said it was hard for the poor children to learn when they were not getting enough food at home, so some of the girls would come to our house for breakfast. My father joked that our home had become a boarding-house.

Having so many people around made it hard to study. I had been delighted to have my own room, and my father had even bought me a dressing table to work on. But now I had two other girls in the room. "I want space!" I'd cry. But then I felt guilty, as I knew we were lucky. I thought back to the children working on the rubbish heap. I kept seeing the dirty face of the girl from the dump and continued to pester my father to give them places at our school.

He tried to explain that those children were breadwinners, so if they went to school, even for free, the whole family would go hungry. However, he got a wealthy philanthropist, Azaday Khan, to pay for him to produce a leaflet asking, *"Kia hasool e elum in bachun ka haq nahe?"*—"Is education not the right of these children?" My father printed thousands of these leaflets, left them at local meetings and distributed them around town.

By then my father was becoming a well known figure in Swat. Even though he was not a khan or a rich man, people listened to him. They knew he would have something interesting to say at workshops and seminars and wasn't afraid to criticize the authorities, even the army, which was now running our country. He was becoming known to the army too, and friends told him that the local commander had called him "lethal" in public. My father didn't know what exactly the brigadier meant, but in our country, where the army is so powerful, it did not bode well.

One of his pet hates was the "ghost schools." Influential people in remote areas took money from the government for schools which never saw a single pupil. Instead they used the buildings for their *hujras* or even to keep their animals. There was even a case of a man drawing a teacher's pension when he had never taught a day in his life. Aside from corruption and bad government, my father's main concern in those days was the environment. Mingora was expanding quickly— around 175,000 people now called it home— and our once-fresh air was becoming very polluted from all the vehicles and cooking fires. The beautiful trees on our hills and mountains were being chopped down for timber. My father said only around half the town's population had access to safe drinking water and most, like us, had no sanitation. So he and his friends set up something called the Global Peace Council which, despite its name, had very local concerns. The name was ironic and my father often laughed about it, but the organization's aim was serious: to preserve the environment of Swat and promote peace and education among local people.

My father also loved to write poetry, sometimes about love, but often on controversial themes such as honor killings and women's rights. Once he visited Afghanistan for a poetry festival at the Kabul Intercontinental Hotel, where he read a poem about peace. It was mentioned as the most inspiring in the closing speech, and some in the audience asked him to repeat whole stanzas and couplets, exclaiming *"Wah wah"* when a particular line pleased them, which is a bit like "Bravo." Even my grandfather was proud. "Son, may you be the star in the sky of knowledge," he used to say.

We too were proud, but his higher profile meant we didn't see him very much. It was always our mother who shopped for our clothes and took us to hospital if we were ill, even though in our culture, particularly for those of us from villages, a woman is not supposed to do these things alone. So one of my father's nephews would have to go along. When my father was at home, he and his friends sat on the roof at dusk and talked politics endlessly. There was really only one subject—9/11. It might have changed the whole world, but we were living right in the epicenter of everything. Osama bin Laden, the leader of al-Qaeda, had been living in Kandahar when the attack on the World Trade Center happened, and the Americans had sent thousands of troops to Afghanistan to catch him and overthrow the Taliban regime which had protected him.

In Pakistan we were still under a dictatorship, but America needed our help, just as it had in the 1980s to fight the Russians in Afghanistan. Just as the Russian invasion of Afghanistan had changed everything for General Zia, so 9/11 transformed General Musharraf from an international outcast. Suddenly he was being invited to the White House by George W. Bush and to 10 Downing Street by Tony Blair. There was a major problem, however. Our own intelligence service ISI had virtually created the Taliban. Many ISI officers were close to its leaders, having known them for years, and shared some of their beliefs. The ISI's Colonel Imam boasted he had trained 90,000 Taliban fighters and even became Pakistan's consul general in Herat during the Taliban regime.

We were not fans of the Taliban, as we had heard they destroyed girls' schools and blew up giant Buddha statues—we had many Buddhas of our own that we were proud of. But many Pashtuns did not like the bombing of Afghanistan or the way Pakistan was helping the Americans, even if it was only by allowing them to cross our airspace and stopping weapon supplies to the Taliban. We did not know then that Musharraf was also letting the Americans use our airfields.

Some of our religious people saw Osama bin Laden as a hero. In the bazaar you could buy posters of him on a white horse and boxes of sweets with his picture on them. These clerics said 9/11 was revenge on the Americans for what they had been doing to other people around the world, but they ignored the fact that the people in the World Trade Center were innocent and had nothing to do with American policy and that the Holy Quran clearly says it is wrong to kill. Our people see conspiracies behind everything, and many argued that the attack was actually carried out by Jews as an excuse for America to launch a war on the Muslim world. Some of our newspapers printed stories that no Jews went to work at the World Trade Center that day. My father said this was rubbish.

Musharraf told our people that he had no choice but to cooperate with the Americans. He said they had told him "Either you are with us, or you are with the terrorists," and threatened to "bomb us back to the Stone Age" if we stood against them. But we weren't exactly cooperating, as the ISI was still arming Taliban fighters and giving their leaders sanctuary in Quetta. They even persuaded the Americans to let them fly hundreds of Pakistani fighters out of northern Afghanistan. The ISI chief asked the Americans to hold off their attack on Afghanistan until he had gone to Kandahar to ask the Taliban leader Mullah Omar to hand over bin Laden; instead he offered the Taliban help.

In our province Maulana Sufi Mohammad, who had fought in Afghanistan against the Russians, issued a fatwa against the US. He held a big meeting in Malakand, where our ancestors had fought the British. The Pakistani government didn't stop him. The governor of our province issued a statement that anyone who wanted to fight in Afghanistan against NATO forces was free to do so. Some 12,000 young men from Swat went to help the Taliban. Many never came back. They were most likely killed, but as there is no proof of death, their wives can't be declared widows. It's very hard on them. My father's close friend Wahid Zaman's brother and brother-in-law were among the many who went to Afghanistan. Their wives and children are still waiting for them. I remember visiting them and feeling their longing. Even so, it all seemed far far away from our peaceful garden valley. Afghanistan is less than a hundred miles away, but to get there you have to go through Bajaur, one of the tribal areas between Pakistan and the border with Afganistan.

Bin Laden and his men fled to the White Mountains of Tora Bora in eastern Afghanistan, where he had built a network of tunnels while fighting the Russians. They escaped through these and over the mountains into Kurram, another tribal agency. What we didn't know then was that bin Laden came to Swat and stayed in a remote village for a year, taking advantage of the *Pashtunwali* hospitality code.

Anyone could see that Musharraf was double-dealing, taking American money while still helping the jihadis—"strategic assets," as the ISI calls them. The Americans say they gave Pakistan billions of dollars to help their campaign against al-Qaeda, but we didn't see a single cent. Musharraf built a mansion by Rawal Lake in Islamabad and bought an apartment in London. Every so often an important American official would complain that we weren't doing enough and then suddenly some big fish would be caught. Khalid Sheikh Mohammad, the mastermind of 9/11, was found in a house just a mile from the army chief's official residence in Rawalpindi. But President Bush kept praising Musharraf, inviting him to Washington and calling him his buddy. My father and his friends were disgusted. They said the Americans always preferred dealing with dictators in Pakistan.

From an early age I was interested in politics and sat on my father's knee listening to everything he and his friends discussed. But I was more concerned with matters closer to home—our own street to be exact. I told my friends at school about the rubbish-dump children and that we should help. Not everyone wanted to, as they said the children were dirty and probably diseased, and their parents would not like them going to school with children like that. They also said it wasn't up to us to sort out the problem. I didn't agree. "We can sit by and hope the government will help, but they won't. If I can help support one or two children and another family supports one or two, then between us we can help them all."

I knew it was pointless appealing to Musharraf. In my experience, if my father couldn't help with matters like these, there was only one option. I wrote a letter to God. "Dear God," I wrote, "I know you see everything, but there are so many things that maybe, sometimes, things get missed, particularly now with the bombing in Afghanistan. But I don't think you would be happy if you saw the children on my road living on a rubbish dump. God, give me strength and courage and make me perfect because I want to make this world perfect. Malala."

The problem was I did not know how to get it to him. Somehow I thought it needed to go deep into the earth, so first I buried it in the garden. Then I thought it would get spoiled, so I put it in a plastic bag. But that didn't seem much use. We like to put sacred texts in flowing waters, so I rolled it up, tied it to a piece of wood, placed a dandelion on top, and floated it in the stream which flows into the Swat River. Surely God would find it there.

7

The Mufti Who Tried to Close Our School

Just in front of the school on Khushal Street, where I was born, was the house of a tall handsome mullah and his family. His name was Ghulamullah and he called himself a *mufti,* which means he is an Islamic scholar and authority on Islamic law, though my father complains that anyone with a turban can call himself a *maulana* or *mufti.* The school was doing well, and my father was building an impressive reception area with an arched entrance in the boys' high school. For the first time my mother could buy nice clothes and even send out for food as she had dreamed of doing back in the village. But all this time the *mufti* was watching. He watched the girls going in and out of our school every day and became angry, particularly as some of the girls were teenagers. "That *maulana* has a bad eye on us," said my father one day. He was right.

Shortly afterward the *mufti* went to the woman who owned the school premises and said, "Ziauddin is running a *haram* school in your building and bringing shame on the *mohalla* [neighborhood]. These girls should be in purdah." He told her, "Take this building back from him and I will rent it for my madrasa. If you do this you will get paid now and also receive a reward in the next world."

She refused and her son came to my father in secret. "This *maulana* is starting a campaign against you," he warned. "We won't give him the building but be careful."

My father was angry. "Just as we say, *'Nim hakim khatrai jan'*—'Half a doctor is a danger to one's life,' so, *'Nim mullah khatrai iman'*—'A mullah who is not fully learned is a danger to faith,'" he said.

I am proud that our country was created as the world's first Muslim homeland, but we still don't agree on what this means. The Quran teaches us *sabar*—patience—but often it feels that we have forgotten the word and think Islam means women sitting at home in purdah or wearing burqas while men do jihad. We have many strands of Islam in Pakistan. Our founder Jinnah wanted the rights of Muslims in India to be recognized, but the majority of people in India were Hindu. It was as if there were a feud between two brothers and they agreed to live in different houses. So British India was divided in August 1947, and an independent Muslim state was born. It could hardly have been a bloodier beginning. Millions of Muslims crossed from India, and Hindus traveled in the other direction. Almost two million of them were killed trying to cross the new border. Many were slaughtered on trains which arrived at Lahore and Delhi full of bloodied corpses. My own grandfather narrowly escaped death in the riots when his train was attacked by Hindus on his way home from Delhi, where he had been studying. Now we are a country of 180 million and more than 96 percent are Muslim. We also have around two million Christians and more than two million Ahmadis, who say they are Muslims though our government says they are not. Sadly those minority communities are often attacked.

Jinnah had lived in London as a young man and trained as a barrister. He wanted a land of tolerance. Our people often quote the famous speech he made a few days before independence: "You are free to go to your temples, you are free to go to your mosques or to any other place of worship in this State of Pakistan. You may belong to any religion or caste or creed—that has nothing to do with the business of the state." My father says the problem is that Jinnah negotiated a piece of real estate for us but not a state. He died of tuberculosis just a year after the creation of Pakistan and we haven't stopped fighting since. We have had three wars against India and what seems like endless killing inside our own country.

We Muslims are split between Sunnis and Shias—we share the same fundamental beliefs and the same Holy Quran, but we disagree over who was the right person to lead our religion when the Prophet, PBUH, died in the seventh century. The man chosen to be the leader or caliph was Abu Bakr, a close friend and adviser of the Prophet, PBUH, and the man he chose to lead prayers as he lay on his deathbed. "Sunni" comes from the Arabic for "one who follows the traditions of the Prophet, PBUH." But a smaller group believed that leadership should have stayed within the family of the Prophet, PBUH, and that Ali, his son-in-law and cousin, should have taken over. They became known as Shias, shortened from Shia-t-Ali, the Party of Ali.

Every year Shias commemorate the killing of

the grandson of the Prophet, PBUH, Hussein Ibn Ali at the battle of Karbala in the year 680 with a festival called Muharram. They whip themselves into a bloody frenzy with metal chains or razor blades on strings until the streets run red. One of my father's friends is a Shia and he cries whenever he talks about Hussein's death at Karbala. He gets so emotional you would think the events had happened just the night before, not more than 1,300 years ago. Our own founder, Jinnah, was a Shia, and Benazir Bhutto's mother was also a Shia from Iran.

Most Pakistanis are Sunnis like us—more than 80 percent—but within that we are again many groups. By far the biggest group is the Barelvis, who are named after a nineteenth-century madrasa in Bareilly, which lies in the Indian state of Uttar Pradesh. Then we have the Deobandi, named after another famous nineteenth-century madrasa in Uttar Pradesh, this time in the village of Deoband. They are very conservative and most of our madrasas are Deobandi. We also have the Ahl-e-Hadith (people of the Hadith), who are Salafists. This group is more Arab-influenced and even more conservative than the others. They are what the West calls fundamentalists. They don't accept our saints and shrines—many Pakistanis are also mystical people and gather at Sufi shrines to dance and worship. Each of these strands has many different sub-groups.

The *mufti* on Khushal Street was a member of Tablighi Jamaat, a Deobandi group that holds a huge rally every year at its headquarters in Raiwind, near Lahore, attended by millions of people. Our last dictator General Zia used to go there, and in the 1980s, under his regime, the Tablighis became very powerful. Many of the imams appointed to preach in army barracks were Tablighis and army officers would often take leave and go on preaching tours for the group.

One night, after the *mufti* had failed to persuade our landlady to cancel our lease, he gathered some of the influential people and elders of our *mohalla* into a delegation and turned up at our door. There were seven people—some other senior Tablighis, a mosque keeper, a former jihadi and a shopkeeper—and they filled our small house.

My father seemed worried and shooed us into the other room, but the house was small, so we could hear every word. "I am representing the Ulema and Tablighian and Taliban," Mullah Ghulamullah said, referring to not just one but two organizations of Muslim scholars to give himself gravitas. "I am representing good Muslims and we all think your girls' school is *haram* and a blasphemy. You should close it. Girls should not be going to school," he continued. "A girl is so sacred she should be in purdah, and so private that there is no lady's name in the Quran, as God doesn't want her to be named."

My father could listen no more. "Maryam is mentioned everywhere in the Quran. Was she not a woman and a good woman at that?"

"No," said the mullah. "She is only there to prove that Isa [Jesus] was the son of Maryam, not the son of God!"

"That may be," replied my father. "But I am pointing out that the Quran names Maryam."

The *mufti* started to object, but my father had had enough. Turning to the group, he said, "When this gentleman passes me on the street, I look to him and greet him, but he doesn't answer, he just bows his head."

The mullah looked down, embarrassed, because greeting someone properly is important in Islam. "You run the *haram* school," he said. "That's why I don't want to greet you."

Then one of the other men spoke up. "I'd heard you were an infidel," he said to my father, "but there are Qurans in your room."

"Of course there are!" replied my father, astonished that his faith would be questioned. "I am a Muslim."

"Let's get back to the subject of the school," said the *mufti,* who could see the discussion was not going his way. "There are men in the reception area of the school, and they see the girls enter, and this is very bad."

"I have a solution," said my father. "The school has another gate. The girls will enter through that."

The *mufti* clearly wasn't happy, as he wanted the school closed altogether. But the elders were happy with this compromise and they left.

My father suspected this would not be the end of the matter. What we knew and they didn't was that the *mufti's* own niece attended the school in secret. So a few days later my father called the *mufti's* elder brother, the girl's father.

"I am very tired of your brother," he said. "What kind of *mufti* is he? He's driving us crazy. Can you help to get him off our backs?"

"I'm afraid I can't help you, Ziauddin," he replied. "I have trouble in my home too. He lives with us and has told his wife that she must observe purdah from us and that our wives must observe purdah from him all in this small space.

Our wives are like sisters to him and his is like a sister to us, but this madman has made our house a hell. I am sorry but I can't help you."

My father was right to think this man was not going to give up—mullahs had become more powerful figures since Zia's rule and campaign of Islamization.

In some ways General Musharraf was very different from General Zia. Though he usually dressed in uniform, he occasionally wore Western suits and he called himself chief executive instead of chief martial law administrator. He also kept dogs, which we Muslims regard as unclean. Instead of Zia's Islamization he began what he called enlightened moderation. He opened up our media, allowing new private TV channels and female newsreaders, as well as showing dancing on television. The celebration of Western holidays such as Valentine's Day and New Year's Eve was allowed. He even sanctioned an annual pop concert on the eve of Independence Day, which was broadcast to the nation. He did something which our democratic rulers hadn't, even Benazir, and abolished the law that stated that for a woman to prove she was raped, she had to produce four male witnesses. He appointed the first woman governor of the state bank and the first women airline pilots and coastguards. He even announced we would have female guards at Jinnah's tomb in Karachi.

However, in our Pashtun homeland of the North West Frontier Province things were very different. In 2002 Musharraf held elections for "controlled democracy." They were strange elections, as the main party leaders Nawaz Sharif and Benazir were in exile. In our province these elections brought what we called a "mullah government" to power. The Muttahida Majlis e-Amal (MMA) alliance was a group of five religious parties including the Jamiat Ulema-e-Islam (JUI), which ran the madrasas where the Taliban were trained. People jokingly referred to the MMA as the Mullah Military Alliance and said they got elected because they had Musharraf's support. But some people supported them because the very religious Pashtuns were angry at the American invasion of Afghanistan and the removal of the Taliban from power there.

Our area had always been more conservative than most of the rest of Pakistan. During the Afghan jihad many madrasas had been built, most of them funded by Saudi money, and many young men had passed through them, as it was free education. That was the start of what my father calls the "Arabization" of Pakistan. Then 9/11 had made this militancy more mainstream. Sometimes when I walked along the main road I saw chalked messages on the sides of buildings. CONTACT US FOR JIHAD TRAINING, they would say, listing a phone number to call. In those days jihadi groups were free to do whatever they wanted. You could see them openly collecting contributions and recruiting men. There was even a headmaster from Shangla who would boast that his greatest success was to send ten boys in Grade 9 for jihad training in Kashmir.

The MMA government banned CD and DVD shops and wanted to create a morality police like the Afghan Taliban had set up. The idea was they would be able to stop a woman accompanied by a man and require her to prove that the man was her relative. Thankfully, our supreme court stopped this. Then MMA activists launched attacks on cinemas and tore down billboards with pictures of women or blacked them out with paint. They even snatched female mannequins from clothing shops. They harassed men wearing Western-style shirts and trousers instead of the traditional shalwar kamiz and insisted women cover their heads. It was as though they wanted to re-move all traces of womankind from public life.

My father's high school opened in 2003. That first year they had boys and girls together, but by 2004 the climate had changed so it was unthink-able to have girls and boys in the same class. That changing climate made Ghulamullah bold. One of the school clerks told my father that the *mufti* kept coming into school and demanding to know why we girls were still using the main entrance. He said that one day, when a male member of staff took a female teacher out to the main road to get a rickshaw, the *maulana* asked, "Why did this man escort her to the road, is he her brother?"

"No," replied the clerk, "he is a colleague."

"That is wrong!" said the *maulana*.

My father told the clerk to call him next time he saw the *maulana*. When the call came, my fa-ther and the Islamic studies teacher went out to confront him.

"Maulana, you have driven me to the wall!" my father said. "Who are you? You are crazy! You need to go to a doctor. You think I enter the school and take my clothes off? When you see a boy and a girl you see a scandal. They are schoolchildren. I think you should go and see Dr. Haider Ali!"

Dr. Haider Ali was a well-known psychiatrist in our area, so to say, "Shall we take you to Dr. Haider Ali?" meant "Are you mad?

The *mufti* went quiet. He took off his turban and put it in my father's lap. For us a turban is a public symbol of chivalry and Pashtun-ness, and for a man to lose his turban is considered a great humiliation. But then he started up again. "I never said those things to your clerk. He is lying."

My father had had enough. "You have no business here," he shouted. "Go away!"

The *mufti* had failed to close our school, but his interference was an indication of how our country was changing. My father was worried. He and his fellow activists were holding endless meetings. These were no longer just about stopping people cutting down trees but also about education and democracy.

In 2004, after resisting pressure from Washington for more than two and a half years, General Musharraf sent the army into the Federally Administered Tribal Areas (FATA), seven agencies that lie along the border with Afghanistan, where the government had little control. The Americans claimed that al-Qaeda militants who had fled from Afghanistan during the US bombing were using the areas as a safe haven, taking advantage of our Pashtun hospitality. From there they were running training camps and launching raids across the border on NATO troops. For us in Swat this was very close to home. One of the agencies, Bajaur, is next to Swat. The people who live in the FATA are all from Pashtun tribes like us Yousafzai, and live on both sides of the border with Afghanistan.

The tribal agencies were created in British times as a buffer zone between Afghanistan and what was then India, and they are still run in the same way, administered by tribal chiefs or elders known as maliks. Unfortunately, the maliks make little difference. In truth the tribal areas are not governed at all. They are forgotten places of harsh rocky valleys where people scrape by on smuggling. (The average annual income is just $250— half the Pakistani average.) They have very few hospitals and schools, particularly for girls, and political parties were not allowed there until recently. Hardly any women from these areas can read. The people are renowned for their fierceness and independence, as you can see if you read any of the old British accounts.

Our army had never before gone into the FATA. Instead they had maintained indirect control in the same way the British had, relying on the Pashtun-recruited Frontier Corps rather than regular soldiers. Sending in the regular army was a tough decision. Not only did our army and ISI have long links with some of the militants, but it also meant our troops would be fighting their own Pashtun brothers. The first tribal area that the army entered was South Waziristan, in March 2004. Predictably the local people saw it as an attack on their way of life. All the men there carry weapons and hundreds of soldiers were killed when the locals revolted.

The army was in shock. Some men refused to fight, not wishing to battle their own people. They retreated after just twelve days and reached what they called a "negotiated peace settlement" with local militant leaders like Nek Mohammad. This involved the army bribing them to halt all attacks and keep out foreign fighters. The militants simply used the cash to buy more weapons and resumed their activities. A few months later came the first attack on Pakistan by a US drone.

On 17 June 2004 an unmanned Predator dropped a Hellfire missile on Nek Mohammad in South Waziristan, apparently while he was giving an interview by satellite phone. He and the men around him were killed instantly. Local people had no idea what it was—back then we did not know that the Americans could do such a thing. Whatever you thought about Nek Mohammad, we were not at war with the Americans and were shocked that they would launch attacks from the sky on our soil. Across the tribal areas people were angry and many joined militant groups or formed *lashkars,* local militias.

Then there were more attacks. The Americans said that bin Laden's deputy Ayman al-Zawahiri was hiding in Bajaur and had taken a wife there. In January 2006 a drone supposedly targeting him landed on a village called Damadola, destroying three houses and killing eighteen people. The Americans said he had been tipped off and escaped. That same year, on 30 October, another US Predator hit a madrasa on a hill near the main town of Khar, killing eighty-two people, many of them young boys. The Americans said it was the al-Qaeda training camp which had featured in the group's videos and that the hill was riddled with tunnels and gun emplacements. Within a few hours of the attack, an influential local cleric called Faqir Mohammad, who had run the madrasa, announced that the deaths would be avenged by suicide bombings against Pakistani soldiers.

My father and his friends were worried and called together local elders and leaders for a peace conference. It was a bitterly cold night in January, but 150 people gathered.

"It's coming here," my father warned. "The fire is reaching the valley. Let's put out the flames of militancy before they reach here."

But no one would listen. Some people even laughed, including a local political leader sitting in the front row.

"Mr. Khan," my father said to him, "you know what happened to the people of Afghanistan. They are now refugees and they're living with us. The same is happening with Bajaur. The same will happen to us, mark my words, and we will have no shelter, no place to migrate to."

But the expression on the man's face was mocking. "Look at this man," he seemed to be saying of my father. "I am a khan. Who would dare kick me out of this area?"

My father came home frustrated. "I have a school, but I am neither a khan nor a political leader. I have no platform," he said. "I am only one small man."

8

The Autumn of the Earthquake

One fine October day when I was still in primary school our desks started to tremble and shake. Our classes were still mixed at that age, and all the boys and girls yelled, "Earthquake!" We ran outside as we had been taught to do. All the children gathered around our teachers as chicks swarm to a mother hen.

Swat lies on a geological fault line and we often had earthquakes, but this felt different. All the buildings around us seemed to be shaking and the rumbling didn't stop. Most of us were crying and our teachers were praying. Miss Rubi, one of my favorite teachers, told us to stop crying and to stay calm; it would soon be over.

Once the shaking had stopped we were all sent home. We found our mother sitting in a chair holding the Quran, reciting verses over and over.

Whenever there is trouble people pray a lot. She was relieved to see us and hugged us, tears streaming down her face. But the aftershocks kept coming all afternoon, so we remained very scared.

We had moved again—we would move seven times by the time I was thirteen—and were living in an apartment building. It was high for Mingora, two stories with a big water tank on the roof. My mother was terrified it would collapse on top of us, so we kept going outside. My father did not get home till late that evening, as he had been busy checking all the other school buildings.

When nightfall came, there were still tremors and my mother was in a state of panic. Every time we felt a tremor we thought it was the Day of Judgment. "We will be buried in our beds!" she cried. She insisted we leave, but my father was exhausted and we Muslims believe our fate is written by God. So he put me and my brothers Khushal and Atal, then just a baby, to bed.

"Go wherever you want," he told my mother and cousin. "I am staying here. If you believe in God you will stay here." I think when there is a great disaster or our lives are in danger we remember our sins and wonder how we will meet God and whether we will be forgiven. But God has also given us the power to forget, so that when the tragedy is over we carry on as normal. I trusted in my father's faith, but I also shared my mother's very real concerns.

That earthquake of 8 October 2005 turned out to be one of the worst in history. It was 7.6 on the Richter Scale and was felt as far away as Kabul and Delhi. Our town of Mingora was largely spared—just a few buildings collapsed— but neighboring Kashmir and the northern areas of Pakistan were devastated. Even in Islamabad buildings collapsed.

It took a while for us to realize how bad it was. When the TV news began to show the devastation we saw that entire villages had been turned to dust. Landslides blocked access to the worst affected parts and all the phones and power lines were down. The earthquake had affected 30,000 square kilometers, an area as big as the American state of Connecticut. The numbers were unbelievable. More than 73,000 people had been killed and 128,000 injured, many of them crippled for life. Around three and a half million people had lost their homes. Roads, bridges, water and power had all gone. Places we had visited like Balakot were almost completely destroyed. Many of those killed were children who like me had been at school that morning. Some 6,400 schools were turned to rubble and 18,000 children lost their lives.

We remembered how scared we had been that morning and started raising money at school. Everyone brought what they could. My father went to everybody he knew, asking for donations of food, clothing and money, and I helped my mother collect blankets. My father raised money from the Swat Association of Private Schools and the Global Peace Council to add to what we had collected at school. The total came to more than one million rupees. A publishing company in Lahore which supplied our schoolbooks sent five trucks of food and other essentials.

We were terribly worried about our family in Shangla, jammed between those narrow mountains. Finally we got news from a cousin. In my father's small village eight people had been killed and many homes destroyed. One of them was the house of the local cleric, Maulana Khadim, which fell down, crushing his four beautiful daughters. I wanted to go to Shangla with my father and the trucks, but he told me it would be too dangerous.

When he returned a few days later he was ashen. He told us that the last part of the journey had been very difficult. Much of the road had collapsed into the river and large boulders had fallen and blocked the way. Our family and friends said they had thought it was the end of the world. They described the roar of rocks sliding down hills and everyone running out of their houses reciting the Quran, the screams as roofs crashed down and the howls of the buffaloes and goats. As the tremors continued they had spent the entire day outdoors and then the night too, huddling together for warmth, even though it was bitterly cold in the mountains.

To start with the only rescue workers who came were a few from a locally based foreign aid agency and volunteers from the Tehrik-e-Nifaz-e-Sharia-e-Mohammadi (TNSM) or Movement for the Enforcement of Islamic Law, the group founded by Sufi Mohammad that had sent men to fight in Afghanistan. Sufi Mohammad had been in jail since 2002 when Musharraf arrested a number of militant leaders after American pressure, but his organization still continued and was being run by his son-in-law Maulana Fazlullah. It was hard for the authorities to reach places like Shangla be-cause most of the roads and bridges had gone and local government had been wiped out throughout the region. We saw an official from the United Nations say on television that it was the "worst lo-gistical nightmare that the UN had ever faced."

General Musharraf called it a "test of the nation" and announced that the army had set up Operation Lifeline—our army likes giving their operations names. There were lots of pictures on the news of army helicopters laden with supplies and tents, but in many of the small valleys the helicopters could not land and the aid packages they dropped often rolled down slopes into rivers. In some places, when the helicopters flew in the locals all rushed underneath them, which meant they could not drop supplies safely.

But some aid did get in. The Americans were quick, as they had thousands of troops and hundreds of helicopters in Afghanistan and could easily fly in supplies and show they were helping us in our hour of need, though some crews covered the American markings on their helicopters, fearing attack. For many in the remote areas it was the first time they had seen a foreigner.

Most of the volunteers came from Islamic charities or organizations, but some of these were fronts for militant groups. The most visible of all was Jamaat-ul-Dawa (JuD), the welfare wing of Lashkar-e-Taiba. LeT had close links to the ISI and was set up to liberate Kashmir, which we believe should be part of Pakistan, not India, as its population is mostly Muslim. The leader of LeT is a fiery professor from Lahore called Hafiz Saeed, who is often on television calling on people to attack India. When the earthquake happened and our government did little to help, JuD set up relief camps patrolled by men with Kalashnikovs and walkie-talkies. Everyone knows these men belonged to LeT, and soon their black and white banners with crossed swords were flying everywhere in the mountains and valleys. In the town of Muzaffarabad in Azad Kashmir the JuD even set up a large field hospital with X-ray machines, an operating room, a well-stocked pharmacy and a dental department. Doctors and surgeons offered their services along with thousands of young volunteers.

Earthquake victims praised the activists who had trudged up and down mountains and through shattered valleys carrying medical help to remote regions no one else had bothered with. They helped clear and rebuild destroyed villages as well as leading prayers and burying bodies. Even today, when most of the foreign aid agencies have gone, shattered buildings still line the roadside and people are still waiting for compensation from the government to build new houses, the JuD banners and helpers are still present. My cousin who was studying in the UK said they raised lots of money from Pakistanis living there. People later said that some of this money had been diverted to finance a plot to bomb planes traveling from Britain to the US.

With such a large number of people killed, there were many children orphaned—11,000 of them. In our culture orphans are usually taken in by the extended family, but the earthquake was so bad that entire families had been wiped out or lost everything and were in no position to take in children. The government promised they would all be looked after by the state, but that felt as empty as most government promises. My father heard that many of the boys were taken in by the JuD and housed in their madrasas. In Pakistan, madrasas are a kind of welfare system, as they give free food and lodging, but their teaching does not follow a normal curriculum. The boys learn the Quran by heart, rocking back and forth as they recite. They learn that there is no such thing as science or literature, that dinosaurs never existed and man never went to the moon.

The whole nation was in shock for a long time after the earthquake. Already so unlucky with our politicians and military dictators, now, on top of everything else, we had to deal with a natural disaster. Mullahs from the TNSM preached that the earthquake was a warning from God. If we did not mend our ways and introduce *shariat* or Islamic law, they shouted in their thundering voices, more severe punishment would come.

Part Two

The Valley of Death

 رباب منگیه وخت د تېر شو   د کلي خوا ته طالبان راغلي دینه

Rabab mangia wakht de teer sho
  Da kali khwa ta Talibaan raaghali dena

Farewell Music! Even your sweetest tunes are best
  kept silent
The Taliban on the edge of the village have stilled
  all lips

As a baby.

With my brother Khushal in Mingora.

My father's friend Hidayatullah holding me outside our first school building.

My maternal grandfather, Malik Janser Khan, in Shangla.

My father's childhood home.

My paternal grandfather, Baba, with me and Khushal
in our house in Mingora.

Reading with my brother Khushal.

With Khushal, enjoying the waterfall in Shangla.

A school picnic.

Assembly prayers at Khushal School. *(Copyright © Justin Sutcliffe, 2013)*

At the beginning, people gave lots of money to Fazlullah.

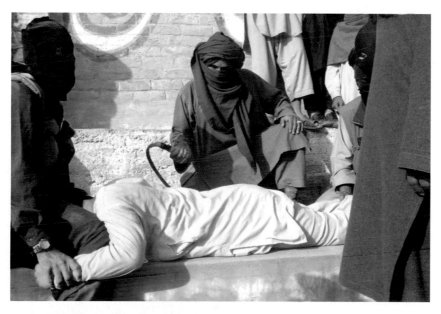

The Taliban publicly whipped people.

Making a speech to honor the people killed in the Haji Baba suicide attack.

Performing in a play at school.

Painting at school.

A picture I painted when I was twelve, just after we came back to Swat from being IDPs. It shows the dream of interfaith harmony.

In our garden in Mingora, building a snowman with Atal.

Visiting Spal Bandi, where my father stayed while he studied.

story - All that glitters is not gold.

stag was once drinking water at a pool.
w his own reflection in the clear water. He
his beautiful horns, but did not like his lean
legs. Suddenly he saw a pack of ____ ds running.
nto the jungle to save his life. Hi ____ on carried
r from hounds, but his ____ s wer ____ bushes.
is efforts, he could not free ____ mself. ____ hounds
d of him, he recognised that hi ____ ly ____ at help
beautiful horns were the cause o ____
All that glitters is not gold.

At school reading a story: "All That Glitters Is Not Gold."

9

Radio Mullah

I was ten when the Taliban came to our valley. Moniba and I had been reading the Twilight books and longed to be vampires. It seemed to us that the Taliban arrived in the night just like vampires. They appeared in groups, armed with knives and Kalashnikovs, and first emerged in Upper Swat, in the hilly areas of Matta. They didn't call themselves Taliban to start with and didn't look like the Afghan Taliban we'd seen in pictures with their turbans and black-rimmed eyes.

These were strange-looking men with long straggly hair and beards and camouflage vests over their shalwar kamiz, which they wore with the trousers well above the ankle. They had jogging shoes or cheap plastic sandals on their feet, and sometimes stockings over their heads with holes for their eyes, and they blew their noses dirtily into the ends of their turbans. They wore black badges which said SHARIAT YA SHAHADAT— SHARIA LAW OR MARTYRDOM—and sometimes black turbans, so people called them Tor Patki or the Black-Turbaned Brigade. They looked so dark and dirty that my father's friend described them as "people deprived of baths and barbers."

Their leader was Maulana Fazlullah, a 28-year-old who used to operate the pulley chair to cross the Swat River and whose right leg dragged because of childhood polio. He had studied in the madrasa of Maulana Sufi Mohammad, the founder of the TNSM, and married his daughter. When Sufi Mohammad was imprisoned in a round-up of militant leaders in 2002, Fazlullah had taken over the movement's leadership. It was shortly before the earthquake that Fazlullah had appeared in Imam Deri, a small village just a few miles outside Mingora on the other side of the Swat River, and set up his illegal radio station.

In our valley we received most of our information from the radio because so many had no TV or were illiterate. Soon everyone seemed to be talking about the radio station. It became known as Mullah FM, and Fazlullah as the Radio Mullah. It broadcast every night from eight to ten and again in the morning from seven to nine.

In the beginning Fazlullah was very wise. He introduced himself as an Islamic reformer and an interpreter of the Quran. My mother is very devout, and to start with she liked Fazlullah. He used his station to encourage people to adopt good habits and abandon practices he said were bad. He said men should keep their beards but give up smoking and using the tobacco they liked to chew. He said people should stop using heroin, and *chars,* which is our word for hashish. He told people the correct way to do their ablutions for prayers—which body part to wash first. He even told people how they should wash their private parts.

Sometimes his voice was reasonable, like when adults are trying to persuade you to do something you don't want to, and sometimes it was scary and full of fire. Often he would weep as he spoke of his love for Islam. Usually he spoke for a while, then his deputy Shah Douran came on air, a man who used to sell snacks from a tricycle in the bazaar. They warned people to stop listening to music, watching movies and dancing. Sinful acts like these had caused the earthquake, Fazlullah thundered, and if people didn't stop they would again invite the wrath of God. Mullahs often misinterpret the Quran and Hadith when they teach them in our country, as few people understand the original Arabic. Fazlullah exploited this ignorance.

"Is he right, *Aba?*" I asked my father. I remembered how frightening the earthquake had been.

"No, *Jani,*" he replied. "He is just fooling people."

My father said the radio station was the talk of the staffroom. By then our schools had about seventy teachers, around forty men and thirty women. Some of the teachers were anti-Fazlullah, but many supported him. People thought that he was a good interpreter of the Holy Quran and admired his charisma. They liked his talk of bringing back Islamic law, as everyone was frustrated with the Pakistani justice system, which had replaced ours when we were merged into the country. Cases such as land disputes, common in our area, which used to be resolved quickly now took ten years to come to court. Everyone was fed up with the corrupt government officials sent into the valley. It was almost as if they thought Fazlullah would re-create our old princely state from the time of the *wali*.

Within six months people were getting rid of their TVs, DVDs and CDs. Fazlullah's men collected them into huge heaps on the streets and set them on fire, creating clouds of thick black smoke that reached high into the sky. Hundreds of CD and DVD shops closed voluntarily and their owners were paid compensation by the Taliban. My brothers and I were worried, as we loved our TV, but my father reassured us that we were not getting rid of it. To be safe we moved it into a cupboard and watched it with the volume low. The Taliban were known to listen at people's doors then force their way in, take the TVs and smash them to pieces on the street. Fazlullah hated the Bollywood movies we so loved, which he denounced as un-Islamic. Only the radio was allowed, and all music except for Taliban songs was declared *haram*.

One day my father went to visit a friend in hospital and found lots of patients listening to cassettes of Fazlullah's sermons. "You must meet Maulana Fazlullah," people told him. "He's a great scholar."

"He's actually a high school drop-out whose real name isn't even Fazlullah," my father retorted, but they wouldn't listen. My father became depressed because people had begun to embrace Fazlullah's words and his religious romanticism. "It's ridiculous," my father would say, "that this so-called scholar is spreading ignorance."

Fazlullah was particularly popular in remote areas where people remembered how TNSM volunteers had helped during the earthquake when the government was nowhere to be seen. On some mosques they set up speakers connected to radios so his broadcasts could be heard by everyone in the village and in the fields. The most popular part of his show came every evening when he would read out people's names. He'd say, "Mr. So-and-so was smoking *chars* but has stopped because it's sinful," or, "Mr. X has kept his beard and I congratulate him," or, "Mr. Y voluntarily closed down his CD shop." He told them they would have their reward in the hereafter. People liked to hear their names on the radio; they also liked to hear which of their neighbors were sinful so they could gossip: "Have you heard about So-and-so?"

Mullah FM made jokes about the army. Fazlullah denounced Pakistani government officials as "infidels" and said they were opposed to bringing in sharia law. He said that if they did not implement it, his men would "enforce it and tear them to pieces." One of his favorite subjects was the injustice of the feudal system of the khans. Poor people were happy to see the khans getting their come-uppance. They saw Fazlullah as a kind of Robin Hood and believed that when Fazlullah took over he would give the khans' land to the poor. Some of the khans fled. My father was against "khanism," but he said the Taliban were worse.

My father's friend Hidayatullah had become a government official in Peshawar and warned us, "This is how these militants work. They want to win the hearts and minds of the people, so they first see what the local problems are and target those responsible, and that way they get the support of the silent majority. That's what they did in Waziristan when they went after kidnappers and bandits. After, when they get power, they behave like the criminals they once hunted down."

Fazlullah's broadcasts were often aimed at women. He must have known that many of our men were away from home, working in coal mines in the south or on building sites in the Gulf. Sometimes he would say, "Men, go outside now. I am talking to the women." Then he'd say, "Women are meant to fulfill their responsibilities in the home. Only in emergencies can they go outside, but then they must wear the veil." Sometimes his men would display the fancy clothes that they said they had taken from "decadent women" to shame them.

My friends at school said their mothers listened

to the Radio Mullah although our headmistress Madam Maryam told us not to. At home we only had my grandfather's old radio, which was broken, but my mother's friends all listened and told her what they heard. They praised Fazlullah and talked of his long hair, the way he rode a horse and behaved like the Prophet, PBUH. Women would tell him their dreams and he would pray for them. My mother enjoyed these stories, but my father was horrified.

I was confused by Fazlullah's words. In the Holy Quran it is not written that men should go outside and women should work all day in the home. In our Islamic studies class at school we used to write essays entitled "How the Prophet (PBUH) Lived." We learned that the first wife of the Prophet, PBUH, was a businesswoman called Khadijah. She was forty, fifteen years older than him, and she had been married before, yet he still married her. I also knew from watching my own mother that Pashtun women are very powerful and strong. Her mother, my grandmother, had looked after all eight children alone after my grandfather had an accident and broke his pelvis and could not leave his bed for eight years.

A man goes out to work, he earns a wage, he comes back home, he eats, he sleeps. That's what he does. Our men think earning money and ordering around others is where power lies. They don't think power is in the hands of the woman who takes care of everyone all day long, and gives birth to their children. In our house my mother managed everything because my father was so busy. It was my mother who would wake up early in the morning, iron our school clothes, make our breakfast and teach us how to behave. It was my mother who would go to the market, shop for us and cook. All those things she did.

In the first year of the Taliban I had two operations, one to take out my appendix and the other to remove my tonsils. Khushal had his appendix out too. It was my mother who took us to hospital; my father just visited us and brought ice cream. Yet my mother still believed it was written in the Quran that women should not go out and women should not talk to men other than relatives they cannot marry. My father would say to her, "Pekai, purdah is not only in the veil, purdah is in the heart."

Lots of women were so moved by what Fazlullah said that they gave him gold and money, particularly in poor villages or households where the husbands were working abroad. Tables were set up for the women to hand over their wedding bangles and necklaces and women queued up to do so or sent their sons. Some gave their life savings, believing that this would make God happy. He began building a vast red-brick headquarters in Imam Deri complete with a madrasa, a mosque and walls and levees to protect it from the Swat River. No one knew where he got the cement and iron bars from, but the workforce was local. Every village had to take turns sending their men for a day to help build it. One day one of our Urdu teachers, Nawab Ali, told my father, "I won't be coming to school tomorrow." When my father asked why, he explained it was his village's turn to work on Fazlullah's buildings.

"Your prime responsibility is to teach the students," replied my father.

"No, I have to do this," said Nawab Ali.

My father came home fuming. "If people volunteered in the same way to construct schools or roads or even clear the river of plastic wrappers, by God, Pakistan would become a paradise within a year," he said. "The only charity they know is to give to mosque and madrasa."

A few weeks later the same teacher told him that he could no longer teach girls, as "the *maulana* doesn't like it."

My father tried to change his mind. "I agree

that female teachers should educate girls," he said. "But first we need to educate our girls so they can become teachers!"

One day Sufi Mohammad proclaimed from jail that there should be no education for women, even at girls' madrasas. "If someone can show any example in history where Islam allows a female madrasa, they can come and piss on my beard," he said. Then the Radio Mullah turned his attention to schools. He began speaking against school administrators and congratulating girls by name who left school. "Miss So-and-so has stopped going to school and will go to heaven," he'd say, or, "Miss X of Y village has stopped education at Class 5. I congratulate her." Girls like me who still went to school he called buffaloes and sheep.

My friends and I couldn't understand why it was so wrong. "Why don't they want girls to go to school?" I asked my father.

"They are scared of the pen," he replied.

Then another teacher at our school, a math teacher with long hair, also refused to teach girls. My father fired him, but some other teachers were worried and sent a delegation to his office. "Sir, don't do this," they pleaded. "These are bad days. Let him stay and we will cover for him."

Every day it seemed a new edict came. Fazlullah closed beauty parlors and banned shaving, so there was no work for barbers. My father, who has only a moustache, insisted he would not grow a beard for the Taliban. The Taliban told women not to go to the bazaar. I didn't mind not going to the Cheena Bazaar. I didn't enjoy shopping, unlike my mother, who liked beautiful clothes even though we didn't have much money. My mother always told me, "Hide your face—people are looking at you."

I would reply, "It doesn't matter; I'm also looking at them," and she'd get so cross.

My mother and her friends were upset about not being able to go shopping, particularly in the days before the Eid holidays, when we beautify ourselves and go to the stalls lit up by fairy lights that sell bangles and henna. All of that stopped. The women would not be attacked if they went to the markets, but the Taliban would shout at them and threaten them until they stayed at home. One Talib could intimidate a whole village. We children were cross too. Normally there are new film releases for the holidays, but Fazlullah had closed the DVD shops. Around this time my mother also got tired of Fazlullah, especially when he began to preach against education and insist that those who went to school would also go to hell.

Next Fazlullah began holding a *shura,* a kind of local court. People liked this, as justice was speedy, unlike in Pakistani courts, where you could wait years and have to pay bribes to be heard. People began going to Fazlullah and his men to resolve grievances about anything from business matters to personal feuds. "I had a thirty-year-old problem and it's been resolved in one go," one man told my father. The punishments decreed by Fazlullah's *shura* included public whippings, which we had never seen before. One of my father's friends told him he had seen three men publicly flogged after the *shura* had found them guilty of involvement in the abduction of two women. A stage was set up near Fazlullah's center, and after going to hear him give Friday prayers, hundreds of people gathered to watch the floggings, shouting *"Allahu akbar!"*— "God is great!" with each lash. Sometimes Fazlullah appeared galloping in on a black horse.

His men stopped health workers giving polio drops, saying the vaccinations were an American plot to make Muslim women infertile so that the people of Swat would die out. "To cure a disease before its onset is not in accordance with sharia law," said Fazlullah on the radio. "You will not find a single child to drink a drop of the vaccine anywhere in Swat."

Fazlullah's men patrolled the streets looking for offenders against his decrees just like the Taliban morality police we had heard about in Afghanistan. They set up volunteer traffic police called Falcon Commandos, who drove through the streets with machine guns mounted on top of their pick-up trucks.

Some people were happy. One day my father ran into his bank manager. "One good thing Fazlullah is doing is banning ladies and girls from going to the Cheena Bazaar, which saves us men money," he said. Few spoke out. My father complained that most people were like our local barber, who one day grumbled to my father that he had only eighty rupees in his till, less than a tenth of what his takings used to be. Just the day before the barber had told a journalist that the Taliban were good Muslims.

After Mullah FM had been on air for about a year, Fazlullah became more aggressive. His brother Maulana Liaquat, along with three of Liaquat's sons, were among those killed in an American drone attack on the madrasa in Bajaur at the end of October 2006. Eighty people were killed, including boys as young as twelve, some of whom had come from Swat. We were all horrified by the attack and people swore revenge. Ten days later a suicide bomber blew himself up in the army barracks at Dargai, on the way from Islamabad to Swat, and killed forty-two Pakistani soldiers. At that time suicide bombings were rare in Pakistan—there were six in total that year—and it was the biggest attack that had ever been carried out by Pakistani militants.

At Eid we usually sacrifice animals like goats or sheep. But Fazlullah said, "On this Eid two-legged animals will be sacrificed." We soon saw what he meant. His men began killing khans and political activists from secular and nationalist parties, especially the Awami National Party (ANP). In January 2007 a close friend of one of my father's friends was kidnapped in his village by eighty masked gunmen. His name was Malak Bakht Baidar. He was from a wealthy khan family and the local vice president of the ANP. His body was found dumped in his family's ancestral graveyard. His legs and arms had all been broken. It was the first targeted killing in Swat, and people said it was because he had helped the army find Taliban hideouts.

The authorities turned a blind eye. Our provincial government was still made up of mullah parties who wouldn't criticize anyone who claimed to be fighting for Islam. At first we thought we were safe in Mingora, the biggest town in Swat. But Fazlullah's headquarters were just a few miles away, and even though the Taliban were not near our house they were in the markets, in the streets and in the hills. Danger began to creep closer.

During Eid we went to our family village as usual. I was in my cousin's car, and as we drove through a river where the road had been washed away we had to stop at a Taliban checkpoint. I was in the back with my mother. My cousin quickly gave us his music cassettes to hide in our purses. The Taliban were dressed in black and carried Kalashnikovs. They told us, "Sisters, you are bringing shame. You must wear burqas."

When we arrived back at school after Eid, we saw a letter taped to the gate. "Sir, the school you are running is Western and infidel," it said. "You teach girls and have a uniform that is un-Islamic. Stop this or you will be in trouble and your children will weep and cry for you." It was signed, "Fedayeen of Islam."

My father decided to change the boys' uniform from shirt and trousers to shalwar kamiz, baggy pyjama-like trousers and a long T-shirt. Ours remained a royal-blue shalwar kamiz with a white *dupatta,* or headscarf, and we were advised to keep our heads covered coming in and out of school.

His friend Hidayatullah told him to stand firm. "Ziauddin, you have charisma; you can speak up and organize against them," he said. "Life isn't just about taking in oxygen and giving out carbon dioxide. You can stay there accepting everything from the Taliban or you can make a stand against them."

My father told us what Hidayatullah had said. He then wrote a letter to the *Daily Azadi,* our local newspaper. "To the *Fedayeen* of Islam [or Islamic sacrificers], this is not the right way to implement Islam," he wrote. "Please don't harm my children, because the God you believe in is the same God they pray to every day. You can take my life but please don't kill my schoolchildren." When my father saw the newspaper he was very unhappy. The letter had been buried on an inside page and the editor had published his name and the address of the school, which my father had not expected him to do. But lots of people called to congratulate him. "You have put the first stone in standing water," they said. "Now we will have the courage to speak."

10

Toffees, Tennis Balls and the Buddhas of Swat

First the Taliban took our music, then our Buddhas, then our history. One of our favorite things was going on school trips. We were lucky to live in a paradise like Swat with so many beautiful places to visit—waterfalls, lakes, the ski resort, the *wali's* palace, the Buddha statues, the tomb of Akhund of Swat. All these places told our special story. We would talk about the trips for weeks beforehand, then, when the day finally came, we dressed up in our best clothes and piled into buses along with pots of chicken and rice for a picnic. Some of us had cameras and took photographs. At the end of the day my father would make us all take turns standing on a rock and tell stories about what we had seen. When Fazlullah came there were no more school trips. Girls were not supposed to be seen outside.

The Taliban destroyed the Buddhist statues and stupas where we played, which had been there for thousands of years and were a part of our history from the time of the Kushan kings. They believed any statue or painting was *haram,* sinful and therefore prohibited. One black day they even dynamited the face of the Jehanabad Buddha, which was carved into a hillside just half an hour's drive from Mingora and towered twenty-three feet into the sky. Archaeologists say it was almost as important as the Buddhas of Bamiyan, which the Afghan Taliban blew up.

It took them two goes to destroy it. The first time they drilled holes in the rock and filled them with dynamite, but that didn't work. A few weeks later, on 8 October 2007, they tried again. This time they obliterated the Buddha's face, which had watched over the valley since the seventh century. The Taliban became the enemy of fine arts, culture and our history. The Swat museum moved its collection away for safekeeping. The Taliban destroyed everything old and brought nothing new. They took over the Emerald Mountain with its mine and began selling the beautiful stones to buy their ugly weapons. They took money from the people who chopped down our precious trees for timber and then demanded more money to let their trucks pass.

Their radio coverage spread across the valley and neighboring districts. Though we still had our television they had switched off the cable channels. Moniba and I could no longer watch our favorite Bollywood shows like *Shararat* or *Making Mischief*. It seemed like the Taliban didn't want us to do anything. They even banned one of our favorite board games, called Carrom, in which we flick counters across a wooden board. We heard stories that the Taliban would hear children laughing and burst into the room and smash the boards. We felt like the Taliban saw us as little dolls to control, telling us what to do and how to dress. I thought if God wanted us to be like that He wouldn't have made us all different.

One day we found our teacher Miss Hammeda in floods of tears. Her husband was a policeman in the small town of Matta, and Fazlullah's men had stormed in and some police officers had been killed, including her husband. It was the first Taliban attack on the police in our valley. Soon they had taken over many villages. The black and white flags of Fazlullah's TNSM started appearing on police stations. The militants would enter villages with megaphones and the police would flee.

In a short time they had taken over fifty-nine villages and set up their own parallel administrations. Policemen were so scared of being killed that they took out ads in the newspapers to announce they had left the force.

All this happened and nobody did a thing. It was as though everyone were in a trance. My father said people had been seduced by Fazlullah. Some joined his men, thinking they would have better lives. My father tried to counter their propaganda, but it was hard. "I have no militants and no FM radio," he joked. He even dared to enter the Radio Mullah's own village one day to speak at a school. He crossed the river in one of the metal boxes suspended from a pulley that we use as makeshift bridges. On the way he saw smoke so high it touched the clouds, the blackest smoke he'd ever seen. At first he thought it might be a brick factory, but as he approached he saw bearded figures in turbans burning TVs and computers.

In the school my father told the people, "I saw your villagers burning these things. Don't you realize the only ones who will profit are the companies in Japan, who will just make more?"

Someone came up to him and whispered, "Don't speak any more in this way—it's risky."

Meanwhile the authorities, like most people, did nothing.

It felt as though the whole country were going mad. The rest of Pakistan was preoccupied with something else—the Taliban had moved right into the heart of our nation's capital, Islamabad. We saw pictures on the news of what people were calling the Burqa Brigade—young women and girls like us in burqas with sticks, attacking CD and DVD shops in bazaars in the center of Islamabad.

The women were from Jamia Hafsa, the biggest female madrasa in our country and part of Lal Masjid—the Red Mosque in Islamabad. It was built in 1965 and got its name from its red walls. It's just a few blocks from parliament and the headquarters of ISI, and many government officials and military used to pray there. The mosque has two madrasas, one for girls and one for boys, which had been used for years to recruit and train volunteers to fight in Afghanistan and Kashmir. It was run by two brothers, Abdul Aziz and Abdul Rashid, and had become a center for spreading propaganda about bin Laden, whom Abdul Rashid had met in Kandahar when visiting Mullah Omar. The brothers were famed for their fiery sermons and attracted thousands of worshippers, particularly after 9/11. When President Musharraf agreed to help America in the "War on Terror," the mosque broke off its long links with the military and became a center of protest against the government. Abdul Rashid was even accused of being part of a plot to blow up Musharraf's convoy in Rawalpindi in December 2003. Investigators said the explosives used had been stored in Lal Masjid. But a few months later he was cleared.

When Musharraf sent troops into the FATA, starting with Waziristan in 2004, the brothers led a campaign declaring the military action un-Islamic. They had their own website and pirate FM station on which they broadcast, just like Fazlullah.

Around the same time as our Taliban were emerging in Swat, the girls of the Red Mosque madrasa began terrorizing the streets of Islamabad. They raided houses they claimed were being used as massage centers, they kidnapped women they said were prostitutes and closed down DVD shops, again making bonfires of CDs and DVDs. When it suits the Taliban, women can be vocal and visible. The head of the madrasa was Umme Hassan, the wife of the elder brother, Abdul Aziz, and she even boasted she had trained many of her girls to become suicide bombers. The mosque also set up its own courts to dispense Islamic justice, saying the state had failed. Their militants kidnapped policemen and ransacked government buildings.

The Musharraf government didn't seem to know what to do. This was perhaps because the military had been so attached to the mosque. But by the middle of 2007 the situation was so bad that people began to worry the militants could take over the capital. It was almost unbelievable—Islamabad is usually a quiet orderly place, very different from the rest of our country. Finally, on the evening of 3 July, commandos with tanks and armored personnel carriers surrounded the mosque. They cut off the electricity in the area, and as dusk fell there was a sudden burst of gunfire and explosions. The troops blasted holes in the wall surrounding the mosque and fired mortars at the compound as helicopter gunships hovered overhead. Over loudspeakers they called for the girls to surrender.

Many of the militants in the mosque had fought in Afghanistan or Kashmir. They barricaded themselves and the madrasa students inside concrete bunkers with sandbags. Worried parents

gathered outside, calling their daughters on mobile phones, begging them to come out. Some of
the girls refused, saying their teachers had taught
them that to become a martyr is a glorious thing.

The next evening a small group of girls
emerged. Hidden among them was Abdul Aziz,
disguised in a burqa, along with his daughter.
But his wife and younger brother stayed inside,
along with many students, and there were daily
exchanges of gunfire between the militants and
the troops outside. The militants had RPGs and
petrol bombs made from Sprite bottles. The siege
went on until late on 9 July, when the commander of the special forces outside was killed by a
sniper in one of the minarets. The military finally
lost patience and stormed the compound.

They called it Operation Silence although it was
very loud. Never had there been such a battle in
the heart of our capital. Commandos fought from
room to room for hours until they finally tracked
Abdul Rashid and his followers to a basement
where they killed him. By nightfall on 10 July,
when the siege was finally over, around a hundred people had been killed including several soldiers and a number of children. The news showed
shocking pictures of the wreckage, blood and broken glass everywhere, and dead bodies. We all

watched in horror. Some of the students at the two madrasas were from Swat. How could something like that happen in our capital city and in a mosque? A mosque is a sacred place for us.

It was after the Red Mosque siege that the Swat Taliban changed. On 12 July—which I remember because it was my birthday—Fazlullah gave a radio address that was quite different from his previous ones. He raged against the Lal Masjid attack and vowed to avenge the death of Abdul Rashid. Then he declared war on the Pakistani government.

This was the start of real trouble. Fazlullah could now carry out his threats and mobilize support for his Taliban in the name of Lal Masjid. A few days later they attacked an army convoy traveling in the direction of Swat and killed thirteen soldiers. The backlash wasn't just in Swat. There was an enormous protest by tribesmen in Bajaur and a wave of suicide bombings across the country. There was one ray of hope—Benazir Bhutto was returning. The Americans were worried that their ally General Musharraf was too unpopular in Pakistan to be effective against the Taliban, so they had helped broker an unlikely power-sharing deal. The plan was that Musharraf would finally take off his uniform and be a civilian president, supported by Benazir's party. In return he would drop corruption charges against her and her husband and agree to hold elections, which everyone assumed would result in Benazir becoming prime minister. No Pakistani, including my father, thought this deal would work, as Musharraf and Benazir hated each other.

Benazir had been in exile since I was two years old, but I had heard so much about her from my father and was very excited that she would return and we might have a woman leader once more. It was because of Benazir that girls like me could think of speaking out and becoming politicians. She was our role model. She symbolized the end of dictatorship and the beginning of democracy as well as sending a message of hope and strength to the rest of the world. She was also our only political leader to speak out against the militants and even offered to help American troops hunt for bin Laden inside Pakistani borders.

Some people obviously did not like that. On 18 October 2007 we were all glued to the TV as she walked down the steps of the plane in Karachi and wept as she stepped onto Pakistani soil after almost nine years in exile. When she paraded on an open-top bus through the streets, hundreds of thousands of people flocked to see her. They had traveled from all over the country and many of them were carrying small children. Some released white doves, one of which flew to perch on Benazir's shoulder. The crowds were so large that the bus moved at a walking pace. We stopped watching after a while, as it was obviously going to take hours.

I had gone to bed when just before midnight the militants struck. Benazir's bus was blown up in a wave of orange flame. My father told me the news when I woke up the next morning. He and his friends were in such a state of shock that they had not gone to bed. Luckily, Benazir survived because she had gone downstairs to an armored compartment to rest her feet just before the explosions, but 150 people had been killed. It was the biggest bomb ever to have gone off in our country. Many of the dead were students who had made a human chain around the bus. They called themselves Martyrs for Benazir. At school that day everyone was subdued, even those who had opposed Benazir. We were devastated but also thankful that she had survived.

About a week later the army came to Swat, making lots of noise with their jeeps and helicopters. We were at school when the helicopters first arrived and were very excited. We ran outside and they threw toffees and tennis balls down to us, which we rushed to catch. Helicopters were a rare sight in Swat, but since our house was close to the local army headquarters they sometimes flew right over us. We used to hold competitions for who would collect the most toffees.

One day a man from along the street came and told us that it had been announced in the mosques that there would be a curfew the next day. We didn't know what a curfew was and were anxious. There was a hole in the wall to our neighbors' house, Safina's family, through which we used to communicate with them, and we knocked on the wall so they would come to the hole. "What does it mean this curfew?" we asked. When they explained, we didn't even come out of our rooms because we thought something bad might happen. Later the curfew took over our lives.

We heard on the news that Musharraf had sent 3,000 troops into our valley to confront the Taliban. They occupied all government and private buildings which they thought were of strategic importance. Until then it had seemed as if the rest of Pakistan were ignoring what was happening in Swat. The following day a suicide bomber attacked another army truck in Swat, killing seventeen soldiers and thirteen civilians. Then all that night we heard *dar dar dar,* the boom of cannons and machine guns from the hills. It was hard to sleep.

On the TV the next day we heard that fighting had erupted in the hills to the north. School was closed and we stayed at home, trying to understand what was going on. The fighting was taking place outside Mingora though we could still hear gunfire. The military said it had killed more than a hundred militants, but then on the first day of November around 700 Taliban overran an army position at Khwazakhela. Some fifty men deserted from the Frontier Corps and another forty-eight were captured and then paraded around. Fazlullah's men humiliated them by taking their uniforms and guns and giving them each 500 rupees to make their way back. The Taliban then took two police stations in Khwazakhela and moved on to Madyan, where more police officers gave up their weapons. Very quickly the Taliban controlled most of Swat outside Mingora.

On 12 November Musharraf ordered 10,000 more troops into our valley with additional helicopter gunships. The army was everywhere. They even camped on the golf course, their big guns trained on the hillsides. They then launched an operation against Fazlullah which later became known as the first battle of Swat. It was the first time the army had launched an operation against its own people outside the FATA. Police once tried to capture Fazlullah when he was speaking at a gathering, but a giant sandstorm blew up and he managed to escape. This added to his mystery and spiritual reputation.

The militants did not give up easily. Instead they advanced to the east and on 16 November captured Alpuri, the main town of Shangla. Again local police fled without a fight. People there said Chechens and Uzbeks were among the fighters. We worried about our family in Shangla, though my father said the village was too remote for the Taliban to bother with and local people had made it clear they would keep them out. The Pakistan army had far more men and heavy weapons, so they quickly managed to recapture the valley. They took Imam Deri, the headquarters of Fazlullah. The militants fled to the forests and by early December the army said they had cleared most areas. Fazlullah retreated into the mountains.

But they did not drive the Taliban away. "This will not last," my father predicted.

Fazlullah's group was not the only one causing

havoc. All across northwestern Pakistan different militant groups had emerged led by people from various tribal groups. About a week after the battle of Swat, forty Taliban leaders from across our province met in South Waziristan to declare war on Pakistan. They agreed to form a united front under the banner of Tehrik-i-Taliban-Pakistan (TTP), or the Pakistan Taliban, and claimed to have 40,000 fighters between them. They chose as their leader a man in his late thirties called Baitullah Mehsud, who had fought in Afghanistan. Fazlullah was made chief of the Swat sector.

When the army arrived we thought that the fighting would soon stop, but we were wrong. There was much more to come. The Taliban targeted not only politicians, MPs and the police, but also people who were not observing purdah, wearing the wrong length of beard or the wrong kind of shalwar kamiz.

On 27 December Benazir Bhutto addressed an election rally in Liaquat Bagh, the park in Rawalpindi where our first prime minister, Liaquat Ali, was assassinated. "We will defeat the forces of extremism and militancy with the power of the people," she declared to loud cheers. She was in a special bulletproof Toyota Land Cruiser, and as it left the park she stood up on the seat and popped her head through the sunroof to wave to supporters. Suddenly there was the crack of gunfire and an explosion, as a suicide bomber blew himself up by the side of her vehicle. Benazir slid back down. The Musharraf government later said she hit her head on the roof handle; other people said she had been shot.

We were watching the TV when the news came through. My grandmother said, "Benazir will become *shaheed*," meaning she would die an honorable death. We all started crying and praying for her. When we learned she was dead, my heart said to me, *Why don't you go there and fight for women's rights?* We were looking forward to democracy and now people asked, "If Benazir can die, nobody is safe." It felt as if my country were running out of hope.

Musharraf blamed Benazir's death on Baitullah Mehsud, the TTP leader, and released a transcript of an intercepted phone call that was supposed to be between him and a fellow militant discussing the attack. Baitullah denied responsibility, which was unusual for the Taliban.

We used to have Islamic studies teachers—*qari sahibs*—who came to our home to teach the Quran to me and other local children. By the time the Taliban came I had finished my recitation of the complete Quran, what we call *Khatam ul-Quran,* much to the delight of *Baba,* my grandfather the cleric. We recite in Arabic, and most people don't actually know what the verses mean, but I had also started learning them in translation. To my horror one *qari sahib* tried to justify Benazir's assassination. "It was a very good job she was killed," he said. "When she was alive she was useless. She was not following Islam properly. If she had lived there would have been anarchy."

I was shocked and told my father. "We don't have any option. We are dependent on these mullahs to learn the Quran," he said. "But you just use him to learn the literal meaning of the words; don't follow his explanations and interpretation. Only learn what God says. His words are divine messages, which you are free and independent to interpret."

11

The Clever Class

It was school that kept me going in those dark days. When I was in the street it felt as though every man I passed might be a Talib. We hid our school bags and our books in our shawls. My father always said that the most beautiful thing in a village in the morning is the sight of a child in a school uniform, but now we were afraid to wear them.

We had moved up to high school. Madam Maryam said no one wanted to teach our class, as we asked so many questions. We liked to be known as the clever girls. When we decorated our hands with henna for holidays and weddings, we drew calculus and chemical formulae instead of flowers and butterflies. My rivalry with Malka-e-Noor continued, but after the shock of being beaten by her when she first joined our school,

187

I worked hard and had managed to regain my position on the school honors board for first in class. She usually came second and Moniba third. The teachers told us examiners first looked at how much we had written, then presentation. Moniba had the most beautiful writing and presentation of the three of us, but I always told her she did not trust herself enough. She worked hard, as she worried that if she got low marks her male relatives might use it as an excuse to stop her education. I was weakest in math—once I got zero in a test—but I worked hard at it. My chemistry teacher, Sir Obaidullah (we called all our teachers Sir or Miss), said I was a born politician because, at the start of oral exams, I would always say, "Sir, can I just say you are the best teacher and yours is my favorite class."

Some parents complained that I was being favored because my father owned the school, but people were always surprised that despite our rivalry we were all good friends and not jealous of each other. We also competed in what we call board exams. These would select the best students from private schools in the district, and one year Malka-e-Noor and I got exactly the same marks. We did another paper at school to see who would get the prize and again we got equal marks. So people wouldn't think I was getting special treatment, my father arranged for us to do papers at another school, that of his friend Ahmad Shah. Again we got the same, so we both got the prize.

There was more to school than work. We liked performing plays. I wrote a sketch based on *Romeo and Juliet* about corruption. I played Romeo as a civil servant interviewing people for a job. The first candidate is a beautiful girl, and he asks her very easy questions such as "How many wheels does a bicycle have?" When she replies, "Two," he says, "You are so brilliant." The next candidate is a man, so Romeo asks him impossible things like "Without leaving your chair tell me the make of the fan in the room above us." "How could I possibly know?" asks the candidate. "You're telling me you have a PhD and you don't know!" replies Romeo. He decides to give the job to the girl.

The girl was played by Moniba, of course, and another classmate, Attiya, played the part of my assistant to add some salt, pepper and masala with her witty asides. Everyone laughed a lot. I like to mimic people, and in breaks my friends used to beg me to impersonate our teachers, particularly Sir Obaidullah. With all the bad stuff going on in those days, we needed small, small reasons to laugh.

The army action at the end of 2007 had not got rid of the Taliban. The army had stayed in Swat and were everywhere in the town, yet Fazlullah still broadcast every day on the radio, and throughout 2008 the situation was even worse than before with bomb blasts and killings. All we talked about in those days was the army and the Taliban and the feeling that we were caught between the two. Attiya used to tease me by saying, "Taliban is good, army not good." I replied, "If there is a snake and a lion coming to attack us, what would we say is good, the snake or lion?"

Our school was a haven from the horrors outside. All the other girls in my class wanted to be doctors, but I decided I wanted to be an inventor and make an anti-Taliban machine which would sniff them out and destroy their guns. But of course at school we were under threat too, and some of my friends dropped out. Fazlullah kept broadcasting that girls should stay at home, and his men had started blowing up schools, usually during nighttime curfew when the children were not there.

The first school to be blown up was Shawar Zangay, a government girls' primary school in Matta. We couldn't believe anyone would do such a thing. Then many more bombings followed, almost every day. Even in Mingora, there were explosions. Twice bombs went off when I was in the kitchen, so close by that the whole house rattled and the fan above the window fell down. I became very scared of going into the kitchen and would only run in and out.

On the last day of February 2008 I was in the kitchen when we heard an enormous blast. It was ear-shatteringly loud and obviously close by. As we always did, we called to each other to make sure we were all safe. "*Khaista, pisho, bhabi, Khushal, Atal!*" Then we heard sirens, one after another, as if all the ambulances of Mingora were passing. A suicide bomber had struck in the basketball court at Haji Baba High School. Funeral prayers had been under way for a popular local police officer, Javid Iqbal, who had been killed by a suicide bomber in a remote area while trying to escape from the Taliban. He was from Mingora, and his body had been brought back for the funeral and a police salute. Now the Taliban had bombed the mourners. More than fifty-five people were killed, including Javid Iqbal's young son and many people we knew. Ten members of Moniba's family were there and were either killed or injured. Moniba was devastated and the whole town was in shock. There were condolences in every mosque.

"Are you scared now?" I asked my father.

"At night our fear is strong, *Jani*," he told me, "but in the morning, in the light, we find our courage again." And this is true for my family. We were scared, but our fear was not as strong as our courage. "We must rid our valley of the Taliban, and then no one has to feel this fear," he said.

In times of crisis we Pashtuns resort to the old trusted ways, so in 2008 elders in Swat created an assembly called the Qaumi Jirga to challenge Fazlullah. Three local men, Mukhtar Khan Yousafzai, Khurshid Kakajee and Zahid Khan, went from *hujra* to *hujra* persuading elders to join together. The senior elder was a white-bearded man of seventy-four called Abdul Khan Khaliq who had been one of the queen's bodyguards when she had visited Swat to stay with our *wali*. Even though my father was not an elder or a khan, he was chosen as spokesperson, as he was not afraid to speak out. Though he was more poetic in Pashto, he could speak our national language, Urdu, and English fluently, which meant he was an effective communicator outside Swat as well as inside.

Every day, on behalf of the Swat Council of

Elders, he was at seminars or on the media challenging Fazlullah. "What are you doing?" he would ask. "You are playing havoc with our lives and our culture."

My father would say to me, "Any organization which works for peace, I will join. If you want to resolve a dispute or come out from conflict, the very first thing is to speak the truth. If you have a headache and tell the doctor you have a stomachache, how can the doctor help? You must speak the truth. The truth will abolish fear."

When he met his fellow activists, particularly his old friends Ahmad Shah, Mohammad Farooq and Zahid Khan, I often went with him. Ahmad Shah also had a school, where Mohammad Farooq worked, and they would sometimes gather on his lawn. Zahid Khan was a hotel owner and had a big *hujra*. When they came to our house I would bring them tea, then sit quietly listening as they discussed what to do. "Malala is not just the daughter of Ziauddin," they would say; "she is the daughter of all of us."

They went back and forth to Peshawar and Islamabad and gave lots of interviews on the radio, particularly to the Voice of America and the BBC, taking turns so there would always be one of them available. They told people that what was happening in Swat was not about Islam. My father said the Taliban presence in Swat was not possible without the support of some in the army and the bureaucracy. The state is meant to protect the rights of its citizens, but it's a very difficult situation when you can't tell the difference between state and non-state and can't trust the state to protect you against non-state.

Our military and ISI are very powerful and most people did not like to voice these things publicly, but my father and many of his friends were not scared. "What you are doing is against our people and against Pakistan," he would say. "Don't support Talibanization, it's inhuman. We are told that Swat is being sacrificed for the sake of Pakistan, but no one and nothing should be sacrificed for the state. A state is like a mother, and a mother never deserts or cheats her children."

He hated the fact that most people would not speak up. In his pocket he kept a poem written by Martin Niemöller, who had lived in Nazi Germany.

First they came for the communists,
and I didn't speak out because I wasn't a
* communist.*

Then they came for the socialists,
and I didn't speak out because I wasn't a
*   socialist.*
Then they came for the trade unionists,
and I didn't speak out because I wasn't a trade
*   unionist.*
Then they came for the Jews,
and I didn't speak out because I was not a Jew.
Then they came for the Catholics,
and I didn't speak out because I was not a
*   Catholic.*
Then they came for me,
and there was no one left to speak for me.

I knew he was right. If people were silent, nothing would change.

At school my father organized a peace march and encouraged us to speak out against what was happening. Moniba put it well. "We Pashtuns are a religion-loving people," she said. "Because of the Taliban, the whole world is claiming we are terrorists. This is not the case. We are peace-loving. Our mountains, our trees, our flowers—everything in our valley is about peace." A group of us girls gave an interview on ATV Khyber, the only privately owned Pashto television channel, about girls dropping out of school due to militancy. Teachers helped us beforehand on how to respond to questions. I wasn't the only one to be interviewed. When we were eleven and twelve, we did them together, but as we turned thirteen or fourteen, my friends' brothers and fathers didn't allow them because they had entered puberty and should observe purdah, and also they were afraid.

One day I went on Geo, which is one of the biggest news channels in our country. There was a wall of screens in their office. I was astonished to see so many channels. Afterward I thought, *The media needs interviews. They want to interview a small girl, but the girls are scared, and even if they're not, their parents won't allow it. I have a father who isn't scared, who stands by me. He said, "You are a child and it's your right to speak."* The more interviews I gave, the stronger I felt and the more support we received. I was only eleven, but I looked older, and the media seemed to like hearing from a young girl. One journalist called me *takra jenai*—a "bright shining young lady" and another said I was *pakha jenai*—wise beyond my years. In my heart was the belief that God would protect me. If I am speaking for my rights, for the rights of girls, I am not doing anything wrong. It's my duty to do so. God wants to see how we behave in such situations. There is a saying in the Quran, "The falsehood has to go and the truth will prevail." *If one man, Fazlullah, can destroy everything, why can't one girl change it?* I wondered. I prayed to God every night to give me strength.

The media in Swat were under pressure to give positive coverage to the Taliban—some even respectfully called the Taliban spokesman Muslim Khan *School Dada,* when in reality he was destroying schools. But many local journalists were unhappy about what was happening to their valley and they gave us a powerful platform, as we would say things they didn't dare to.

We didn't have a car, so we went by rickshaw, or one of my father's friends would take us to the interviews. One day my father and I went to Peshawar to appear on a BBC Urdu talk show hosted by a famous columnist called Wasatullah Khan. We went with my father's friend Fazal Maula and his daughter. Two fathers and two daughters. To represent the Taliban they had Muslim Khan, who wasn't in the studio. I was a bit nervous, but I knew it was important, as many people all over Pakistan would be listening. "How dare the Taliban take away my basic right to education?" I said. There was no response from Muslim Khan because his phone interview had been prerecorded. How can a recording respond to live questions?

Afterward people congratulated me. My father laughed and said I should go into politics. "Even as a toddler you talked like a politician," he teased. But I never listened to my interviews. I knew these were very small steps.

Our words were like the eucalyptus blossoms of spring tossed away on the wind. The destruction of schools continued. On the night of 7 October 2008 we heard a series of faraway blasts. The next morning we learned that masked militants had entered the Sangota Convent School for girls and the Excelsior College for boys and blown them up using improvised explosive devices (IEDs). The teachers had already been evacuated, as they had received threats earlier. These were famous schools, particularly Sangota, which dated from the time of the last *wali* and was well known for academic excellence. They were also big—Excelsior had over 2,000 pupils and Sangota had 1,000. My father went there after the bombings and found the buildings completely razed to the ground. He gave interviews to TV reporters amid broken bricks and burned books and returned home horrified. "It's all just rubble," he said.

Yet my father remained hopeful and believed there would be a day when there was an end to the destruction. What really depressed him was the looting of the destroyed schools—the furniture, the books, the computers, were all stolen by local people. He cried when he heard this. "They are vultures jumping on a dead body."

The next day he went on a live show on the Voice of America and angrily condemned the attacks. Muslim Khan, the Taliban spokesman, was on the phone. "What was so wrong with these two schools that you should bomb them?" my father asked him.

Muslim Khan said that Sangota was a convent school teaching Christianity and that Excelsior was coeducational, teaching girls and boys together. "Both things are false!" replied my father. "Sangota school has been there since the 1960s and never converted anyone to Christianity—in fact some of them converted to Islam. And Excelsior is only coeducational in the primary section."

Muslim Khan didn't answer. "What about their own daughters?" I asked my father. "Don't they want them to learn?"

Our headmistress, Madam Maryam, had studied at Sangota, and her younger sister Ayesha was a pupil there, so she and some of the other Sangota girls transferred to our school. The monthly school fees were never enough to cover all our outgoings, so the extra fees were welcome, but my father was unhappy. He went everywhere he could demanding the reconstruction of both schools. Once he spoke at a big gathering and held up an audience member's baby girl and said, "This girl is our future. Do we want her to be ignorant?" The crowd agreed that they would sacrifice themselves before giving up their daughters' education. The new girls had horrible stories. Ayesha told us how one day on the way home from Sangota she had seen a Taliban holding up the severed head of a policeman by its hair, blood dripping from the neck. The Sangota girls were also very bright, which meant more competition. One of them, Rida, was excellent at making speeches. She became a good friend of mine and of Moniba's, which sometimes caused fights, as three is a tricky number. Moniba often brought food to school and would just bring one spare fork. "Are you my friend or Rida's?" I asked Moniba.

She laughed and said, "We are all three good friends."

By the end of 2008, around 400 schools had been destroyed by the Taliban. We had a new government under President Asif Zardari, the widower of Benazir, but they didn't seem to care about Swat. I told people things would be different if Zardari's own daughters were at school in Swat. There were suicide bombings all over the country: even the Marriott Hotel in Islamabad had been blown up.

In Swat it was safer in the town than in the remote areas, and many of our family came from the countryside to stay with us. The house was small and got very crowded with the cousins who already lived with us. There was little to do. We couldn't play cricket in the street or on the roof like we used to. We played marbles in the yard over and over again. I fought nonstop with my brother Khushal, and he would go crying to our mother. Never in history have Khushal and Malala been friends.

I liked doing my hair in different styles and would spend ages in the bathroom in front of the mirror trying out looks I had seen in movies. Until I was eight or nine my mother used to cut my hair short like my brothers' because of lice and also to make it easier to wash and brush, as it would get messed up under my shawl. But finally I had persuaded her to let me grow it to my shoulders. Unlike Moniba's, which is straight, my hair is wavy, and I liked to twist it into curls or tie it into plaits. "What are you doing in there *pisho?*" my mother would shout. "Our guests need the bathroom and everyone is having to wait for you."

One of the worst times was the fasting month of Ramadan in 2008. During Ramadan no food or drink can pass a Muslim's lips in daylight hours. The Taliban bombed the power station, so we had no electricity, then a few days later they blasted the pipeline, so we had no gas either. The price of the gas cylinders we used to buy from the market doubled, so my mother had to cook on a fire like we did in the village. She didn't complain—food needed to be cooked and she cooked it, and there were others worse off than us. But there was no clean water and people started dying from cholera. The hospital could not cope with all the patients and had to erect big tents outside to treat people.

Though we had no generator at home, my father bought one to install at the school, and fresh water was pumped from a borehole, which all the children in the neighborhood went to collect. Every day there would be lines of people waiting to fill jugs, bottles and drums. One of the neighbors got frightened. "What are you doing?" he asked. "If the Taliban find out you're giving water in the month of Ramadan they will bomb us!"

My father replied that people would die either of thirst or bombings.

The days when we used to go for trips or for picnics seemed like a dream. No one would venture from their homes after sunset. The terrorists even blew up the ski lift and the big hotel in Malam Jabba where tourists used to stay. A holiday paradise turned into a hell where no tourist would venture.

Then, at the end of 2008, Fazlullah's deputy Maulana Shah Dauran announced on the radio that all girls' schools would close. From 15 January girls must not go to school, he warned. First I thought it was a joke. "How can they stop us from going to school?" I asked my friends. "They don't have the power. They are saying they will destroy the mountain, but they can't even control the road."

The other girls didn't agree with me. "Who will stop them?" they asked. "They have already blown up hundreds of schools and no one has done anything."

My father used to say the people of Swat and the teachers would continue to educate our children until the last room, the last teacher and the last student was alive. My parents never once suggested I should withdraw from school, ever. Though we loved school, we hadn't realized how important education was until the Taliban tried to stop us. Going to school, reading and doing our homework wasn't just a way of passing time, it was our future.

That winter it snowed and we built snow bears but without much joy. In winter the Taliban used to disappear into the mountains, but we knew they would be back and had no idea what was coming next. We believed school would start again. The Taliban could take our pens and books, but they couldn't stop our minds from thinking.

12

The Bloody Square

The bodies would be dumped in the square at night so that everyone would see them the next morning on their way to work. There was usually a note pinned to them saying something like "This is what happens to an army agent" or "Do not touch this body until 11 a.m. or you will be next." On some of the nights of the killings there would also be earthquakes, which made people even more scared, as we connect every natural disaster with a human disaster.

They killed Shabana on a bitterly cold night in January 2009. She lived in Banr Bazaar, a narrow street in our town of Mingora which is famous for its dancers and musicians. Shabana's father said a group of men had knocked at her door and asked her to dance for them. She went to put on her dancing clothes, and when she returned to dance for them, they pulled out their guns and threatened to slit her throat. This happened after the 9 p.m. curfew and people heard her screaming, "I promise I'll stop! I promise I won't sing and dance again. Leave me, for God's sake! I am a woman, a Muslim. Don't kill me!" Then shots rang out and her bullet-ridden body was dragged to Green Chowk. So many bodies had been left there that people started calling it the Bloody Square.

We heard about Shabana's death the next morning. On Mullah FM, Fazlullah said she deserved to die for her immoral character and any other girls found performing in Banr Bazaar would be killed one by one. We used to be proud of our music and art in Swat, but now most of the dancers fled to Lahore or to Dubai. Musicians took out ads in the papers saying they had stopped playing and pledging to live pious lives to appease the Taliban.

People used to talk about Shabana's bad character, but our men both wished to see her dance and also despised her because she was a dancer. A khan's daughter can't marry a barber's son and a barber's daughter can't marry a khan's son. We Pashtuns love shoes but don't love the cobbler; we love our scarves and blankets but do not respect the weaver. Manual workers made a great contribution to our society but received no recognition, and this is the reason so many of them joined the Taliban—to finally achieve status and power.

So people loved to see Shabana dance but didn't respect her, and when she was murdered they said nothing. Some even agreed with her killing, out of fear of the Taliban or because they were in favor of them. "Shabana was not a Muslim," they said. "She was bad, and it was right that she was killed."

I can't say that was the worst day. Around the time of Shabana's murder every day seemed like the worst day; every moment was the worst. The bad news was everywhere: this person's place bombed, this school blown up, public whippings. The stories were endless and overwhelming. A couple of weeks after Shabana's murder, a teacher in Matta was killed when he refused to pull his shalwar above the ankle the way the Taliban wore theirs. He told them that nowhere in Islam is this required. They hanged him and then they shot his father.

I couldn't understand what the Taliban were trying to do. "They are abusing our religion," I said in interviews. "How will you accept Islam if I put a gun to your head and say Islam is the true religion? If they want every person in the world to be Muslim, why don't they show themselves to be good Muslims first?"

Regularly my father would come home shaken up due to the terrible things he had witnessed and heard about, such as policemen beheaded, their heads paraded through the town. Even those who had defended Fazlullah at the start, believing his men were the real standard-bearers of Islam, and given him their gold, began to turn against him. My father told me about a woman who had donated generously to the Taliban while her husband was working abroad. When he came back and found out she had given away her gold he was furious. One night there was a small explosion in their village and the wife cried. "Don't cry," said her husband. "That is the sound of your earrings and nose studs. Now listen to the sound of your lockets and bangles."

Yet still so few people spoke out. My father's old rival in college politics Ihsan ul-Haq Haqqani had become a journalist in Islamabad and organized a conference on the situation in Swat. None of the lawyers and academics he invited from Swat to speak turned up. Only my father and some journalists went. It seemed that people had decided the Taliban were here to stay and they had better get along with them. "When you are in the

Taliban you have 100 percent life security," people would say. That's why they volunteered their young men. The Taliban would come to peoples' houses, demanding money to buy Kalashnikovs, or they would ask them to hand over their sons to fight with them. Many of the rich fled. The poor had no choice but to stay and survive the best they could. So many of our men had gone to the mines or to the Gulf to work, leaving their families fatherless, the sons were easy prey.

The threats began to come closer to home. One day Ahmad Shah received a warning from unknown people that they would kill him, so for a while he left for Islamabad to try to raise awareness there of what was happening to our valley. One of the worst things about that period was when we started to doubt one another. Fingers were even pointed at my father. "Our people are being killed, but this Ziauddin is so outspoken and he's still alive! He must be a secret agent!" Actually he had been threatened too but hadn't told us. He had given a press conference in Peshawar demanding that the military act against the Taliban and go after their commanders. Afterward people told him his name was heard on Mullah FM in a threat from Shah Douran.

My father brushed it off. But I was worried. He

was outspoken and involved in so many groups and committees that he often wouldn't come home till midnight. He started to sleep at one of his friend's houses to protect us in case the Taliban came for him. He couldn't bear the thought of being killed in front of us. I could not sleep until he returned and I could lock the gate. When he was at home my mother would place a ladder in the back yard up to the outside wall so he could get down to the street below if he was in sudden danger. He laughed at the idea. "Maybe Atal the squirrel could make it but not me!"

My mother was always trying to think up plans for what she would do if the Taliban came. She thought of sleeping with a knife under her pillow. I said I could sneak into the toilet and call the police. My brothers and I thought of digging a tunnel. Once again I prayed for a magic wand to make the Taliban disappear.

One day I saw my little brother Atal digging furiously in the garden. "What are you doing?" I asked him. "Making a grave," he said. Our news bulletins were full of killings and death, so it was natural for Atal to think of coffins and graves. Instead of hide-and-seek and cops and robbers, children were now playing army vs. Taliban. They made rockets from branches and used sticks for Kalashnikovs; these were their sports of terror.

There was no one to protect us. Our own deputy commissioner, Syed Javid, was going to Taliban meetings, praying in their mosque and leading their meetings. He became a perfect Talib. One target of the Taliban were non-governmental organizations, or NGOs, which they said were anti-Islam. When the NGOs received threatening letters from the Taliban and went to the DC to ask for his help, he wouldn't even listen to them. Once in a meeting my father challenged him: "Whose orders are you representing? Fazlullah's or the government's?" We say in Arabic, "People follow their king." When the highest authority in your district joins the Taliban, then Talibanization becomes normal.

We like conspiracy theories in Pakistan and we had many. Some believed the authorities were deliberately encouraging the Taliban. They said the army wanted the Taliban in Swat because the Americans wanted to use an air base there to launch their drones. With the Taliban in the valley, our government could say to the Americans, we can't help you because we have our own problems. It was also a way to answer growing American criticism that our military was helping the Taliban rather than trying to stop them.

Now our government could respond, "You say we are taking your money and aiding these terrorists, but if that's the case why are they attacking us too?"

"The Taliban obviously have the support of unseen forces," said my father. "But what's happening is not simple, and the more you want to understand, the more complex it becomes."

That year, 2008, the government even released Sufi Mohammad, the founder of the TNSM, from prison. He was said to be more moderate than his son-in-law Fazlullah, and there was hope that he would make a peace deal with the government to impose sharia law in Swat and release us from Taliban violence. My father was in favor of this. We knew this would not be the end, but my father argued that if we had *shariat* the Taliban would have nothing more to fight for. They should then put down their arms and live like ordinary men. If they did not, he said, this would expose them for what they really were.

The army still had their guns trained on the mountains overlooking Mingora. We would lie in bed listening to them *boom boom* all night. They would stop for five, ten or fifteen minutes and then start again the moment we drifted off to sleep. Sometimes we covered our ears or buried our heads under pillows, but the guns were close by and the noise was too loud to block out. Then the morning after, on TV, we would hear of more Taliban killings and wonder what the army was doing with all its booming cannons and why they could not even stop the daily broadcasts on Mullah FM.

Both the army and the Taliban were powerful. Sometimes their roadblocks were less than a kilometer apart on the same main roads. They would stop us but seemed unaware of each other's presence. It was unbelievable. No one understood why we were not being defended. People would say they were two sides of the same coin. My father said we common people were like chaff caught between the two stones of a water mill. But he still wasn't afraid. He said we should continue to speak out.

I am only human, and when I heard the guns my heart used to beat very fast. Sometimes I was very afraid, but I said nothing, and it didn't mean I would stop going to school. But fear is very powerful and in the end it was this fear that had made people turn against Shabana. Terror had made people cruel. The Taliban bulldozed both our Pashtun values and the values of Islam.

I tried to distract myself by reading Stephen

Hawking's *A Brief History of Time,* which answered big questions such as how the universe began and whether time could run backward. I was only eleven years old and already I wished it could.

We Pashtuns know the stone of revenge never decays, and when you do something wrong you will face the music. *But when would that be?* we continually asked ourselves.

13

The Diary of Gul Makai

It was during one of those dark days that my father received a call from his friend Abdul Hai Kakar, a BBC radio correspondent based in Peshawar. He was looking for a female teacher or a schoolgirl to write a diary about life under the Taliban. He wanted to show the human side of the catastrophe in Swat. Initially Madam Maryam's younger sister Ayesha agreed, but her father found out and refused his permission saying it was too risky.

When I overheard my father talking about this, I said, "Why not me?" I wanted people to know what was happening. Education is our right, I said. Just as it is our right to sing. Islam has given us this right and says that every girl and boy should go to school. The Quran says we should seek knowledge, study hard and learn the mysteries of our world.

I had never written a diary before and didn't know how to begin. Although we had a computer, there were frequent power cuts and few places had Internet access. So Hai Kakar would call me in the evening on my mother's mobile. He used his wife's phone to protect us, as he said his own phone was bugged by the intelligence services. He would guide me, asking me questions about my day, and asking me to tell him small anecdotes or talk about my dreams. We would speak for half an hour or forty-five minutes in Urdu, even though we are both Pashtun, as the blog was to appear in Urdu and he wanted the voice to be as authentic as possible. Then he wrote up my words and once a week they would appear on the BBC Urdu website. He told me about Anne Frank, a thirteen-year-old Jewish girl who hid from the Nazis with her family in Amsterdam during the war. He told me she kept a diary about their lives all cramped together, about how they spent their days and about her own feelings. It was very sad, as in the end the family was betrayed and arrested and Anne died in a concentration camp when she was only fifteen. Later her diary was published and is a very powerful record.

Hai Kakar told me it could be dangerous to use my real name and gave me the pseudonym

Gul Makai, which means "cornflower" and is the name of the heroine in a Pashtun folk story. It's a kind of *Romeo and Juliet* story in which Gul Makai and Musa Khan meet at school and fall in love. But they are from different tribes, so their love causes a war. However, unlike Shakespeare's play their story doesn't end in tragedy. Gul Makai uses the Quran to teach her elders that war is bad and they eventually stop fighting and allow the lovers to unite.

My first diary entry appeared on 3 January 2009 under the heading I AM AFRAID: "I had a terrible dream last night filled with military helicopters and Taliban. I have had such dreams since the launch of the military operation in Swat." I wrote about being afraid to go to school because of the Taliban edict and looking over my shoulder all the time. I also described something that happened on my way home from school: "I heard a man behind me saying, 'I will kill you.' I quickened my pace and after a while I looked back to see if he was following me. To my huge relief I saw he was speaking on his phone, he must have been talking to someone else."

It was thrilling to see my words on the website. I was a bit shy to start with, but after a while I got to know the kind of things Hai Kakar wanted me to talk about and became more confident. He liked personal feelings and what he called my "pungent sentences" and also the mix of everyday family life with the terror of the Taliban.

I wrote a lot about school, as that was at the center of our lives. I loved my royal-blue school uniform, but we were advised to wear plain clothes instead and hide our books under our shawls. One extract was called DO NOT WEAR COLORFUL CLOTHES. In it I wrote, "I was getting ready for school one day and was about to put on my uniform when I remembered the advice of our principal, so that day I decided to wear my favorite pink dress."

I also wrote about the burqa. When you're very young, you love the burqa because it's great for dressing up. But when you are made to wear it, that's a different matter. Also it makes walking difficult! One of my diary entries was about an incident that happened when I was out shopping with my mother and cousin in the Cheena Bazaar: "There we heard gossip that one day a woman was wearing a shuttlecock burqa and fell over. When a man tried to help her she refused and said. 'Don't help me, brother, as this will bring immense pleasure to Fazlullah.' When we entered the shop we were going to, the shopkeeper laughed and told us he got scared thinking we might be suicide bombers, as many suicide bombers wore the burqa."

At school people started talking about the diary. One girl even printed it out and brought it in to show my father.

"It's very good," he said with a knowing smile.

I wanted to tell people it was me, but the BBC correspondent had told me not to, as it could be dangerous. I didn't see why, as I was just a child, and who would attack a child? But some of my friends recognized incidents in it. And I almost gave the game away in one entry when I said, "My mother liked my pen name Gul Makai and joked to my father we should change my name...I also like the name because my real name means 'grief-stricken.'"

The diary of Gul Makai received attention further afield. Some newspapers printed extracts. The BBC even made a recording of it using another girl's voice, and I began to see that the pen and the words that come from it can be much more powerful than machine guns, tanks or helicopters. We were learning how to struggle. And we were learning how powerful we are when we speak.

Some of our teachers stopped coming to school.

One said he had been ordered by Mullah Fazlullah to help build his center in Imam Deri. Another said he'd seen a beheaded corpse on the way in and could no longer risk his life to teach. Many people were scared. Our neighbors said the Taliban were instructing people to make it known to the mosque if their daughters were unmarried so they could be married off, probably to militants.

By the start of January 2009 there were only ten girls in my class when once there had been twenty-seven. Many of my friends had left the valley so they could be educated in Peshawar, but my father insisted we would not leave. "Swat has given us so much. In these tough days we must be strong for our valley," he said.

One night we all went for dinner at the house of my father's friend Dr. Afzal, who runs a hospital. After dinner, when the doctor was driving us home, we saw masked Taliban on both sides of the road carrying guns. We were terrified. Dr. Afzal's hospital was in an area that had been taken over by the Taliban. The constant gunfire and curfews had made it impossible for the hospital to function, so he had moved it to Barikot. There had been an outcry, and the Taliban spokesman Muslim Khan had called on the doctor to reopen it. He had asked for my father's advice. My father told him, "Don't accept good things from bad people." A hospital protected by the Taliban was not a good idea, so he refused.

Dr. Afzal did not live far from us, so once we were safely home, my father insisted on going back with him in case he was targeted by the Taliban. As he and my father drove back, Dr. Afzal nervously asked him, "What names shall we give if they stop us?"

"You are Dr. Afzal and I am Ziauddin Yousafzai," replied my father. "These bloody people. We haven't done anything wrong. Why should we change our names—that's what criminals do."

Fortunately the Taliban had disappeared. We all breathed a big sigh of relief when my father phoned to say they were safe.

I didn't want to give in either. But the Taliban's deadline was drawing closer: girls had to stop going to school. How could they stop more than 50,000 girls from going to school in the twenty-first century? I kept hoping something would happen and the schools would remain open. But finally the deadline was upon us. We were determined that the Khushal School bell would be the last to stop ringing. Madam Maryam had even got married so she could stay in Swat. Her family had moved to Karachi to get away from the conflict and, as a woman, she could not live alone.

Wednesday 14 January was the day my school closed, and when I woke up that morning I saw TV cameras in my bedroom. A Pakistani journalist called Irfan Ashraf was following me around, even as I said my prayers and brushed my teeth.

I could tell my father was in a bad mood. One of his friends had persuaded him to participate in a documentary for the *New York Times* website to show the world what was happening to us. A few weeks before, we had met the American video journalist Adam Ellick in Peshawar. It was a funny meeting, as he conducted a long interview with my father in English and I didn't say a word. Then he asked if he could talk to me and began asking questions using Irfan as an interpreter. After about ten minutes of this he realized from my facial expressions that I could understand him perfectly. "You speak English?" he asked me.

"Yes, I was just saying there is a fear in my heart," I replied.

Adam was astonished. "What's wrong with you people?" he asked Irfan and my father. "She speaks better English than the rest of you and you're translating for her!" We all laughed.

The original idea for the documentary had been to follow my father on the last day of school, but at the end of the meeting Irfan asked me, "What would you do if there comes a day when you can't go back to your valley and school?" I said this wouldn't happen. Then he insisted and I started to weep. I think it was then that Adam decided he should focus on me.

Adam could not come to Swat because it was too dangerous for foreigners. When Irfan and a cameraman arrived in Mingora, our uncle, who was staying with us, said over and over that it was too risky to have cameras in our house. My father also kept telling them to hide the cameras. But they had come a long way and it's hard for us as Pashtuns to refuse hospitality. Besides my father knew this could be our megaphone to the outside world. His friend had told him it would make far more impact than him roaming from pillar to post.

I had done a lot of television interviews and enjoyed speaking into the microphone so much that my friends would tease me. But I had never done anything like this. "Be natural," Irfan told me. That wasn't easy with a camera trained on me everywhere I went even as I brushed my teeth. I showed them the uniform I couldn't wear and told them I was scared that if the Taliban caught me going to school they would throw acid in my face, as they had to girls in Afghanistan.

We had a special assembly that final morning, but it was hard to hear with the noise of helicopters overhead. Some of us spoke out against what was happening in our valley. The bell rang for the very last time, and then Madam Maryam announced it was winter vacation. But unlike in other years no date was announced for the start of next term. Even so, some teachers still gave us homework. In the yard I hugged all my friends. I looked at the honors board and wondered if my name would ever appear on it again. Exams were due in March, but how could they take place? Coming first didn't matter if you couldn't study at all. When someone takes away your pens you realize quite how important education is.

Before I closed the school door I looked back as if it were the last time I would ever be at school. That's the closing shot in one part of the documentary. In reality I went back inside. My friends and I didn't want that day to end, so we decided to stay on for a while longer. We went to the primary school where there was more space to run around and played cops and robbers. Then we played mango mango, where you make a circle and sing, then when the song stops everyone has to freeze. Anyone who moves or laughs is out.

We came home from school late that day. Usually we leave at 1 p.m., but that day we stayed till three. Before we left, Moniba and I had an argument over something so silly I can't remember what it was. Our friends couldn't believe it. "You two always argue when there's an important occasion!" they said. It wasn't a good way to leave things.

I told the documentary makers, "They cannot stop me. I will get my education if it's at home, school or somewhere else. This is our request to the world—to save our schools, save our Pakistan, save our Swat."

When I got home, I cried and cried. I didn't want to stop learning. I was only eleven years old, but I felt as though I had lost everything. I had told everyone in my class that the Taliban wouldn't go through with it. "They're just like our politicians—they talk the talk, but they won't do anything," I'd said. But then they went ahead and closed our school and I felt embarrassed. I couldn't control myself. I was crying, my mother was crying, but my father insisted, "You will go to school."

For him the closing of the schools also meant the loss of business. The boys' school would re-open after the winter holidays, but the loss of the girls' school represented a big cut in our income. More than half the school fees were overdue and my father spent the last day chasing money to pay the rent, the utility bills and the teachers' salaries.

That night the air was full of artillery fire and I woke up three times. The next morning everything had changed. I began to think that maybe I should go to Peshawar or abroad or maybe I could ask our teachers to form a secret school in our home, as some Afghans had done during Taliban rule. Afterward I went on as many radio and TV channels as possible. "They can stop us going to school, but they can't stop us learning," I said. I sounded hopeful, but in my heart I was worried. My father and I went to Peshawar and visited lots of places to tell people what was happening. I spoke of the irony of the Taliban wanting female teachers and doctors for women yet not letting girls go to school to qualify for these jobs.

Once Muslim Khan had said girls should not go to school and learn Western ways. This from a man who had lived so long in America! He insisted he would have his own education system. "What would Muslim Khan use instead of the stethoscope and the thermometer?" my father asked. "Are there any Eastern instruments which will treat the sick?" The Taliban is against education because they think that when a child reads a book or learns English or studies science he or she will become Westernized.

But I said, "Education is education. We should learn everything and then choose which path to follow." Education is neither Eastern nor Western, it is human.

My mother used to tell me to hide my face when I spoke to the media because at my age I should be in purdah and she was afraid for my safety. But she never banned me from doing anything. It was a time of horror and fear. People often said the Taliban might kill my father but not me. "Malala is a child," they would say, "and even the Taliban don't kill children."

But my grandmother wasn't so sure. Whenever my grandmother saw me speaking on television, or leaving the house, she would pray, "Please God make Malala like Benazir Bhutto but do not give her Benazir's short life."

After my school closed down I continued to write the blog. Four days after the ban on girls' schools, five more were destroyed. "I am quite surprised," I wrote, "because these schools had closed, so why did they also need to be destroyed? No one has gone to school following the Taliban's deadline. The army is doing nothing about it. They are sitting in their bunkers on top of the hills. They slaughter goats and eat with pleasure." I also wrote about people going to watch the floggings announced on Mullah FM, and the fact that the police were nowhere to be seen.

One day we got a call from America, from a student at Stanford University. Her name was Shiza Shahid and she came from Islamabad. She had seen the *New York Times* documentary *Class Dismissed in Swat Valley* and tracked us down. We saw then the power of the media and she became a great support to us. My father was almost bursting with pride at how I came across on the documentary. "Look at her," he told Adam Ellick. "Don't you think she is meant for the skies?" Fathers can be very embarrassing.

Adam took us to Islamabad. It was the first time I had ever visited. Islamabad was a beautiful place with nice white bungalows and broad roads, though it has none of the natural beauty of Swat. We saw the Red Mosque where the siege had taken place, the wide, wide Constitution Avenue leading to the white-colonnaded buildings of the Parliament House and the Presidency, where Zardari now lived. General Musharraf was in exile in London.

We went to shops where I bought school books and Adam bought me DVDs of American TV programs like *Ugly Betty*, which was about a girl with big braces and a big heart. I loved it and dreamed of one day going to New York and working on a magazine like her. We visited the Lok Virsa museum, and it was a joy to celebrate our national heritage once again. Our own museum in Swat had closed. On the steps outside an old man was selling popcorn. He was a Pashtun like us, and when my father asked if he was from Islamabad he replied, "Do you think Islamabad can ever belong to us Pashtuns?" He said he came from Mohmand, one of the tribal areas, but had to flee because of a military operation. I saw tears in my parents' eyes.

Lots of buildings were surrounded by concrete blocks, and there were checkpoints for incoming vehicles to guard against suicide bombs. When our bus hit a pothole on the way back my brother Khushal, who had been asleep, jerked awake. "Was that a bomb blast?" he asked. This was the fear that filled our daily lives. Any small disturbance or noise could be a bomb or gunfire.

On our short trips we forgot our troubles in

Swat. But we returned to the threats and danger as we entered our valley once again. Even so, Swat was our home and we were not ready to leave it.

Back in Mingora the first thing I saw when I opened my wardrobe was my uniform, school bag and geometry set. I felt so sad. The visit to Islamabad had been a lovely break, but this was my reality now.

14

A Funny Kind of Peace

When my brothers' schools reopened after the winter break, Khushal said he would rather stay at home like me. I was cross. "You don't realize how lucky you are!" I told him. It felt strange to have no school. We didn't even have a television set, as someone had stolen ours while we were in Islamabad, using my father's "getaway" ladder to get inside.

Someone gave me a copy of *The Alchemist* by Paulo Coelho, a fable about a shepherd boy who travels to the Pyramids in search of treasure when all the time it's at home. I loved that book and read it over and over again. "When you want something all the universe conspires in helping you achieve it," it says. I don't think that Paulo Coelho had come across the Taliban or our useless politicians.

What I didn't know was that Hai Kakar was holding secret talks with Fazlullah and his commanders. He had got to know them in interviews, and was urging them to rethink their ban on girls' education.

"Listen, Maulana," he told Fazlullah. "You killed people, you slaughtered people, you beheaded people, you destroyed schools and still there was no protest in Pakistan. But when you banned girls' education people spoke out. Even the Pakistan media, which has been so soft on you till now, is outraged."

The pressure from the whole country worked, and Fazlullah agreed to lift the ban for girls up to ten years old—Year 4. I was in Year 5 and some of us pretended we were younger than we were. We started going to school again, dressed in ordinary clothes and hiding our books under our shawls. It was risky, but it was the only ambition I had back then. We were lucky too that Madam Maryam was brave and resisted the pressure to stop working. She had known my father since she was ten and they trusted each other completely—she used to signal to him to wind up when he spoke for too long, which was often!

"The secret school is our silent protest," she told us.

I didn't write anything about it in my diary. If they had caught us they would have flogged or even slaughtered us as they had Shabana. Some people are afraid of ghosts, some of spiders or snakes—in those days we were afraid of our fellow human beings.

On the way to school I sometimes saw the Taliban with their caps and long dirty hair. Most of the time they hid their faces. They were awkward, horrible-looking. The streets of Mingora were very empty, as a third of the inhabitants had left the valley. My father said you couldn't really blame people for leaving, as the government had no power. There were now 12,000 army troops in the region—four times as many as their estimates of the Taliban—along with tanks, helicopters and sophisticated weapons. Yet 70 percent of Swat was under Taliban control.

About a week after we had returned to school, on 16 February 2009, we were woken one night by the sound of gunfire. Our people traditionally fire rifles in celebration of births and weddings, but even that had stopped during the conflict. So at first we thought we were in danger. Then we heard the news. The gunfire was in celebration. A peace deal had been struck between the Taliban and the provincial government, which was now under the control of the ANP, not the mullahs. The government had agreed to impose sharia law throughout Swat and in return the militants would stop fighting. The Taliban agreed to a ten-day truce and, as a peace gesture, released a Chinese telephone engineer who they had kidnapped six months before.

We were happy too—my father and I had often spoken in favor of a peace deal—but we questioned how it would work. People hoped that the Taliban would settle down, go back to their homes, and live as peaceful citizens. They convinced themselves that the *shariat* in Swat would be different from the Afghan version—we would still have our girls' schools and there would be no morality police. Swat would be Swat just with a different justice system. I wanted to believe this, but I was worried. I thought, *Surely how the system works depends on the people overseeing it? The Taliban.*

And it was hard to believe it was all over! More than a thousand ordinary people and police had been killed. Women had been kept in purdah, schools and bridges had been blown up, businesses had closed. We had suffered barbaric public courts and violent justice and had lived in a constant state of fear. And now it was all to stop.

A Funny Kind of Peace

At breakfast I suggested to my brothers that we should talk of peace now and not of war. As ever, they ignored me and carried with on their war games. Khushal had a toy helicopter and Atal a pistol made of paper, and one would shout, "Fire!" and the other, "Take position." I didn't care. I went and looked at my uniform, happy that I would soon be able to wear it openly. A message came from our headmistress that exams would take place in the first week of March. It was time to get back to my books.

Our excitement did not last long. Just two days later I was on the roof of the Taj Mahal Hotel giving an interview about the peace deal to a well-known reporter called Hamid Mir when we got the news that another TV reporter we knew had been killed. His name was Musa Khan Khel, and he had often interviewed my father. That day he had been covering a peace march led by Sufi Mohammad. It wasn't really a march but a cavalcade of cars. Afterward Musa Khan's body was found nearby. He had been shot several times and his throat partly slit. He was twenty-eight years old.

My mother was so upset when we told her that she went to bed in tears. She was worried that violence had returned to the valley so soon after the peace deal. Was the deal merely an illusion? she wondered.

A few days later, on 22 February, a "permanent ceasefire" was announced by Deputy Commissioner Syed Javid at the Swat Press Club in Mingora. He appealed to all Swatis to return. The Taliban spokesman Muslim Khan then confirmed they had agreed an indefinite ceasefire. President Zardari would sign the peace deal into law. The government also agreed to pay compensation to the families of victims.

Everyone in Swat was jubilant, but I felt the happiest because it meant school would reopen properly. The Taliban said girls could go to school after the peace agreement but they should be veiled and covered. We said OK, if that's what you want, as long as we can live our lives.

Not everyone was happy about the deal. Our American allies were furious. "I think the Pakistan government is basically abdicating to the Taliban and the extremists," said Hillary Clinton, the US secretary of state. The Americans were worried the deal meant surrender. The Pakistani newspaper *Dawn* wrote in an editorial that the deal sent "a disastrous signal—fight the state militarily and it will give you what you want and get nothing in return."

But none of those people had to live here. We needed peace whoever brought it. In our case it happened to be a white-bearded militant called Sufi Mohammad. He made a "peace camp" in Dir and sat there in our famous mosque, Tabligh Markaz, like the master of our land. He was the guarantor that the Taliban would lay down their arms and there would be peace in the valley. People visited him to pay homage and kiss his hand because they were tired of war and suicide bombings.

In March I stopped writing my blog, as Hai Kakar thought there was not much more to say. But to our horror things didn't change much. If anything the Taliban became even more barbaric. They were now state-sanctioned terrorists. We were disillusioned and disappointed. The peace deal was merely a mirage. One night the Taliban held what we call a flag march near our street and patrolled the roads with guns and sticks as if they were the army.

They were still patrolling the Cheena Bazaar. One day my mother went shopping with my cousin, as she was getting married and wanted to buy things for her wedding. A Talib accosted them and blocked their way. "If I see you again wearing a scarf but no burqa I will beat you," he said. My mother is not easily scared and remained composed. "Yes, OK. We will wear burqas in future," she told him. My mother always covers her head, but the burqa is not part of our Pashtun tradition.

We also heard that Taliban had attacked a shopkeeper because an unaccompanied woman was looking at the lipsticks in his beauty shop. "There is a banner in the market saying women are not allowed to be in your shop unaccompanied by a male relative and you have defied us," they said. He was badly beaten and nobody helped him.

One day I saw my father and his friends watching a video on his phone. It was a shocking scene. A teenage girl wearing a black burqa and red trousers was lying face down on the ground being flogged in broad daylight by a bearded man in a black turban. "Please stop it!" she begged in Pashto in between screams and whimpers as each blow was delivered. "In the name of Allah, I am dying!"

You could hear the Taliban shouting, "Hold her down. Hold her hands down." At one point during the flogging her burqa slips and they stop for a moment to adjust it then carry on beating her. They hit her thirty-four times. A crowd had gathered but did nothing. One of the woman's relatives even volunteered to help hold her down.

A few days later the video was everywhere. A woman film-maker in Islamabad got hold of it and it was shown on Pakistan TV over and over, and then around the world. People were rightly outraged, but this reaction seemed odd to us, as it showed they had no idea of the awful things going on in our valley. I wished their outrage extended to the Taliban's banning of girls' education. Prime Minister Yusuf Raza Gilani called for an inquiry and made a statement saying the flogging of the girl was against the teachings of Islam. "Islam teaches us to treat women politely," he said.

Some people even claimed the video was fake. Others said that the flogging had taken place in January, before the peace deal, and had been released now to sabotage it. But Muslim Khan confirmed it was genuine. "She came out of her house with a man who was not her husband, so we had to punish her," he said. "Some boundaries cannot be crossed."

Around the same time in early April another well known journalist called Zahid Hussain came to Swat. He went to visit the DC at his official residence and found him hosting what appeared to be a celebration of the Taliban takeover. There were several senior Taliban commanders with armed escorts including Muslim Khan, and even Faqir Mohammad, the leader of the militants in Bajaur, who were in the middle of a bloody fight with the army. Faqir had a $200,000 bounty on his head yet there he was sitting in a government official's house having dinner. We also heard that an army brigadier went to prayers led by Fazlullah.

"There cannot be two swords in one sheath," said one of my father's friends. "There cannot be two kings in one land. Who is in charge here— the government or Fazlullah?"

But we still believed in peace. Everyone was looking forward to a big outside public meeting on 20 April when Sufi Mohammad would address the people of Swat.

We were all at home that morning. My father and brothers were standing outside when a group of teenage Taliban went past playing victory songs on their mobiles. "Oh look at them, *Aba*," said Khushal. "If I had a Kalashnikov I would kill them."

It was a perfect spring day. Everyone was excited because they hoped Sufi Mohammad would proclaim peace and victory and ask the

Taliban to lay down their arms. My father didn't attend the gathering. He watched it from the roof of Sarosh Academy, the school run by his friend Ahmad Shah where he and other activists often gathered in the evenings. The roof overlooked the stage, so some media had set up their cameras there.

There was a huge crowd—between 30,000 and 40,000 people—wearing turbans and singing Taliban and jihadi songs. "It was complete Talibanization humming," said my father. Liberal progressives like him did not enjoy the singing and chanting. They thought it was toxic, especially at times like this.

Sufi Mohammad was sitting on the stage with a long queue of people waiting to pay homage. The meeting started with recitations from the Chapter of Victory—a *surah* from the Quran—followed by speeches from different leaders in the five districts of our valley—Kohistan, Malakand, Shangla, Upper Dir and Lower Dir. They were all very enthusiastic, as each one was hoping to be made the *amir* of his district so he could be in charge of imposing *shariat*. Later these leaders would be killed or thrown in jail, but back then they dreamed of power. So everyone spoke with great authority, celebrating like the Prophet,

PBUH, when he conquered Mecca, though his speech was one of forgiveness not cruel victory.

Then it was Sufi Mohammad's turn. He was not a good speaker. He was very old and seemed in poor health and rambled on for forty-five minutes. He said totally unexpected things as if he had someone else's tongue in his mouth, described Pakistan's courts as un-Islamic and said, "I consider Western democracy a system imposed on us by the infidels. Islam does not allow democracy or elections."

Sufi Mohammad said nothing about education. He didn't tell the Taliban to lay down their arms and leave the *hujras*. Instead he appeared to threaten the whole nation. "Now wait, we are coming to Islamabad," he shouted.

We were shocked. It was like when you pour water onto a blazing fire—the flames are suddenly extinguished. People were bitterly disappointed and started abusing him. "What did that devil say?" people asked. "He's not for peace; he wants more killing." My mother put it best. "He had the chance to be the hero of history but didn't take it," she said. Our mood on the way home was the exact opposite of what we had felt on the way to the meeting.

That night my father spoke on Geo TV and

told Kamran Khan that people had had high hopes but were disappointed. Sufi Mohammad didn't do what he should have done. He was supposed to seal the peace deal with a speech calling for reconciliation and an end to violence.

People had different conspiracy theories about what had happened. Some said Sufi Mohammad had gone mad. Others said he had been ordered to deliver this speech and been warned, "If you don't, there are four or five suicide bombers who will blast you and everyone there." People said he had looked uneasy on stage before he spoke. They muttered about hidden hands and unseen forces. *What does it matter?* I wondered. *The point is we are a Taliban state.*

My father was again busy speaking at seminars on our troubles with the Taliban. At one the information minister for our province said Talibanization was the result of our country's policy of training militants and sending them to Afghanistan, first to fight the Russians, then to fight the Americans. "If we had not put guns in the hands of madrasa students at the behest of foreign powers we would not be facing this bloodbath in the tribal areas and Swat," he said.

It soon became clear that the Americans had been right in their assessment of the deal. The

Taliban believed the Pakistani government had given in and they could do what they liked. They streamed into Buner, the next district to the southeast of Swat and only sixty-five miles from Islamabad. People in Buner had always resisted the Taliban, but they were ordered by the local authorities not to fight. As the militants arrived with their RPGs and guns, the police abandoned their posts, saying the Taliban had "superior weapons," and people fled. The Taliban set up *shariat* courts in all districts and broadcast sermons from mosques calling on the local youth to join them.

Just as they had in Swat, they burned TV sets, pictures, DVDs and tapes. They even took control of the famous shrine of a Sufi saint, Pir Baba, which was a pilgrimage site. People would visit to pray for spiritual guidance, cures for their ailments and even happy marriages for their children. But now it was locked and bolted.

People in the lower districts of Pakistan became very worried as the Taliban moved toward the capital. Everyone seemed to have seen the video of the girl in the black burqa being flogged and were asking, "Is this what we want in Pakistan?" Militants had killed Benazir, blown up the country's best-known hotel, killed thousands of people in suicide bombings and beheadings and destroyed hundreds of schools. What more would it take for the army and government to resist them?

In Washington the government of President Obama had just announced it was sending 21,000 more troops to Afghanistan to turn around the war against the Taliban. But now they seemed to be more alarmed about Pakistan than Afghanistan. Not because of girls like me and my school but because our country has more than 200 nuclear warheads and they were worried about who was going to control them. They talked about stopping their billions of dollars in aid and sending troops instead.

At the start of May our army launched Operation True Path to drive the Taliban out of Swat. We heard they were dropping hundreds of commandos from helicopters into the mountains in the north. More troops appeared in Mingora too. This time they would clear the town. They announced over megaphones that all residents should leave.

My father said we should stay. But the gunfire kept us awake most nights. Everyone was in a continuous state of anxiety. One night we were woken up by screaming. We had recently got some pets—three white chickens and a white rabbit that one of Khushal's friends had given him and which we let wander around the house. Atal was only five then and really loved that rabbit, so it used to sleep under my parents' bed. But it used to wee everywhere, so that night we put it outside. Around midnight a cat came and killed it. We all heard the rabbit's agonized cries. Atal would not stop weeping. "Let the sun come and I will teach that cat a lesson tomorrow," he said. "I will kill him." It seemed like a bad omen.

15

Leaving the Valley

Leaving the valley was harder than anything I had done before. I remembered the *tapa* my grandmother used to recite: "No Pashtun leaves his land of his own sweet will. Either he leaves from poverty or he leaves for love." Now we were being driven out for a third reason the *tapa* writer had never imagined—the Taliban.

Leaving our home felt like having my heart ripped out. I stood on our roof looking at the mountains, the snow-topped Mount Elum where Alexander the Great had reached up and touched Jupiter. I looked at the trees all coming into leaf. The fruit of our apricot tree might be eaten by someone else this year. Everything was silent, pin-drop silent. There was no sound from the river or the wind; even the birds were not chirping.

I wanted to cry because I felt in my heart I

might never see my home again. The documentary makers had asked me how I would feel if one day I left Swat and never came back. At the time I had thought it was a stupid question, but now I saw that everything I could not imagine happening had happened. I thought my school would not close and it had. I thought we would never leave Swat and we were just about to. I thought Swat would be free of the Taliban one day and we would rejoice, but now I realized that might not happen. I started to cry. It was as if everyone had been waiting for someone else to start. My cousin's wife, Honey, started weeping, then all of us were crying. But my mother was very composed and courageous.

I put all my books and notebooks in my school bag then packed another bag of clothes. I couldn't think straight. I took the trousers from one set and the top from another, so I had a bag of things which didn't match. I didn't take any of my school awards or photos or personal belongings, as we were traveling in someone else's car and there was little room. We didn't own anything expensive like a laptop or jewelry—our only valuable items had been our TV, a fridge and a washing machine. We didn't lead a life of luxury—we Pashtuns prefer to sit on floors rather than chairs. Our house has holes in the walls, and every plate and cup is cracked.

My father had resisted leaving till the end. But then some of my parents' friends had lost a relative in gunfire, so they went to the house to offer prayers of condolences even though nobody was really venturing out. Seeing their grief made my mother determined to leave. She told my father, "You don't have to come, but I am going and I will take the children to Shangla." She knew he couldn't let her go alone. My mother had had enough of the gunfire and tension and called Dr. Afzal and begged him to persuade my father to leave. He and his family were going, so they offered us a lift. We didn't have a car, so we were lucky that our neighbors, Safina and her family, were also leaving and could fit some of us in their car while the rest would go with Dr. Afzal.

On 5 May 2009 we became IDPs. Internally displaced persons. It sounded like a disease.

There were a lot of us—not just us five but also my grandmother, my cousin, his wife, Honey, and their baby. My brothers also wanted to take their pet chickens—mine had died because I washed it in cold water on a winter's day. It wouldn't revive even when I put it in a shoebox in the house to keep it warm and got everyone in the neighborhood to pray for it. My mother refused to let the chickens come. What if they make a mess in the car? she asked. Atal suggested we buy them nappies! In the end we left them with a lot of water and corn. She also said I must leave my school bag because there was so little room. I was horrified. I went and whispered Quranic verses over the books to try and protect them.

Finally everyone was ready. My mother, father, grandmother, my cousin's wife and baby and my brothers all squashed into the back of Dr. Afzal's van along with his wife and children. There were children in the laps of adults and smaller children in their laps. I was luckier—there were fewer people in Safina's car—but I was devastated by the loss of my school bag. Because I had packed my books separately, I had had to leave them all behind.

We all said *surahs* from the Quran and a special prayer to protect our sweet homes and school. Then Safina's father put his foot on the pedal and away we drove out of the small world of our street, home and school and into the unknown. We did not know if we would ever see our town again. We had seen pictures of how the army had flattened everything in an operation against militants in Bajaur and we thought everything we knew would be destroyed.

The streets were jam-packed. I had never seen them so busy before. There were cars everywhere, as well as rickshaws, mule carts and trucks laden with people and their belongings. There were even motorbikes with entire families balanced on them. Thousands of people were leaving with just the clothes they had on their backs. It felt as if the whole valley were on the move. Some people believe that the Pashtuns descend from one of the lost tribes of Israel, and my father said, "It is as though we are the Israelites leaving Egypt, but we have no Moses to guide us." Few people knew where they were going, they just knew they had to leave. This was the biggest exodus in Pashtun history.

Usually there are many ways out of Mingora, but the Taliban had cut down several huge apple trees and used them to block some routes, so everyone was squashed onto the same road. We were an ocean of people. The Taliban patrolled the roads with guns and watched us from the tops of buildings. They were keeping the cars in lines but with weapons not whistles. "Traffic Taliban," we joked to try and keep our spirits up. At regular intervals along the road we passed army and Taliban checkpoints side by side. Once again the army was seemingly unaware of the Taliban's presence.

"Maybe they have poor eyesight," we laughed, "and can't see them."

The road was heaving with traffic. It was a long slow journey and we were all very sweaty crammed in together. Usually car journeys are an adventure for us children, as we rarely go anywhere. But this was different. Everyone was depressed.

Inside Dr. Afzal's van my father was talking to the media, giving a running commentary on the exodus from the valley. My mother kept telling him to keep his voice down for fear the Taliban would hear him. My father's voice is so loud my mother often jokes that he doesn't need to make phone calls, he can just shout.

Finally we got through the mountain pass at Malakand and left Swat behind. It was late afternoon by the time we reached Mardan, which is a hot and busy city.

My father kept insisting to everyone, "In a few days we will return. Everything will be fine." But we knew that was not true.

In Mardan there were already big camps of white UNHCR tents like those for Afghan refugees in Peshawar. We weren't going to stay in the camps because it was the worst idea ever. Almost two million of us were fleeing Swat and you couldn't have fitted two million people in those camps. Even if there was a tent for us, it was far too hot inside and there was talk that diseases like cholera were spreading. My father said he had heard rumors that some Taliban were even hiding inside the camps and harassing the women.

Those who could, stayed in the homes of local people or with family and friends. Amazingly three quarters of all the IDPs were put up by the people of Mardan and the nearby town of Swabi. They opened the doors of their homes, schools and mosques to the refugees. In our culture women are expected not to mix with men they are not related to. In order to protect women's purdah, men in families hosting the refugees even slept away from their own homes. They became voluntary IDPs. It was an astonishing example of Pashtun hospitality. We were convinced that if the exodus had been managed by the government many more would have died of hunger and illness.

As we had no relatives in Mardan we were planning to make our way to Shangla, our family village. So far we had driven in the opposite direction, but we had had to take the only lift we could get out of Swat.

We spent that first night in the home of Dr. Afzal. My father then left us to go to Peshawar and alert people to what was happening. He promised to meet us later in Shangla. My mother tried very hard to persuade him to come with us, but he refused. He wanted the people of Peshawar and Islamabad to be aware of the terrible conditions in which IDPs were living and that the military were doing nothing. We said good-bye and were terribly worried we wouldn't see him again.

The next day we got a lift to Abbottabad, where my grandmother's family lived. There we met up with my cousin Khanjee, who was heading north like us. He ran a boys' hostel in Swat and was taking seven or eight boys to Kohistan by coach. He was going to Besham, from where we would need another lift to take us to Shangla.

It was nightfall by the time we reached Besham, as many roads were blocked. We spent the night in a cheap dirty hotel while my cousin tried to arrange a van to take us to Shangla. A man came near my mother and she took her shoe off and hit him once then twice and he ran away. She had hit him so hard that when she looked at the shoe it was broken. I always knew my mother was a strong woman but I looked at her with new respect.

It was not easy to get from Besham to our village and we had to walk twenty-five kilometers carrying all our things. At one point we were stopped by the army, who told us we could go no further and must turn back. "Our home is in Shangla. Where will we go?" we begged. My grandmother started crying and saying her life had never been so bad. Finally, they let us through. The army and their machine guns were everywhere. Because of the curfew and the checkpoints there was not one other vehicle on the road that didn't belong to the military. We were afraid that the army wouldn't know who we were and would shoot us.

When we reached the village our family was astonished to see us. Everyone believed the Taliban would return to Shangla, so they couldn't understand why we hadn't remained in Mardan.

We stayed in my mother's village, Karshat, with my uncle Faiz Mohammad and his family. We had to borrow clothes from our relatives, as we hadn't brought much. I was happy to be with my cousin Sumbul, who is a year older than me. Once we were settled I started going to school with her. I was in Year 6 but started in Year 7 to be with Sumbul. There were only three girls in that year, as most of the village girls of that age do not go to school, so we were taught with boys, as they didn't have enough room or staff to teach just three girls separately. I was different from the other girls, as I didn't cover my face and I used to talk to every teacher and ask questions. But I tried to be obedient and polite, always saying, "Yes, sir."

It took over half an hour to walk to school, and because I am bad at getting up in the morning the second day we were late. I was shocked when the teacher hit my hand with a stick to punish me, but then decided that at least it meant they were accepting me and not treating me differently. My uncle even gave me pocket money to buy snacks at school—they sold cucumber and watermelon not sweets and crisps like in Mingora.

One day at school there was a parents' day and prize-giving ceremony, and all the boys were encouraged to make speeches. Some of the girls also took part, but not in public. Instead we spoke into a microphone in our classrooms and our voices were then projected into the main hall. But I was used to speaking in public, so I came out and in front of all the boys I recited one *naat*, a poem in which I praised the Prophet, PBUH. Then I asked the teacher if I could read some more poetry. I read a poem about working hard to achieve your heart's desires. "A diamond must be cut many times before it yields even a tiny jewel," I said. After that I spoke of my namesake, Malalai of Maiwand, who had strength and power equal to hundreds and thousands of brave men because her few lines of poetry changed everything so the British were defeated.

People in the audience seemed surprised and I wondered whether they thought I was showing off or whether they were asking themselves why I wasn't wearing a veil.

It was nice being with my cousins, but I missed my books. I kept thinking of my school bag at home with copies of *Oliver Twist* and *Romeo and Juliet* waiting to be read and the *Ugly Betty* DVDs on the shelf. But now we were living our own drama. We had been so happy, then something very bad had come into our lives and we were now waiting for our happy ending. When I complained about my books my brothers whined about their chickens.

We'd heard on the radio that the army had started the battle for Mingora. They had parachuted in soldiers and there had been hand-to-hand fighting in the streets. The Taliban were using hotels and government buildings as bunkers. After four days the military took three squares including Green Chowk, where the Taliban used to display the beheaded bodies of their victims. Then they captured the airport and in a week they had taken back the city.

We continued to worry about my father. In Shangla it was hard to find a mobile phone signal. We had to climb onto a huge boulder in a field, and even then we rarely had more than one bar of reception, so we hardly ever spoke to him. But after we had been in Shangla for about six weeks, my father said we could travel to Peshawar, where he had been staying in one room with three friends.

It was very emotional to see him again. Then, a complete family once more, we traveled down to Islamabad, where we stayed with the family of Shiza, the lady who had called us from Stanford. While we were there we heard that Ambassador Richard Holbrooke, the American envoy to Pakistan and Afghanistan, was holding a meeting in the Serena Hotel about the conflict, and my father and I managed to get inside.

We almost missed it, as I hadn't set the alarm properly, so my father was barely speaking to me.

Holbrooke was a big gruff man with a red face, but people said he had helped bring peace to Bosnia. I sat next to him and he asked me how old I was. "I am twelve," I replied trying to look as tall as possible. "Respected Ambassador, I request you, please help us girls to get an education," I asked.

He laughed. "You already have lots of problems and we are doing lots for you," he replied. "We have pledged billions of dollars in economic aid; we are working with your government on providing electricity, gas...but your country faces a lot of problems."

I did an interview with a radio station called Power 99. They liked it very much and told us they had a guesthouse in Abbottabad where we could all go. We stayed there for a week and to my joy I heard Moniba was also in Abbottabad, as was one of our teachers and another friend. Moniba and I had not spoken since our fight on the last day before becoming IDPs. We arranged to meet in a park, and I brought her Pepsi and biscuits. "It was all your fault," she told me. I agreed. I didn't mind; I just wanted to be friends.

Our week at the guesthouse soon ended and we went to Haripur, where one of my aunts lived. It was our fourth city in two months. I knew we were better off than those who lived in the camps, queuing for food and water for hours under the hot sun, but I missed my valley. It was there I spent my twelfth birthday. Nobody remembered. Even my father forgot, he was so busy hopping about. I was upset and recalled how different my eleventh birthday had been. I had shared a cake with my friends. There were balloons and I had made the same wish I was making on my twelfth birthday, but this time there was no cake and there were no candles to blow out. Once again I wished for peace in our valley.

Part Three

Three Girls, Three Bullets

سر د په لوړه تیګه کیږده   پردي وطن دي په کښی نشته بالختونه

Sir de pa lowara tega kegda
  Praday watan de paki nishta balakhtona

O Wayfarer! Rest your head on the stony cobblestone
  It is a foreign land—not the city of your kings!

16

The Valley of Sorrows

It all seemed like a bad dream. We had been away from our valley for almost three months and as we drove back past Churchill's Picket, past the ancient ruins on the hill and the giant Buddhist stupa, we saw the wide Swat River and my father began to weep. Swat seemed to be under complete military control. The vehicle we were in had even had to pass through an explosives check before we could head up the Malakand Pass. Once we got over the other side and down into the valley it seemed there were army checkpoints everywhere and soldiers had made nests for their machine guns on so many of the rooftops.

As we drove through villages we saw buildings in ruins and burned-out vehicles. It made me think of old war movies or the video games my brother Khushal loves to play. When we reached

Mingora we were shocked. The army and Taliban had fought street to street and almost every wall was pockmarked with bullet holes. There was the rubble of blown-up buildings which the Taliban had used as hideouts, and piles of wreckage, twisted metal and smashed-up signs. Most of the shops had heavy metal shutters; those that didn't had been looted. The city was silent and emptied of people and traffic as if a plague had descended. The strangest sight of all was the bus station. Usually it's a complete confusion of Flying Coaches and rickshaws, but now it was completely deserted. We even saw plants growing up through the cracks in the paving. We had never seen our city like this.

At least there was no sign of the Taliban.

It was 24 July 2009, a week after our prime minister had announced that the Taliban had been cleared out. He promised that the gas supply had been restored and that the banks were reopening, and called on the people of Swat to return. In the end as many as half of its 1.8 million population had left our valley. From what we could see, most of them weren't convinced it was safe to return.

As we drew close to home we all fell silent, even my little brother, Atal the chatterbox. Our home was near Circuit House, the army headquarters, so we were worried it might have been destroyed in the shelling. We'd also heard that many homes had been looted. We held our breath as my father unlocked the gate. The first thing we saw was that in the three months we'd been away the garden had become a jungle.

My brothers immediately rushed off to check on their pet chickens. They came back crying. All that remained of the chickens was a pile of feathers and the bones of their small bodies entangled as if they had died in an embrace. They had starved to death.

I felt so sad for my brothers, but I had to check on something of my own. To my joy I found my school bag still packed with my books, and I gave thanks that my prayers had been answered and that they were safe. I took out my books one by one and just stared at them. Math, physics, Urdu, English, Pashto, chemistry, biology, *Islamiyat,* Pakistan studies. Finally I would be able to return to school without fear.

Then I went and sat on my bed. I was overwhelmed.

We were lucky our house had not been broken into. Four or five of the houses on our street had been looted and TVs and gold jewelry had been taken. Safina's mother next door had deposited her gold in a bank vault for safe keeping and even that had been looted.

My father was anxious to check on the school. I went with him. We found that the building opposite the girls' school had been hit by a missile, but the school itself looked intact. For some reason my father's keys would not work, so we found a boy who climbed over the wall and opened it from the inside. We ran up the steps anticipating the worst.

"Someone has been in here," my father said as soon as we entered the courtyard. There were cigarette stubs and empty food wrappers all over the floor. Chairs had been upended and the space was a mess. My father had taken down the Khushal School sign and left it in the courtyard. It was leaning against the wall and I screamed as we lifted it. Underneath were the rotting heads of goats. It looked like the remains of someone's dinner.

Then we went into the classrooms. Anti-Taliban slogans were scrawled all over the walls. Someone had written ARMY ZINDABAD (Long live the army) on a whiteboard in permanent marker. Now we knew who had been living there. One soldier had even written corny love poems in one of my classmate's diaries. Bullet casings littered the floor. The soldiers had made a hole in the wall through which you could see the city below. Maybe they had even shot at people through that hole. I felt sorry that our precious school had become a battlefield.

While we were looking around we heard someone banging on the door downstairs. "Don't open it, Malala!" my father ordered.

In his office my father found a letter left by the army. It blamed citizens like us for allowing the Taliban to control Swat. "We have lost so many of the precious lives of our soldiers and this is due to your negligence. Long live Pak Army," he read.

"This is typical," he said. "We people of Swat were first seduced by the Taliban, then killed by them and now blamed for them. Seduced, killed and blamed."

In some ways the army did not seem very different from the militants. One of our neighbors told us he had even seen them leaving the bodies of dead Taliban in the streets for all to see. Now their helicopters flew in pairs overhead like big black buzzing insects, and when we walked home we stayed close to the walls so they wouldn't see us.

We heard that thousands of people had been arrested including boys as young as eight who had been brainwashed to train for suicide bombing missions. The army was sending them to a special camp for jihadis to de-radicalize them. One of the people arrested was our old Urdu teacher who had refused to teach girls and had instead gone to help Fazlullah's men collect and destroy CDs and DVDs.

Fazlullah himself was still at large. The army had destroyed his headquarters in Imam Deri and then claimed to have him surrounded in the mountains of Peochar. Then they said he was badly injured and that they had his spokesman, Muslim Khan, in custody. Later the story changed and they reported that Fazlullah had escaped into Afghanistan and was in the province of Kunar. Some people said that Fazlullah had been captured but that the army and the ISI couldn't agree on what to do with him. The army had wanted to imprison him, but the intelligence service had prevailed and taken him to Bajaur so that he could slip across the border to Afghanistan.

Muslim Khan and another commander called Mehmud seemed to be the only members of the Taliban leadership who were in custody—all the others were still free. As long as Fazlullah was still around I was afraid the Taliban would regroup and return to power. At night I sometimes had nightmares, but at least his radio broadcasts had stopped.

My father's friend Ahmad Shah called it a "controlled peace, not a durable peace." But gradually people returned to the valley because Swat is beautiful and we cannot bear to be away from it for long.

Our school bell rang again for the first time on 1 August. It was wonderful to hear that sound and run through the doorway and up the steps as we used to. I was overjoyed to see all my old friends. We had so many stories from our time as IDPs. Most of us had stayed with friends or family, but some had been in the camps. We knew we were lucky. Many children had to have their classes in tents because the Taliban had destroyed their schools. And one of my friends, Sundus, had lost her father, who had been killed in an explosion.

It seemed like everyone knew I had written the BBC diary. Some thought my father had done it for me, but Madam Maryam, our principal, told them, "No. Malala is not just a good speaker but also a good writer."

That summer there was only one topic of conversation in my class. Shiza Shahid, our friend from Islamabad, had finished her studies in Stanford and invited twenty-seven girls from the Khushal School to spend a few days in the capital seeing the sights and taking part in workshops to help us get over the trauma of living under the Taliban. Those from my class were me, Moniba, Malka-e-Noor, Rida, Karishma and Sundus, and we were chaperoned by my mother and Madam Maryam.

We left for the capital on Independence Day, 14 August, and traveled by bus, everyone brimming with excitement. Most of the girls had only ever left the valley when we became IDPs. This was different and very much like the holidays we read about in novels. We stayed in a guesthouse and did lots of workshops on how to tell our stories so people outside would know what was going on in our valley and help us. Right from the first session I think Shiza was surprised how strong-willed and vocal we all were. "It's a room full of Malalas!" she told my father.

We also had fun doing things like going to the park and listening to music, which might seem ordinary for most people but in Swat had become acts of political protest. And we saw the sights. We visited the Faisal Mosque at the base of the Margalla Hills, which was built by the Saudis for millions of rupees. It is huge and white and looks like a shimmering tent suspended between minarets. We went on our first ever visit to the theater to see an English play called *Tom, Dick and Harry* and had art classes. We ate at restaurants and had our first visit to a McDonald's. There were lots of firsts although I had to miss a meal in a Chinese restaurant because I was on a TV show called *Capital Talk*. To this day I still haven't got to try duck pancakes!

Islamabad was totally different from Swat. It was as different for us as Islamabad is from New York. Shiza introduced us to women who were lawyers and doctors and also activists, which showed us that women could do important jobs yet still keep their culture and traditions. We saw women in the streets without purdah, their heads completely uncovered. I stopped wearing my shawl over my head in some of the meetings, thinking I had become a modern girl. Later I realized that simply having your head uncovered isn't what makes you modern!

We were there one week and predictably Moniba and I quarreled. She saw me gossiping with a girl in the year above and told me, "Now you are with Resham and I am with Rida."

Shiza wanted to introduce us to influential people. In our country of course this often means the military. One of our meetings was with Major

General Athar Abbas, the chief spokesman for the army and its head of public relations. We drove to Islamabad's twin city of Rawalpindi to see him in his office. Our eyes widened when we saw that the army headquarters was so much neater than the rest of the city with perfect green lawns and blossoming flowers. Even the trees were all the same size with the trunks painted white to exactly halfway up—we didn't know why. Inside the HQ we saw offices with banks of televisions, men monitoring every channel, and one officer showed my father a thick file of cuttings which contained every mention of the army in that day's papers. He was amazed. The army seemed much more effective at PR than our politicians.

We were taken into a hall to wait for the general. On the walls were photographs of all our army chiefs, the most powerful men in our country including dictators like Musharraf and scary Zia. A servant with white gloves brought us tea and biscuits and small meat samosas that melted in our mouths. When General Abbas came in we all stood up.

He began by telling us about the military operation in Swat, which he presented as a victory. He said 128 soldiers and 1,600 terrorists had been killed in the operation.

After he finished we could ask questions. We had been told to prepare questions in advance and I had made a list of seven or eight. Shiza had laughed and said he wouldn't be able to answer so many. I sat in the front row and was the first to be called on. I asked, "Two or three months ago you told us Fazlullah and his deputy were shot and injured, and then you said they were in Swat and sometimes you say they're in Afghanistan. How did they get there? If you have so much information, why can't you catch them?"

His reply went on for about ten to fifteen minutes and I couldn't work out what his answer was! Then I asked about reconstruction. "The army must do something for the future of the valley, not just focus on the military operation," I said.

Moniba asked something similar. "Who will reconstruct all these buildings and schools?" she wanted to know.

The general replied in a very military way. "After the operation, first we will have recovery, then rehabilitation, then hold and transfer to civil authorities."

All of us girls made it clear that we wanted to see the Taliban brought to justice, but we weren't very convinced this would happen.

Afterward General Abbas gave some of us his

visiting cards and told us to contact him if we ever needed anything.

On the last day we all had to give a speech at the Islamabad Club about our experiences in the valley under Taliban rule. When Moniba spoke she couldn't control her tears. Soon everyone was weeping. We had enjoyed a glimpse of a different life in Islamabad. In my speech I told the audience that until I had watched the English play I had no idea there were so many talented people in Pakistan. "Now we realize we don't need to watch Indian movies," I joked. We'd had a wonderful time, and when we got back to Swat I felt so hopeful about the future I planted a mango seed in the garden during Ramadan, as they are a favorite fruit to eat after breaking the fast.

But my father had a big problem. While we had been IDPs and for all the months the school had been closed he had collected no fees, but the teachers still expected to be paid. Altogether that would be over one million rupees. All the private schools were in the same boat. One school gave its teachers salaries for a month, but most didn't know what to do, as they couldn't afford to pay. The teachers at the Khushal School demanded something. They had their own expenses, and one of them, Miss Hera, was about to get married and had been relying on her salary to help pay for the ceremony.

My father was in a fix. Then we remembered General Abbas and his visiting card. It was because of the army operation to expel the Taliban that we had all had to leave and found ourselves in this situation now. So Madam Maryam and I wrote an email to General Abbas explaining the situation. He was very kind and sent us 1,100,000 rupees so my father could pay everyone three months' back pay. The teachers were so happy. Most had never received so much money at once. Miss Hera called my father in tears, grateful that her wedding could go ahead as planned.

This didn't mean we went easy on the army. We were very unhappy about the army's failure to capture the Taliban leadership, and my father and I continued to give lots of interviews. We were often joined by my father's friend Zahid Khan, a fellow member of the Swat Qaumi Jirga. He was also the president of the All Swat Hotels Association, so he was particularly eager for life to go back to normal in order so that tourists could return. Like my father he was very outspoken and had been threatened too. One night in November 2009 he had had a very narrow escape. Zahid

Khan was returning to his home from a meeting with army officials at Circuit House late at night when he was ambushed. Fortunately, many of his family live in the same area and they exchanged fire with the attackers, forcing them to flee.

Then on 1 December 2009 there was a suicide attack on a well-known local ANP politician and member of the Khyber Pakhtunkwa assembly, Dr. Shamsher Ali Khan. He had been greeting friends and constituents for Eid at his *hujra,* just a mile from Imam Deri where Fazlullah's headquarters had been, when the bomb went off. Dr. Shamsher had been an outspoken critic of the Taliban. He died on the spot and nine other people were injured. People said the bomber was about eighteen years old. The police found his legs and other parts of his body.

A couple of weeks after that our school was asked to take part in the District Child Assembly Swat, which had been set up by the charity Unicef and by the Khpal Kor (My Home) Foundation for orphans. Sixty students from all over Swat had been chosen as members. They were mostly boys although eleven girls from my school went along. The first meeting was in a hall with lots of politicians and activists. We held an election for speaker and I won! It was strange to stand up there on the stage and have people address me as Madam Speaker, but it felt good to have our voices heard. The assembly was elected for a year and we met almost every month. We passed nine resolutions calling for an end to child labor and asking for help to send the disabled and street children to school, as well as for the reconstruction of all the schools destroyed by the Taliban. Once the resolutions were agreed, they were sent to officials and a handful were even acted on.

Moniba, Ayesha and I also started learning about journalism from a British organization called the Institute for War and Peace Reporting, which ran a project called Open Minds Pakistan. It was fun learning how to report issues properly. I had become interested in journalism after seeing how my own words could make a difference and also from watching the *Ugly Betty* DVDs about life at an American magazine. This was a bit different—when we wrote about subjects close to our hearts, these were topics like extremism and the Taliban rather than clothes and hairstyles.

All too soon it was another year of exams. I beat Malka-e-Noor for first place again although it was close. Our headmistress had tried to persuade her to be a school prefect, but she said she couldn't do anything that might distract her from her studies. "You should be more like Malala and do other things," said Madam Maryam. "It's just as important as your education. Work isn't everything." But I couldn't blame her. She really wanted to please her parents, particularly her mother.

It wasn't the same Swat as before—maybe it never would be—but it was returning to normal. Even some of the dancers of Banr Bazaar had moved back, although they were mostly making DVDs to sell, rather than performing live. We enjoyed peace festivals with music and dancing, unheard of under the Taliban. My father organized one of the festivals in Marghazar and invited those who had hosted the IDPs in the lower districts as a thank you. There was music all night long.

Things often seemed to happen around my birthday, and around the time I turned thirteen in July 2010 the rain came. We normally don't have monsoons in Swat and at first we were happy, thinking the rain would mean a good harvest. But it was relentless and so heavy that you couldn't even see the person standing in front of you. Environmentalists had warned that our mountains had been stripped of trees by the Taliban and timber smugglers. Soon muddy floods were raging down the valleys, sweeping away everything in their wake.

We were in school when the floods started and were sent home. But there was so much water that the bridge across the dirty stream was submerged, so we had to find another way. The next bridge we came to was also submerged, but the water wasn't too deep, so we splashed our way across. It smelled foul. We were wet and filthy by the time we got home.

The next day we heard that the school had been flooded. It took days for the water to drain away and when we returned we could see chest-high tide marks on the walls. There was mud, mud, mud everywhere. Our desks and chairs were covered with it. The classrooms smelled disgusting. There was so much damage that it cost my father 90,000 rupees to repair—equivalent to the monthly fees for ninety students.

It was the same story throughout Pakistan. The mighty Indus River, which flows from the Himalayas down through KPK and Punjab to Karachi and the Arabian Sea, and of which we are so proud, had turned into a raging torrent and burst its banks. Roads, crops and entire villages were washed away. Around 2,000 people drowned and 14 million people were affected. Many of them lost their homes and 7,000 schools were destroyed. It was the worst flood in living memory. The head of the United Nations, Ban Ki-moon, called it a "slow-motion tsunami." We read that more lives had been affected and more damage had been caused by the floods than the Asian tsunami, our 2005 earthquake, Hurricane Katrina and the Haiti earthquake combined.

Swat was one of the places most affected. Thirty-four of our forty-two bridges had been washed away, cutting off much of the valley. Electric pylons had been smashed into pieces, so we had no power. Our own street was on a hill, so we were a bit better protected from the overflowing river, but we shivered at the sound of it, a growling heavy-breathing dragon devouring everything in its path. The riverside hotels and restaurants where tourists used to eat trout and enjoy the views were all destroyed. The tourist areas were the hardest hit parts of Swat. Hill station resorts like Malam Jabba, Madyan and Bahrain were devastated, their hotels and bazaars in ruins.

We soon heard from our relatives that the damage in Shangla was unimaginable. The main road to our village from Alpuri, the capital of Shangla, had been washed away, and entire villages were submerged. Many of the houses on the hilly terraces of Karshat, Shahpur and Barkana had been taken by mudslides. My mother's family home,

At the tomb of Jinnah, the founder of Pakistan.

My father and the elders of Swat.

School bombing. *(Copyright © Kh Awais)*

The bus where I was shot. *(Copyright © Asad Hashim / Al Jazeera. Courtesy of Al Jazeera English; AlJazeera.com)*

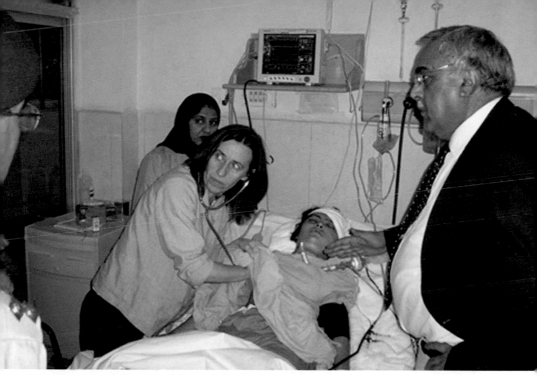

Dr. Fiona and Dr. Javid by my bedside. *(Copyright © University Hospitals Birmingham NHS Foundation Trust; used with the kind permission of the Queen Elizabeth Hospital in Birmingham)*

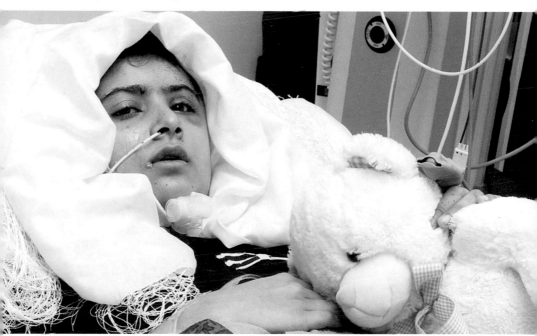

First days in the Birmingham hospital. *(Copyright © University Hospitals Birmingham NHS Foundation Trust; used with the kind permission of the Queen Elizabeth Hospital in Birmingham)*

I am reading in hospital. *(Copyright © University Hospitals Birmingham NHS Foundation Trust; used with the kind permission of the Queen Elizabeth Hospital in Birmingham)*

Our headmistress, Madam Maryam (left), with Shazia, one of the girls who was shot with me.

My friends keep a chair in class for me (far right).

چه شهباز و طرنکچې نه وي
حکمرانه ژوند به ښه وي

Khushal
School & College Swat

Sir Amjad, head of the boys' school, greets my poster every morning.

(Copyright © Justin Sutcliffe, 2013)

Here I am at the UN with Ban Ki-moon, Gordon Brown, family and friends. *(Copyright © UN Photo / Eskinder Debebe; used with the kind permission of the United Nations Photo Library)*

Speaking at the UN on my sixteenth birthday. *(Copyright © UN Photo / Rick Bajornas; used with the kind permission of the United Nations Photo Library)*

With my mother in Medina.

Here we are outside our new home in Birmingham. *(Copyright © Antonio Olmos)*

where Uncle Faiz Mohammad lived, was still standing, but the road it stood on had vanished.

People had desperately tried to protect what little they owned, moving their animals to higher ground, but the floods saturated the corn they had harvested, destroyed the orchards and drowned many of the buffaloes. The villagers were helpless. They had no power, as all their makeshift hydroelectric projects had been smashed to pieces. They had no clean water, as the river was brown with wreckage and debris. So strong was the force of the water that even concrete buildings had been reduced to rubble. The school, hospital and electricity station along the main road were all razed to the ground.

No one could understand how this had happened. People had lived by the river in Swat for 3,000 years and always seen it as our lifeline, not a threat, and our valley as a haven from the outside world. Now we had become "the valley of sorrows," said my cousin Sultan Rome. First the earthquake, then the Taliban, then the military operation, and now, just as we were starting to rebuild, devastating floods arrived to wash all our work away. People were desperately worried that the Taliban would take advantage of the chaos and return to the valley.

My father sent food and aid to Shangla using money collected by friends and the Swat Association of Private Schools. Our friend Shiza and some of the activists we had met in Islamabad came to Mingora and distributed lots of money. But just like during the earthquake, it was mainly volunteers from Islamic groups who were the first to arrive in the more remote and isolated areas with aid. Many said the floods were another reproof from God for the music and dancing we had enjoyed at the recent festivals. The consolation this time, however, was that there was no radio to spread this message!

While all this suffering was going on, while people were losing their loved ones, their homes and their livelihoods, our president, Asif Zardari, was on holiday at a chateau in France. "I am confused, *Aba*," I told my father. "What's stopping each and every politician from doing good things? Why would they not want our people to be safe, to have food and electricity?"

After the Islamic groups the main help came from the army. Not just our army. The Americans also sent helicopters, which made some people suspicious. One theory was that the devastation had been created by the Americans using something called HAARP (High Frequency Active

Auroral Research Program) technology, which causes huge waves under the ocean, thus flooding our land. Then, under the pretext of bringing in aid, they could legitimately enter Pakistan and spy on all our secrets.

Even when the rains finally ceased life was still very difficult. We had no clean water and no electricity. In August we had our first case of cholera in Mingora and soon there was a tent of patients outside the hospital. Because we were cut off from supply routes, what little food was available was extremely expensive. It was the peach and onion season and farmers were desperate to save their harvests. Many of them made hazardous journeys across the churning swollen river on boats made from rubber tires to try to bring their produce to market. When we found peaches for sale we were so happy.

There was less foreign help than there might have been at another time. The rich countries of the West were suffering from an economic crisis, and President Zardari's travels around Europe had made them less sympathetic. Foreign governments pointed out most of our politicians weren't paying any income tax, so it was a bit much to ask hard-pressed taxpayers in their own countries to contribute. Foreign aid agencies were also worried about the safety of their staff after a Taliban spokesperson demanded that the Pakistan government reject help from Christians and Jews. No one doubted they were serious. The previous October, the World Food Program office in Islamabad had been bombed and five aid workers were killed.

In Swat we began to see more signs that the Taliban had never really left. Two more schools were blown up and three foreign aid workers from a Christian group were kidnapped as they returned to their base in Mingora and then murdered. We received other shocking news. My father's friend Dr. Mohammad Farooq, the vice chancellor of Swat University, had been killed by two gunmen who burst into his office. Dr. Farooq was an Islamic scholar and former member of the Jamaat-e-Islami party, and as one of the biggest voices against Talibanization he had even issued a fatwa against suicide attacks.

We felt frustrated and scared once again. When we were IDPs I had thought about becoming a politician and now I knew that was the right choice. Our country had so many crises and no real leaders to tackle them.

17

Praying to Be Tall

When I was thirteen I stopped growing. I had always looked older than I was, but suddenly all my friends were taller than me. I was one of the three shortest girls in my class of thirty. I felt embarrassed when I was with my friends. Every night I prayed to Allah to be taller. I measured myself on my bedroom wall with a ruler and a pencil. Every morning I would stand against it to check if I had grown. But the pencil mark stayed stubbornly at five feet. I even promised Allah that if I could grow just a tiny bit taller I would offer a hundred *raakat nafl,* extra voluntary prayers on top of the five daily ones.

I was speaking at a lot of events, but because I was so short it wasn't easy to be authoritative. Sometimes I could hardly see over the lectern. I did not like high-heeled shoes, but I started to wear them.

One of the girls in my class did not return to school that year. She had been married off as soon as she entered puberty. She was big for her age but was still only thirteen. A while later we heard that she had two children. In class, when we were reciting hydrocarbon formulae during our chemistry lessons, I would daydream about what it would be like to stop going to school and instead start looking after a husband.

We had begun to think about other things besides the Taliban, but it wasn't possible to completely forget. Our army, which already had a lot of strange side businesses, like factories making cornflakes and fertilizers, had started producing soap operas. People across Pakistan were glued to a series on prime-time TV called *Beyond the Call of Duty*, which was supposed to consist of real-life stories of soldiers battling militants in Swat.

Over a hundred soldiers had been killed in the military operation and 900 injured, and they wanted to show themselves as heroes. But though their sacrifice was supposed to have restored government control, we were still waiting for the rule of law. Most afternoons when I came home from school there were women at our house in tears. Hundreds of men had gone missing during the military campaign, presumably picked up by the army or ISI, but no one would say. The women could not get information; they didn't know if their husbands and sons were dead or alive. Some of them were in desperate situations, as they had no way to support themselves. A woman can only remarry if her husband is declared dead, not missing.

My mother gave them tea and food, but that wasn't why they came. They wanted my father's help. Because of his role as spokesman for the Swat Qaumi Jirga, he acted as a kind of liaison between the people and the army.

"I just want to know if my husband is dead or not," pleaded one lady I met. "If they killed him then I can put the children in an orphanage. But now I'm neither a widow nor a wife." Another lady told me her son was missing. The women said the missing men had not collaborated with the Taliban; maybe they had given them a glass of water or some bread when they'd been ordered to do so. Yet these innocent men were being held while the Taliban leaders went free.

There was a teacher in our school who lived just a ten-minute walk from our house. Her brother had been picked up by the army, put in leg irons and tortured, and then kept in a fridge until he died. He'd had nothing to do with the Taliban.

He was just a simple shopkeeper. Afterward the army apologized to her and said they'd been confused by his name and picked up the wrong person.

It wasn't just poor women who came to our house. One day a rich businessman arrived from Muscat in the Gulf. He told my father that his brother and five or six nephews had all disappeared, and he wanted to know if they had been killed or were being held so he knew whether to find new husbands for their wives. One of them was a *maulana* and my father managed to get him freed.

This wasn't just happening in Swat. We heard there were thousands of missing all over Pakistan. Many people protested outside courthouses or put up posters of their missing but got nowhere.

Meanwhile our courts were busy with another issue. In Pakistan we have something called the Blasphemy Law, which protects the Holy Quran from desecration. Under General Zia's Islamization campaign, the law was made much stricter so that anyone who "defiles the sacred name of the Holy Prophet (PBUH)" can be punished by death or life imprisonment.

One day in November 2010 there was a news

report about a Christian woman called Asia Bibi who had been sentenced to death by hanging. She was a poor mother of five who picked fruit for a living in a village in Punjab. One hot day she had fetched water for her fellow workers, but some of them refused to drink it, saying that the water was "unclean" because she was a Christian. They believed that as Muslims they would be defiled by drinking with her. One of them was her neighbor, who was angry because she said Asia Bibi's goat had damaged her water trough. They had ended up in an argument, and of course just as in our arguments at school there were different versions of who said what. One version was that they tried to persuade Asia Bibi to convert to Islam. She replied that Christ had died on the cross for the sins of Christians and asked what the Prophet Mohammad (PBUH) had done for Muslims. One of the fruit pickers reported her to the local imam, who informed the police. She spent more than a year in jail before the case went to court and she was sentenced to death.

Since Musharraf had allowed satellite television, we now had lots of channels. Suddenly we could witness these events on television. There was outrage around the world and all the talk shows covered the case. One of the few people who spoke out for Asia Bibi in Pakistan was the governor of Punjab, Salman Taseer. He himself had been a political prisoner as well as a close ally of Benazir. Later on he became a wealthy media mogul. He went to visit Asia Bibi in jail and said that President Zardari should pardon her. He called the Blasphemy Law a "black law," a phrase which was repeated by some of our TV anchors to stir things up. Then some imams at Friday prayers in the largest mosque in Rawalpindi condemned the governor.

A couple of days later, on 4 January 2011, Salman Taseer was gunned down by one of his own bodyguards after lunch in an area of fashionable coffee bars in Islamabad. The man shot him twenty-six times. He later said that he had done it for God after hearing the Friday prayers in Rawalpindi. We were shocked by how many people praised the killer. When he appeared in court even lawyers showered him with rose petals. Meanwhile the imam at the late governor's mosque refused to perform his funeral prayers and the president did not attend his funeral.

Our country was going crazy. How was it possible that we were now garlanding murderers?

Shortly after that my father got another death threat. He had spoken at an event to commemorate the third anniversary of the bombing of the Haji Baba High School. At the event my father had spoken passionately. "Fazlullah is the chief of all devils!" he shouted. "Why hasn't he been caught?" Afterward people told him to be very careful. Then an anonymous letter came to our house addressed to my father. It started with *"Asalaamu alaikum"*—"Peace be upon you"—but it wasn't peaceful at all. It went on, "You are the son of a religious cleric, but you are not a good Muslim. The mujahideen will find you wherever you go." When my father received the letter he seemed worried for a couple of weeks, but he refused to give up his activities and was soon distracted by other things.

In those days it seemed like everyone was talking about America. Where once we used to blame our old enemy India for everything, now it was the US. Everyone complained about the drone attacks which were happening in the FATA almost every week. We heard lots of civilians were being killed. Then a CIA agent called Raymond Davis shot and killed two men in Lahore who had approached his car on a motorbike. He said they had attempted to rob him. The Americans claimed he was not CIA but an ordinary diplomat, which made everyone very suspicious. Even we schoolchildren know that ordinary diplomats don't drive around in unmarked cars carrying Glock pistols.

Our media claimed Davis was part of a vast secret army that the CIA had sent to Pakistan because they didn't trust our intelligence agencies. He was said to be spying on a militant group called Lashkar-e-Taiba based in Lahore that had helped our people a lot during the earthquake and floods. They were thought to be behind the terrible Mumbai massacre of 2008. The group's main objective was to liberate Kashmir's Muslims from Indian rule, but they had recently also become active in Afghanistan. Other people said Davis was really spying on our nuclear weapons.

Raymond Davis quickly became the most famous American in Pakistan. There were protests all over the country. People imagined our bazaars were full of Raymond Davises, gathering intelligence to send back to the States. Then the widow of one of the men Davis had murdered took rat poison and killed herself, despairing of receiving justice.

It took weeks of back and forth between Washington and Islamabad, or rather army headquarters in Rawalpindi, before the case was finally resolved.

What they did was like our traditional *jirgas*—the Americans paid "blood money" amounting to $2.3 million and Davis was quickly spirited out of court and out of the country. Pakistan then demanded that the CIA send home many of its contractors and stopped approving visas. The whole affair left a lot of bad feeling, particularly because on 17 March, the day after Davis was released, a drone attack on a tribal council in North Waziristan killed about forty people. The attack seemed to send the message that the CIA could do as it pleased in our country.

One Monday I was about to measure myself against the wall to see if I had miraculously grown in the night when I heard loud voices next door. My father's friends had arrived with news that was hard to believe. During the night American special forces called Navy SEALs had carried out a raid in Abbottabad, one of the places we'd stayed as IDPs, and had found and killed Osama bin Laden. He had been living in a large walled compound less than a mile from our military academy. We couldn't believe the army had been oblivious to bin Laden's whereabouts. The newspapers said that the cadets even did their training in the field alongside his house. The compound had twelve-foot-high walls topped with barbed wire. Bin Laden lived on the top floor with his youngest wife, a Yemeni woman named Amal. Two other wives and his eleven children lived below them. An American senator said that the only thing missing from bin Laden's hideaway was a "neon sign."

In truth, lots of people in Pashtun areas live in walled compounds because of purdah and privacy, so the house wasn't really unusual. What was odd was that the residents never went out and the house had no phone or Internet connections. Their food was brought in by two brothers who also lived in the compound with their wives. They acted as couriers for bin Laden. One of the wives was from Swat!

The SEALs had shot bin Laden in the head and his body had been flown out by helicopter. It didn't sound as though he had put up a fight. The two brothers and one of bin Laden's grown-up sons had also been killed, but bin Laden's wives and other children had been tied up and left behind and were then taken into Pakistani custody. The Americans dumped bin Laden's body at sea. President Obama was very happy, and on TV we watched big celebrations take place outside the White House.

At first we assumed our government had known and been involved in the American operation. But we soon found out that the Americans had gone it alone. This didn't sit well with our people. We were supposed to be allies and we had lost more soldiers in their War on Terror than they had. They had entered the country at night, flying low and using special quiet helicopters, and had blocked our radar with electronic interference. They had only announced their mission to the army chief of staff, General Ashfaq Kayani, and President Zardari after the event. Most of the army leadership learned about it on TV.

The Americans said they had no choice but to do it like that because no one really knew which side the ISI was on and someone might have tipped off bin Laden before they reached him. The director of the CIA said Pakistan was "either involved or incompetent. Neither place is a good place to be."

My father said it was a shameful day. "How could a notorious terrorist be hiding in Pakistan and remain undetected for so many years?" he asked. Others were asking the same thing.

You could see why anyone would think our intelligence service must have known bin Laden's location. ISI is a huge organization with agents everywhere. How could he have lived so close to the capital—just sixty miles away? And for so long! Maybe the best place to hide is in plain sight, but he had been living in that house since the 2005 earthquake. Two of his children were even born in the Abbottabad hospital. And he'd been in Pakistan for more than nine years. Before Abbottabad he'd been in Haripur and before that hidden away in our own Swat Valley, where he met Khalid Sheikh Mohammad, the mastermind of 9/11.

The way bin Laden was found was like something out of the spy movies my brother Khushal likes. To avoid detection he used human couriers rather than phone calls or emails. But the Americans had discovered one of his couriers, tracked the number plate of his car, and followed it from Peshawar to Abbottabad. After that they monitored the house with a kind of giant drone that has X-ray vision, which spotted a very tall bearded man pacing around the compound. They called him the Pacer.

People were intrigued by the new details that came every day, but they seemed angrier at the American incursion than at the fact that the world's biggest terrorist had been living on our soil. Some newspapers ran stories saying that the Americans had actually killed bin Laden years before this and kept his body in a freezer. The story was that they had then planted the body in Abbottabad and faked the raid to embarrass Pakistan.

We started to receive text messages asking us to rally in the streets and show our support of the army. "We were there for you in 1948, 1965 and 1971," said one message, referring to our three wars with India. "Be with us now when we have been stabbed in the back." But there were also text messages which ridiculed the army. People asked how we could be spending $6 billion a year on the military (seven times more than we were spending on education) if four American helicopters could just sneak in under our radar? And if they could do it, what was to stop the Indians next door? "Please don't honk, the army is sleeping," said one text and "Second-hand Pakistani radar for sale... can't detect US helicopters but gets cable TV just fine," said another.

General Kayani and General Ahmad Shuja Pasha, the head of ISI, were called to testify in parliament, something that had never happened. Our country had been humiliated and we wanted to know why.

We also learned that American politicians were furious that bin Laden had been living under our noses when all along they had imagined he was hiding in a cave. They complained that they had given us $20 billion over an eight-year period to cooperate and it was questionable which side we were on. Sometimes it felt as though it was all about the money. Most of it had gone to the army; ordinary people received nothing.

A few months after that, in October 2011, my father told me he had received an email informing him I was one of five nominees for the international peace prize of KidsRights, a children's advocacy group based in Amsterdam. My name had been put forward by Archbishop Desmond Tutu from South Africa. He was a great hero of my father for his fight against apartheid. My father was disappointed when I didn't win, but I pointed out to him that all I had done was speak out; we didn't have an organization doing practical things like the award winners had.

Shortly after that I was invited by the chief minister of Punjab, Shahbaz Sharif, to speak in Lahore at an education gala. He was building a network of new schools he calls Daanish Schools and giving free laptops to students, even if they did have his picture on their screens when you switched them on. To motivate students in all provinces he was giving cash awards to girls and boys who scored well in their exams. I was presented with a check for half a million rupees, about $4,500, for my campaign for girls' rights.

I wore pink to the gala and for the first time talked publicly about how we had defied the Taliban edict and carried on going to school secretly. "I know the importance of education because my pens and books were taken from me by force," I said. "But the girls of Swat are not afraid of anyone. We have continued with our education."

Then I was in class one day when my classmates said, "You have won a big prize and half a million rupees!" My father told me the government had awarded me Pakistan's first ever National Peace Prize. I couldn't believe it. So many journalists thronged to the school that day that it turned into a news studio.

The ceremony was on 20 December 2011 at the prime minister's official residence, one of the big white mansions on the hill at the end of Constitution Avenue which I had seen on my trip to Islamabad. By then I was used to meeting politicians. I was not nervous though my father tried to intimidate me by saying Prime Minister Gilani came from a family of saints. After the PM presented me with the award and check, I presented him with a long list of demands. I told him that we wanted our schools rebuilt and a girls' university in Swat. I knew he would not take my demands seriously, so I didn't push very hard. I thought, *One day I will be a politician and do these things myself.*

It was decided that the prize should be awarded annually to children under eighteen years old and be named the Malala Prize in my honor. I noticed my father was not very happy with this. Like most Pashtuns he is a bit superstitious. In Pakistan we don't have a culture of honoring people while they are alive, only the dead, so he thought it was a bad omen.

I know my mother didn't like the awards because she feared I would become a target, as I was becoming more well known. She herself would never appear in public. She refused even to be photographed. She is a very traditional woman and this is our centuries-old culture. Were she to break that tradition, men and women would talk against her, particularly those in our own family. She never said she regretted the work my father and I had undertaken, but when I won prizes, she said, "I don't want awards, I want my daughter. I wouldn't exchange a single eyelash of my daughter for the whole world."

My father argued that all he had ever wanted was to create a school in which children could learn. We had been left with no choice but to get involved in politics and campaign for education. "My only ambition," he said, "is to educate my children and my nation as much as I am able. But when half of your leaders tell lies and the other half is negotiating with the Taliban, there is nowhere to go. One has to speak out."

When I returned home I was greeted with the news that there was a group of journalists who wanted to interview me at school and that I should wear a nice outfit. First I thought of wearing a very beautiful dress, but then I decided to wear something more modest for the interview, as I wanted people to focus on my message and not my clothes. When I arrived at school I saw all my friends had dressed up. "Surprise!" they shouted when I walked in. They had collected money and organized a party for me with a big white cake on which was written *Success Forever* in chocolate icing. It was wonderful that my friends wanted to share in my success. I knew that any of the girls in my class could have achieved what I had achieved if they had had their parents' support.

"Now you can get back to schoolwork," said Madam Maryam as we finished off the cake. "Exams in March!"

But the year ended on a sad note. Five days after I got the award, Aunt Babo, my mother's eldest sister, died suddenly. She wasn't even fifty years old. She was diabetic and had seen a TV ad for a doctor in Lahore with some miracle treatment and persuaded my uncle to take her there. We don't know what the doctor injected her with, but she went into shock and died. My father said the doctor was a charlatan and this was why we needed to keep struggling against ignorance.

I had amassed a lot of money by the end of that year—half a million rupees each from the prime minister, the chief minister of Punjab, the chief minister of our state Khyber Pakhtunkhwa and the Sindh government. Major General Ghulam Qamar, the local army commander, also gave our school 100,000 rupees to build a science laboratory and a library. But my fight wasn't over. I was reminded of our history lessons, in which we learned about the loot or bounty an army enjoys when a battle is won. I began to see the awards and recognition just like that. They were little jewels without much meaning. I needed to concentrate on winning the war.

My father used some of the money to buy me a new bed and cabinet and pay for tooth implants for my mother and a piece of land in Shangla. We decided to spend the rest of the money on people who needed help. I wanted to start an education foundation. This had been on my mind ever since I'd seen the children working on the rubbish mountain. I still could not shake the image of the black rats I had seen there, and the girl with matted hair who had been sorting rubbish. We held a conference of twenty-one girls and made our priority education for every girl in Swat with a particular focus on street children and those in child labor.

As we crossed the Malakand Pass I saw a young girl selling oranges. She was scratching marks on a piece of paper with a pencil to account for the oranges she had sold, as she could not read or write. I took a photo of her and vowed I would do everything in my power to help educate girls just like her. This was the war I was going to fight.

18

The Woman and the Sea

Aunt Najma was in tears. She had never seen the sea before. My family and I sat on the rocks, gazing across the water, breathing in the salt tang of the Arabian Sea. It was such a big expanse, surely no one could know where it ended. At that moment I was very happy. "One day I want to cross this sea," I said.

"What is she saying?" asked my aunt, as if I were talking about something impossible. I was still trying to get my head around the fact that she had been living in the seaside city of Karachi for thirty years and yet had never actually laid eyes on the ocean. Her husband would not take her to the beach, and even if she had somehow slipped out of the house, she would not have been able to follow the signs to the sea because she could not read.

I sat on the rocks and thought about the fact that

across the water were lands where women were free. In Pakistan we had had a woman prime minister and in Islamabad I had met those impressive working women, yet the fact was that we were a country where almost all the women depend entirely on men. My headmistress Maryam was a strong educated woman, but in our society she could not live on her own and come to work. She had to be living with a husband, brother or parents.

In Pakistan when women say they want independence, people think this means we don't want to obey our fathers, brothers or husbands. But it does not mean that. It means we want to make decisions for ourselves. We want to be free to go to school or to go to work. Nowhere is it written in the Quran that a woman should be dependent on a man. The word has not come down from the heavens to tell us that every woman should listen to a man.

"You are a million miles away, *Jani*," said my father, interrupting my thoughts. "What are you dreaming about?"

"Just about crossing oceans, *Aba*," I replied.

"Forget all that!" shouted my brother Atal. "We're at the beach and I want to go for a camel ride!"

It was January 2012 and we were in Karachi as guests of Geo TV after the Sindh government announced they were renaming a girls' secondary school on Mission Road in my honor. My brother Khushal was now at school in Abbottabad, so it was just me, my parents and Atal. We flew to Karachi, and it was the first time any of us had ever been on a plane. The journey was just two hours, which I found incredible. It would have taken us at least two days by bus. On the plane we noticed that some people could not find their seats because they could not read letters and numbers. I had a window seat and could see the deserts and mountains of our land below me. As we headed south the land became more parched. I was already missing the green of Swat. I could see why when our people go to Karachi to work they always want to be buried in the cool of our valley.

Driving from the airport to the hostel, I was amazed by the number of people and houses and cars. Karachi is one of the biggest cities on earth. It was strange to think it was just a port of 300,000 people when Pakistan was created. Jinnah lived there and made it our first capital, and it was soon flooded by millions of Muslim refugees from India known as *mohajirs* which means "immigrants" and speak Urdu. Today it has around twenty million people. It's actually the largest

Pashtun city in the world, even though it's far from our lands; between five and seven million Pashtuns have gone there to work.

Unfortunately, Karachi had also become a very violent city and there is always fighting between the *mohajirs* and Pashtuns. The *mohajir* areas we saw all seemed very organized and neat whereas the Pashtun areas were dirty and chaotic. The *mohajirs* almost all support a party called the MQM led by Altaf Hussain, who lives in exile in London and communicates with his people by Skype. The MQM is a very organized movement, and the *mohajir* community sticks together. By contrast we Pashtuns are very divided, some following Imran Khan because he is Pashtun, a khan and a great cricketer, some Maulana Fazlur Rehman because his party JUI is Islamic, some the secular ANP because it's a Pashtun nationalist party, and some the PPP of Benazir Bhutto or the PML(N) of Nawaz Sharif.

We went to the Sindh assembly, where I was applauded by all the members. Then we went to visit some schools including the one that was being named after me. I made a speech about the importance of education and also talked about Benazir Bhutto, as this was her city. "We must all work together for the rights of girls," I said. The children sang for me and I was presented with a painting of me looking up at the sky. It was both odd and wonderful to see my name on a school just like my namesake, Malalai of Maiwand, after whom so many schools in Afghanistan are named. In the next school holidays my father and I planned to go and talk to parents and children in the distant hilly areas of Swat about the importance of learning to read and write. "We will be like preachers of education," I said.

Later that day we visited my aunt and uncle. They lived in a very small house and so at last my father understood why they had refused to take him in when he was a student. On the way we passed through Aashiqan e-Rasool Square and were shocked to see a picture of the murderer of Governor Salman Taseer decorated with garlands of rose petals as though he were a saint. My father was angry. "In a city of twenty million people is there not one person who will take this down?"

There was one important place we had to include in our visit to Karachi besides our outings to the sea or the huge bazaars, where my mother bought lots of clothes. We needed to visit the mausoleum of our founder and great leader Mohammad Ali Jinnah. This is a very peaceful building of white marble and somehow seemed separate from the hustle and bustle of the city. It felt sacred to us. Benazir was on her way there to make her first speech on her return to Pakistan when her bus was blown up.

The guard explained that the tomb in the main room under a giant chandelier from China did not contain Jinnah's body. The real tomb is on the floor below, where he lies alongside his sister Fatima, who died much later. Next to it is the tomb of our first prime minister, Liaquat Ali Khan, who was assassinated.

Afterward we went into the small museum at the back, which had displays of the special white bow ties Jinnah used to order from Paris, his three-piece suits tailored in London, his golf clubs and a special traveling box with drawers for twelve pairs of shoes including his favorite two-tone brogues. The walls were covered with photographs. In the ones from the early days of Pakistan you could easily see from his thin sunken face that Jinnah was dying. His skin looked paper-thin. But at the time it was kept a secret. Jinnah smoked fifty cigarettes a day. His body was riddled with TB and lung cancer when Lord Mountbatten, the last British viceroy of India, agreed that India would be divided at independence. Afterward he said that had he known Jinnah was dying he would have delayed and there would have been no Pakistan. As it was, Jinnah died in September 1948, just over a year later. Then, a little more than three years after that, our first prime minister was killed. Right from the start we were an unlucky country.

Some of Jinnah's most famous speeches were displayed. There was the one about people of all religions being free to worship in the new Pakistan. And another where he had spoken about the important role of women. I wanted to see pictures of the women in his life. But his wife died young and was a Parsee, and their only daughter Dina stayed in India and married a Parsee, which didn't sit very well in the new Muslim homeland. Now she lives in New York. So most of the pictures I found were of his sister Fatima.

It was hard to visit that place and read those speeches without thinking that Jinnah would be very disappointed in Pakistan. He would probably say that this was not the country he had wanted. He wished us to be independent, to be tolerant, to be kind to each other. He wanted everyone to be free whatever their beliefs.

"Would it have been better if we had not become independent but stayed part of India?" I asked my father. It seemed to me that before

Pakistan there was endless fighting between Hindus and Muslims. Then even when we got our own country there was still fighting, but this time it was between *mohajirs* and Pashtuns and between Sunnis and Shias. Instead of celebrating each other, our four provinces struggle to get along. Sindhis often talk of separation and in Baluchistan there is an ongoing war which gets talked about very little because it is so remote. Did all this fighting mean we needed to divide our country yet again?

When we left the museum some young men with flags were protesting outside. They told us they were Seraiki speakers from southern Punjab and wanted their own province.

There seemed to be so many things about which people were fighting. If Christians, Hindus or Jews are really our enemies, as so many say, why are we Muslims fighting with each other? Our people have become misguided. They think their greatest concern is defending Islam and are being led astray by those like the Taliban who deliberately misinterpret the Quran. We should focus on practical issues. We have so many people in our country who are illiterate. And many women have no education at all. We live in a place where schools are blown up. We have no reliable electricity supply. Not a single day passes without the killing of at least one Pakistani.

One day a lady called Shehla Anjum turned up at our hostel. She was a Pakistani journalist living in Alaska and wanted to meet me after she had seen the documentary about us on the *New York Times* website. She chatted with me for a while, then with my father. I noticed she had tears in her eyes. Then she asked my father, "Did you know, Ziauddin, that the Taliban have threatened this innocent girl?" We didn't know what she was talking about, so she went on the Internet and showed us that the Taliban had that day issued threats against two women—Sha Begum, an activist in Dir, and me, Malala. "These two are spreading secularism and should be killed," it said. I didn't take it seriously, as there are so many things on the Internet and I thought we would have heard from elsewhere if it were real.

That evening my father received a call from the family who had been sharing our home for the last eighteen months. Their previous home had a mud roof which leaked in the rain and we had two spare rooms, so they stayed with us for a nominal rent and their children went to our school for free. They had three children, and we liked them living with us as we all played cops and robbers on the roof. They told my father that the police had turned up at the house and demanded to know whether we had received any threats. When my father heard this, he called the deputy superintendent, who asked him the same thing. My father asked, "Why, have you any information?" The officer asked to see my father when we were back in Swat.

After that my father was restless and could not enjoy Karachi. I could see my mother and father were both very upset. I knew my mother was still mourning my aunt and they had been feeling uneasy about me receiving so many awards, but it seemed to be about more than that. "Why are you like this?" I asked. "You're worried about something but you're not telling us."

Then they told me about the call from home and that they were taking the threats seriously. I don't know why, but hearing I was being targeted did not worry me. It seemed to me that everyone knows they will die one day. My feeling was nobody can stop death; it doesn't matter if it comes from a Talib or cancer. So I should do whatever I want to do.

"Maybe we should stop our campaigning, *Jani*, and go into hibernation for a time," said my father.

"How can we do that?" I replied. "You were the one who said if we believe in something greater than our lives, then our voices will only multiply even if we are dead. We can't disown our campaign!"

People were asking me to speak at events. How could I refuse, saying there was a security problem? We couldn't do that, especially not as proud Pashtuns. My father always says that heroism is in the Pashtun DNA.

Still it was with a heavy heart that we returned to Swat. When my father went to the police they showed him a file on me. They told him that my national and international profile meant I had attracted attention and death threats from the Taliban and that I needed protection. They offered us guards, but my father was reluctant. Many elders in Swat had been killed despite having bodyguards and the Punjab governor had been killed by his own bodyguard. He also thought armed guards would alarm the parents of the students at school, and he didn't want to put others at risk. When he had had threats before he always said, "Let them kill me, but I'll be killed alone."

He suggested sending me to boarding school in Abbottabad like Khushal, but I didn't want to go. He also met the local army colonel, who said being in college in Abbottabad would not really be any safer and that as long as I kept a low profile we would be OK in Swat. So when the government of KPK offered to make me a peace ambassador, my father said it was better to refuse.

At home I started bolting the main gate of our house at night. "She smells the threat," my mother told my father. He was very unhappy. He kept telling me to draw the curtains in my room at night, but I would not.

"*Aba,* this is a very strange situation," I told him. "When there was Talibanization we were safe; now there are no Taliban we are unsafe."

"Yes, Malala," he replied. "Now the Talibanization is especially for us, for those like you and me who continue to speak out. The rest of Swat is OK. The rickshaw drivers, the shopkeepers are all safe. This is Talibanization for particular people, and we are among them."

There was another downside to receiving those awards—I was missing a lot of school. After the exams in March the cup that went into my new cabinet was for second place.

19

A Private Talibanization

"Let's pretend it's a Twilight movie and that we're vampires in the forest," I said to Moniba. We were on a school trip to Marghazar, a beautiful green valley where the air is cool, and there is a tall mountain and a crystal-clear river where we were planning to have a picnic. Nearby was the White Palace Hotel, which used to be the *wali*'s summer residence.

It was April 2012, the month after our exams, so we were all feeling relaxed. We were a group of about seventy girls. Our teachers and my parents were there too. My father had hired three Flying Coaches, but we could not all fit in, so five of us—me, Moniba and three other girls—were in the *dyna,* the school van. It wasn't very comfortable, especially because we also had giant pots of chicken and rice on the floor for the picnic, but it was only half an hour's drive. We had fun, singing songs on the way there. Moniba was looking very beautiful, her skin porcelain-pale. "What skin cream are you using?" I asked her.

"The same one you're using," she replied.

I knew that could not be true. "No. Look at my dark skin and look at yours!"

We visited the White Palace and saw where the queen had slept and the gardens of beautiful flowers. Sadly we could not see the *wali*'s room, as it had been damaged by the floods.

We ran around for a while in the green forest, then took some photographs and waded into the river and splashed each other with water. The drops sparkled in the sun. There was a waterfall down the cliff and for a while we sat on the rocks and listened to it. Then Moniba started splashing me again.

"Don't! I don't want to get my clothes wet!" I pleaded. I walked off with two other girls she didn't like. The other girls stirred things up, what we call "putting masala on the situation." It was a recipe for another argument between Moniba and me. That put me in a bad mood, but I cheered up when we got to the top of the cliff, where lunch was being prepared. Usman Bhai Jan, our driver, made us laugh as usual. Madam Maryam had brought her baby boy and Hannah, her two-year-old, who looked like a little doll but was full of mischief.

Lunch was a disaster. When the school assistants put the pans on the fire to heat up the chicken curry, they panicked that there was not enough food for so many girls and added water from the stream. We said it was "the worst lunch ever." It was so watery that one girl said, "The sky could be seen in the soupy curry."

Like on all our trips my father got us all to stand on a rock and talk about our impressions of the day before we left. This time all anyone talked about was how bad the food was. My father was embarrassed and for once short of words.

The next morning a school worker came with milk, bread and eggs to our house for our breakfast. My father always answered the door, as women must stay inside. The man told him the shopkeeper had given him a photocopied letter.

When my father read it, he went pale. "By God, this is terrible propaganda against our school!" he told my mother. He read it out.

Dear Muslim brothers
There is a school, the Khushal School, which is

*run by an NGO [NGOs have a very bad repu-
tation among religious people in our country so
this was a way to invite people's wrath] and is
a center of vulgarity and obscenity. It is a Hadith of the Holy Prophet, PBUH, that if you see
something bad or evil you should stop it with
your own hand. If you are unable to do that
then you should tell others about it, and if you
can't do that you should think about how bad
it is in your heart. I have no personal quarrel
with the principal but I am telling you what Islam says. This school is a center of vulgarity and
obscenity and they take girls for picnics to different resorts. If you don't stop it you will have
to answer to God on Doomsday. Go and ask the
manager of the White Palace Hotel and he will
tell you what these girls did . . .*

He put down the piece of paper. "It has no sig-
nature. Anonymous."

We sat stunned.

"They know no one will ask the manager," said
my father. "People will just imagine something
terrible went on."

"We know what happened there. The girls did
nothing bad," my mother reassured him.

My father called my cousin Khanjee to find

out how widely the letters had been distributed. He called back with bad news—they had been left everywhere, though most shopkeepers had ignored them and thrown them away. There were also giant posters pasted on the front of the mosque with the same accusations.

At school my classmates were terrified. "Sir, they are saying very bad things about our school," they said to my father. "What will our parents say?"

My father gathered all the girls into the courtyard. "Why are you afraid?" he asked. "Did you do anything against Islam? Did you do anything immoral? No. You just splashed water and took pictures, so don't be scared. This is the propaganda of the followers of Mullah Fazlullah. Down with them! You have the right to enjoy greenery and waterfalls and landscape just as boys do."

My father spoke like a lion, but I could see in his heart he was worried and scared. Only one person came and withdrew his sister from the school, but we knew that was not the end of it. Shortly after that we were told a man who had completed a peace walk from Dera Ismail Khan was coming through Mingora and we wanted to welcome him. I was on the way to meet him with my parents when we were approached by a short man who was frantically talking on two different phones. "Don't go that way," he urged. "There is a suicide bomber over there!" We'd promised to meet the peace walker, so we went by a different route, placed a garland around his neck, then left quickly for home.

All through that spring and summer odd things kept happening. Strangers came to the house asking questions about my family. My father said they were from the intelligence services. The visits became more frequent after my father and the Swat Qaumi Jirga held a meeting in our school to protest against army plans for the people of Mingora and our community defense committees to conduct night patrols. "The army say there is peace," said my father. "So why do we need flag marches and night patrols?"

Then our school hosted a painting competition for the children of Mingora sponsored by my father's friend who ran an NGO for women's rights. The pictures were supposed to show the equality of the sexes or highlight discrimination against women. That morning two men from the intelligence services came to our school to see my father. "What is going on in your school?" they demanded.

"This is a school," he replied. "There's a painting

competition just as we have debating competitions, cookery competitions and essay contests." The men got very angry and so did my father. "Everyone knows me and what I do!" he said. "Why don't you do your real work and find Fazlullah and those whose hands are red with the blood of Swat?"

That Ramadan a friend of my father's in Karachi called Wakeel Khan sent clothes for the poor, which he wanted us to distribute. We went to a big hall to hand them out. Before we had even started, intelligence agents came and asked, "What are you doing? Who brought these outfits?"

On 12 July I turned fourteen, which in Islam means you are an adult. With my birthday came the news that Taliban had killed the owner of the Swat Continental Hotel, who was on a peace committee. He was on his way from home to his hotel in Mingora Bazaar when they ambushed him in a field.

Once again people started worrying that the Taliban were creeping back. But whereas in 2008–9 there were many threats to all sorts of people, this time the threats were specific to those who spoke against militants or the high-handed behavior of the army.

"The Taliban is not an organized force like we imagine," said my father's friend Hidayatullah when they discussed it. "It's a mentality, and this mentality is everywhere in Pakistan. Someone who is against America, against the Pakistan establishment, against English law, he has been infected by the Taliban."

It was late in the evening of 3 August when my father received an alarming phone call from a Geo TV correspondent called Mehboob. He was the nephew of my father's friend Zahid Khan, the hotel owner who had been attacked in 2009. People used to say both Zahid Khan and my father were on the Taliban radar and both would be killed; the only thing they didn't know was which would be killed first. Mehboob told us that his uncle had been on his way to *isha* prayers, the last prayers of the day, at the mosque on the street near his house when he was shot in the face.

When he heard the news my father said the earth fell away from his feet. "It was as if I had been shot," he said. "I was sure it was my turn next."

We pleaded with my father not to go to the hospital, as it was very late and the people who had attacked Zahid Khan might be waiting for him. But he said not to go would be cowardly. He was offered an escort by some fellow political activists, but he thought that it would be too late to go if he waited for them. So he called my cousin to take him. My mother began to pray.

When he got to the hospital only one other member of the *jirga* committee was there. Zahid Khan was bleeding so much it was as if his white beard were bathed in red. But he had been lucky. A man had fired at him three times from close range with a pistol, but Zahid Khan had managed to grab his hand so only the first bullet struck. Strangely it went through his neck and out through his nose. Later he said he remembered a small clean-shaven man just standing there smiling, not even wearing a mask. Then darkness overcame him as if he had fallen into a black hole. The irony was that Zahid Khan had only recently started to walk to the mosque again because he thought it was safe.

After praying for his friend, my father talked to the media. "We don't understand why he's been attacked when they claim there's peace," he said. "It's a big question for the army and administration."

People warned my father to leave the hospital. "Ziauddin, it's midnight and you're here! Don't be stupid!" they said. "You are as vulnerable and as wanted a target as he is. Don't take any more risks!"

Finally Zahid Khan was transferred to Peshawar to be operated on and my father came home. I had not gone to sleep because I was so worried. After that I double-checked all the locks every night.

At home our phone did not stop ringing with people calling to warn my father he could be the next target. Hidayatullah was one of the first to call. "For God's sake be careful," he warned. "It could have been you. They are shooting *jirga* members one by one. You are the spokesman— how can they possibly let you live?"

My father was convinced the Taliban would hunt him down and kill him, but he again refused security from the police. "If you go around with a lot of security the Taliban will use Kalashnikovs or suicide bombers and more people will be killed," he said. "At least I'll be killed alone." Nor would he leave Swat. "Where can I go?" he asked my mother. "I cannot leave the area. I am president of the Global Peace Council, the spokesperson of the council of elders, the president of the Swat Association of Private Schools, director of my school and head of my family."

His only precaution was to change his routine.

One day he would go to the primary school first, another day to the girls' school, the next day to the boys' school. I noticed wherever he went he would look up and down the street four or five times.

Despite the risks, my father and his friends continued to be very active, holding protests and press conferences. "Why was Zahid Khan attacked if there's peace? Who attacked him?" they demanded. "Since we've come back from being IDPs we haven't seen any attacks on army and police. The only targets now are peace-builders and civilians."

The local army commander was not happy. "I tell you there are no terrorists in Mingora," he insisted. "Our reports say so." He claimed that Zahid Khan had been shot because of a dispute over property.

Zahid Khan was in hospital for twelve days, then at home recuperating for a month after having plastic surgery to repair his nose. But he refused to be silent. If anything he became more outspoken, particularly against the intelligence agencies, as he was convinced they were behind the Taliban. He wrote opinion pieces in newspapers saying that the conflict in Swat had been manufactured. "I know who targeted me. What we need to know is who imposed these militants on us," he wrote. He demanded that the chief justice set up a judicial commission to investigate who had brought the Taliban into our valley.

He drew a sketch of his attacker and said the man should be stopped before shooting anyone else. But the police did nothing to find him.

After the threats against me my mother didn't like me walking anywhere and insisted I get a rickshaw to school and take the bus home even though it was only a five-minute walk. The bus dropped me at the steps leading up to our street. A group of boys from our neighborhood used to hang around there. Sometimes there was a boy called Haroon with them, who was a year older than me and used to live on our street. We had played together as children and later he told me he was in love with me. But then a pretty cousin came to stay with our neighbor Safina and he fell in love with her instead. When she said she wasn't interested he turned his attention back to me. After that they moved to another street and we moved into their house. Then Haroon went away to army cadet college.

But he came back for vacations, and one day when I returned home from school he was hanging around on the street. He followed me to the house and put a note inside our gate where I would see it. I told a small girl to fetch it for me. He had written, "Now you have become very popular, I still love you and know you love me. This is my number, call me."

I gave the note to my father and he was angry. He called Haroon and told him he would tell his father. That was the last time I saw him. After that the boys stopped coming to our street, but one of the small boys who played with Atal would call out suggestively, "How is Haroon?" whenever I passed by. I got so fed up with it that one day I told Atal to bring the boy inside. I shouted at him so angrily that he stopped.

I told Moniba what had happened once we were friends again. She was always very careful about interactions with boys because her brothers watched everything. "Sometimes I think it's easier to be a Twilight vampire than a girl in Swat," I sighed. But really I wished that being hassled by a boy was my biggest problem.

20

Who Is Malala?

One morning in late summer when my father was getting ready to go to school he noticed that the painting of me looking at the sky which we had been given by the school in Karachi had shifted in the night. He loved that painting and had hung it over his bed. Seeing it crooked disturbed him. "Please put it straight," he asked my mother in an unusually sharp tone.

That same week our math teacher, Miss Shazia, arrived at school in a hysterical state. She told my father that she'd had a nightmare in which I came to school with my leg badly burned and she had tried to protect it. She begged him to give some cooked rice to the poor, as we believe that if you give rice, even ants and birds will eat the bits that drop to the floor and will pray for us. My father gave money instead and she was distraught, saying that wasn't the same.

We laughed at Miss Shazia's premonition, but then I started having bad dreams too. I didn't say anything to my parents, but whenever I went out I was afraid that Taliban with guns would leap out at me or throw acid in my face, as they had done to women in Afghanistan. I was particularly scared of the steps leading up to our street where the boys used to hang out. Sometimes I thought I heard footsteps behind me or imagined figures slipping into the shadows.

Unlike my father, I took precautions. At night I would wait until everyone was asleep—my mother, my father, my brothers, the other family in our house and any guests we had from our village—then I'd check every single door and window. I'd go outside and make sure the front gate was locked. Then I would check all the rooms, one by one. My room was at the front with lots of windows and I kept the curtains open. I wanted to be able to see everything, though my father told me not to. "If they were going to kill me they would have done it in 2009," I said. But I worried someone would put a ladder against the house, climb over the wall and break in through a window.

Then I'd pray. At night I used to pray a lot. The Taliban think we are not Muslims but we are. We believe in God more than they do and we trust him to protect us. I used to say the *Ayat al-Kursi,* the Verse of the Throne from the second surah of the Quran, the Chapter of the Cow. This is a very special verse and we believe that if you say it three times at night your home will be safe from *shayatin* or devils. When you say it five times your street will be safe, and seven times will protect the whole area. So I'd say it seven times or even more. Then I'd pray to God, "Bless us. First our father and family, then our street, then our whole *mohalla,* then all Swat." Then I'd say, "No, all Muslims." Then, "No, not just Muslims; bless all human beings."

The time of year I prayed most was during exams. It was the one time when my friends and I did all five prayers a day like my mother was always trying to get me to do. I found it particularly hard in the afternoon, when I didn't want to be dragged away from the TV. At exam time I prayed to Allah for high marks though our teachers used to warn us, "God won't give you marks if you don't work hard. God showers us with his blessings, but he is honest as well."

So I studied hard too. Usually I liked exams as

a chance to show what I could do. But when they came around in October 2012 I felt under pressure. I did not want to come second to Malka-e-Noor again as I had in March. Then she had beaten me by not just one or two marks, the usual difference between us, but by five marks! I had been taking extra lessons with Sir Amjad, who ran the boys' school. The night before the exams began I stayed up studying until 3 o'clock in the morning and reread an entire textbook.

The first paper, on Monday, 8 October, was physics. I love physics because it is about truth, a world determined by principles and laws—no messing around or twisting things like in politics, particularly those in my country. As we waited for the signal to start the exam, I recited holy verses to myself. I completed the paper, but I knew I'd made a mistake filling in the blanks. I was so cross with myself I almost cried. It was just one question worth only one mark, but it made me feel that something devastating was going to happen.

When I got home that afternoon I was sleepy, but the next day was Pakistan Studies, a difficult paper for me. I was worried about losing even more marks, so I made myself coffee with milk to drive away the devils of sleep. When my mother came she tried it and liked it and drank the rest.

I could not tell her, "*Bhabi,* please stop it, that's my coffee." But there was no more coffee left in the cupboard. Once again I stayed up late, memorizing the textbook about the history of our independence.

In the morning my parents came to my room as usual and woke me up. I don't remember a single school day on which I woke up early by myself. My mother made our usual breakfast of sugary tea, chapatis and fried egg. We all had breakfast together—me, my mother, my father, Khushal and Atal. It was a big day for my mother, as she was going to start lessons that afternoon to learn to read and write with Miss Ulfat, my old teacher from kindergarten.

My father started teasing Atal, who was eight by then and cheekier than ever. "Look, Atal, when Malala is prime minister, you will be her secretary," he said.

Atal got very cross. "No, no, no!" he said. "I'm no less than Malala. I will be prime minister and she will be my secretary." All the banter meant I ended up being so late I only had time to eat half my egg and no time to clear up.

The Pakistan Studies paper went better than I thought it would. There were questions about how Jinnah had created our country as the first

Muslim homeland and also about the national tragedy of how Bangladesh came into being. It was strange to think that Bangladesh was once part of Pakistan despite being a thousand miles away. I answered all the questions and was confident I'd done well. I was happy when the exam was over, chatting and gossiping with my friends as we waited for Sher Mohammad Baba, a school assistant, to call for us when the bus arrived.

The bus did two trips every day, and that day we took the second one. We liked staying on at school and Moniba said, "As we're tired after the exam, let's stay and chat before going home." I was relieved that the Pakistan Studies exam had gone well, so I agreed. I had no worries that day. I was hungry, but because we were fifteen we could no longer go outside to the street, so I got one of the small girls to buy me a corn cob. I ate a little bit of it then gave it to another girl to finish.

At 12 o'clock *Baba* called us over the loudspeaker. We all ran down the steps. The other girls all covered their faces before emerging from the door and climbed into the back of the bus. I wore my scarf over my head but never over my face.

I asked Usman Bhai Jan to tell us a joke while we were waiting for two teachers to arrive. He has a collection of extremely funny stories. That day instead of a story he did a magic trick to make a pebble disappear. "Show us how you did it!" we all clamored, but he wouldn't.

When everyone was ready he took Miss Rubi and a couple of small children in the front cab with him. Another little girl cried, saying she wanted to ride there too. Usman Bhai Jan said no, there was no room; she would have to stay in the back with us. But I felt sorry for her and persuaded him to let her in the cab.

Atal had been told by my mother to ride on the bus with me, so he walked over from the primary school. He liked to hang off the tailboard at the back, which made Usman Bhai Jan cross, as it was dangerous. That day Usman Bhai Jan had had enough and refused to let him. "Sit inside, Atal Khan, or I won't take you!" he said. Atal had a tantrum and refused, so he walked home in a huff with some of his friends.

Usman Bhai Jan started the *dyna* and we were off. I was talking to Moniba, my wise, nice friend. Some girls were singing, I was drumming rhythms with my fingers on the seat.

Moniba and I liked to sit near the open back so we could see out. At that time of day Haji Baba Road was always a jumble of colored rickshaws, people on foot and men on scooters, all zigzagging and honking. An ice-cream boy on a red tricycle painted with red and white nuclear missiles rode up behind waving at us, until a teacher shooed him away. A man was chopping off chickens' heads, the blood dripping onto the street. I drummed my fingers. Chop, chop, chop. Drip, drip, drip. Funny, when I was little we always said Swatis were so peace-loving it was hard to find a man to slaughter a chicken.

The air smelled of diesel, bread and kebab mixed with the stink from the stream where people still dumped their rubbish and were never going to stop despite all my father's campaigning. But we were used to it. Besides, soon the winter would be here, bringing the snow, which would cleanse and quieten everything.

The bus turned right off the main road at the army checkpoint. On a kiosk was a poster of crazy-eyed men with beards and caps or turbans under big letters saying WANTED TERRORISTS. The picture at the top of a man with a black turban and beard was Fazlullah. More than three years had passed since the military operation to drive the Taliban out of Swat had begun. We were grateful to the army but couldn't understand why they were still everywhere, in machine-gun nests on roofs and manning checkpoints. To even enter our valley people needed official permission.

The road up the small hill is usually busy, as it is a shortcut, but that day it was strangely quiet. "Where are all the people?" I asked Moniba. All the girls were singing and chatting and our voices bounced around inside the bus.

Around that time my mother was probably just going through the doorway into our school for her first lesson since she had left school at age six.

I didn't see the two young men step out into the road and bring the van to a sudden halt. I didn't get a chance to answer their question "Who is Malala?" or I would have explained to them why they should let us girls go to school as well as their own sisters and daughters.

The last thing I remember is that I was thinking about the revision I needed to do for the next day. The sounds in my head were not the *crack, crack, crack* of three bullets, but the *chop, chop, chop, drip, drip, drip* of the man severing the heads of chickens, and them dropping into the dirty street, one by one.

Part Four

Between Life and Death

بنيري به ولي درته نه كړم   توره توپكه ورانه وي ودان كورونه

Khairey ba waley darta na kram
Toora topaka woranawey wadan korona

Guns of Darkness! Why would I not curse you?
You turned love-filled homes into broken debris

21

"God, I Entrust Her to You"

As soon as Usman Bhai Jan realized what had happened he drove the *dyna* to Swat Central Hospital at top speed. The other girls were screaming and crying. I was lying on Moniba's lap, bleeding from my head and left ear. We had only gone a short way when a policeman stopped the van and started asking questions, wasting precious time. One girl felt my neck for a pulse. "She's alive!" she shouted. "We must get her to hospital. Leave us alone and catch the man who did this!"

Mingora seemed like a big town to us, but it's really a small place and the news spread quickly. My father was at the Swat Press Club for a meeting of the Association of Private Schools and had just gone on stage to give a speech when his mobile rang. He recognized the number as the

Khushal School and passed the phone to his friend Ahmad Shah to answer. "Your school bus has been fired on," he whispered urgently to my father.

The color drained from my father's face. He immediately thought, *Malala could be on that bus!* Then he tried to reassure himself, thinking it might be a boy, a jealous lover who had fired a pistol in the air to shame his beloved. He was at an important gathering of about 400 principals who had come from all over Swat to protest against plans by the government to impose a central regulatory authority. As president of their association, my father felt he couldn't let all those people down, so he delivered his speech as planned. But there were beads of sweat on his forehead and for once there was no need for anyone to signal to him to wind it up.

As soon as he had finished, my father did not wait to take questions from the audience and instead rushed off to the hospital with Ahmad Shah and another friend, Riaz, who had a car. The hospital was only five minutes away. They arrived to find crowds gathered outside and photographers and TV cameras. Then he knew for certain that I was there. My father's heart sank. He pushed through the people and ran through the camera flashes into the hospital. Inside I was lying on a trolley, a bandage over my head, my eyes closed, my hair spread out.

"My daughter, you are my brave daughter, my beautiful daughter," he said over and over, kissing my forehead and cheeks and nose. He didn't know why he was speaking to me in English. I think somehow I knew he was there even though my eyes were closed. My father said later, "I can't explain it. I felt she responded." Someone said I had smiled. But to my father it was not a smile, just a small beautiful moment because he knew he had not lost me forever. Seeing me like that was the worst thing that had ever happened to him. All children are special to their parents, but to my father I was his universe. I had been his comrade in arms for so long, first secretly as Gul Makai, then quite openly as Malala. He had always believed that if the Taliban came for anyone, it would be for him, not me. He said he felt as if he had been hit by a thunderbolt. "They wanted to kill two birds with one stone. Kill Malala and silence me forever."

He was very afraid but he didn't cry. There were people everywhere. All the principals from the meeting had arrived at the hospital and there were scores of media and activists; it seemed the whole

343

town was there. "Pray for Malala," he told them. The doctors reassured him that they had done a CT scan which showed that the bullet had not gone near my brain. They cleaned and bandaged the wound.

"O Ziauddin! What have they done?" Madam Maryam burst through the doors. She had not been at school that day but at home nursing her baby when she received a phone call from her brother-in-law checking she was safe. Alarmed, she switched on the TV and saw the headline that there had been a shooting on the Khushal School bus. As soon as she heard I had been shot she called her husband. He brought her to the hospital on the back of his motorbike, something very rare for a respectable Pashtun woman. "Malala, Malala. Do you hear me?" she called.

I grunted.

Maryam tried to find out more about what was going on. A doctor she knew told her the bullet had passed through my forehead, not my brain, and that I was safe. She also saw the two other Khushal girls who had been shot. Shazia had been hit twice, in the left collarbone and palm, and had been brought to the hospital with me. Kainat had not realized she was hurt to start with and had gone home, then discovered she had been grazed by a bullet at the top of her right arm, so her family had brought her in.

My father knew he should go and check on them but did not want to leave my bedside for a minute. His phone kept ringing. The chief minister of KPK was the first person who called. "Don't worry, we will sort everything out," he said. "Lady Reading Hospital in Peshawar is expecting you." But it was the army who took charge. At 3 p.m. the local commander arrived and announced they were sending an army helicopter to take me and my father to Peshawar. There wasn't time to fetch my mother, so Maryam insisted she would go too, as I might need a woman's help. Maryam's family was not happy about this, as she was still nursing her baby boy, who had recently undergone a small operation. But she is like my second mother.

When I was put in the ambulance my father was afraid the Taliban would attack again. It seemed to him that everyone must know who was inside. The helipad was only a mile away, a five-minute drive, but he was scared the whole way. When we got there the helicopter had not arrived, and we waited for what felt like hours to him inside the ambulance. Finally it landed and I was taken on board with my father, my cousin

Khanjee, Ahmad Shah and Maryam. None of them had ever been on a helicopter. As it took off we flew over an army sports gala with patriotic music pounding from speakers. To hear them singing about their love of country gave my father a bad taste. He normally liked singing along, but a patriotic song hardly seemed appropriate when here was a fifteen-year-old girl shot in the head, an almost dead daughter.

Down below, my mother was watching from the roof of our house. When she heard that I had been hurt she was having her reading lesson with Miss Ulfat and struggling to learn words like "book" and "apple." The news at first was muddled and she initially believed I'd been in an accident and had injured my foot. She rushed home and told my grandmother, who was staying with us at the time. She begged my grandmother to start praying immediately. We believe Allah listens more closely to the white-haired. My mother then noticed my half-eaten egg from breakfast. There were pictures of me everywhere receiving the awards she had disapproved of. She sobbed as she looked at them. All around was Malala, Malala.

Soon the house was full of women. In our culture, if someone dies women come to the home of the deceased and the men to the *hujra*—not just family and close friends but everyone from the neighborhood.

My mother was astonished to see all the people. She sat on a prayer mat and recited from the Quran. She told the women, "Don't cry—pray!" Then my brothers rushed into the room. Atal, who had walked home from school, had turned on the television and seen the news that I had been shot. He had called Khushal, and together they joined the weeping. The phone did not stop ringing. People reassured my mother that although I had been shot in the head, the bullet had just skimmed my forehead. My mother was very confused by all the different stories, first that my foot had been injured, then that I had been shot in the head. She thought I would think it strange that she hadn't come to me, but people told her not to go, as I was either dead or about to be moved. One of my father's friends phoned her to tell her I was being taken to Peshawar by helicopter and she should come by road. The worst moment for her was when someone came to the house with my front door keys, which had been found at the scene of the shooting. "I don't want keys, I want my daughter!" my mother cried.

"What use are keys without Malala?" Then they heard the sound of the helicopter.

The helipad was just a mile from our house and all the women rushed up to the roof. "It must be Malala!" they said. As they watched the helicopter fly overhead, my mother took her scarf off her head, an extremely rare gesture for a Pashtun woman, and lifted it up to the sky, holding it in both hands as if it were an offering. "God, I entrust her to You," she said to the heavens. "We didn't accept security guards—You are our protector. She was under Your care and You are bound to give her back."

Inside the helicopter I was vomiting blood. My father was horrified, thinking this meant I had internal bleeding. He was starting to lose hope. But then Maryam noticed me trying to wipe my mouth with my scarf. "Look, she is responding!" she said. "That's an excellent sign."

When we landed in Peshawar, they assumed we'd be taken to Lady Reading Hospital, where there was a very good neurosurgeon called Dr. Mumtaz who had been recommended. Instead they were alarmed to be taken to CMH, the Combined Military Hospital. CMH is a large sprawling brick hospital with 600 beds and dates from British rule. There was a lot of construction going on to build a new tower block. Peshawar is the gateway to the FATA and since the army went into those areas in 2004 to take on the militants, the hospital had been very busy tending wounded soldiers and victims of the frequent suicide bombs in and around the city. As in much of our country, there were concrete blocks and checkpoints all around CMH to protect it from suicide bombers.

I was rushed to the Intensive Care Unit, which is in a separate building. Above the nurses' station the clock showed it was just after 5 p.m. I was wheeled into a glass-walled isolation unit and a nurse put me on a drip. In the next room was a soldier who had been horrifically burned in an IED attack and had a leg blown off. A young man came in and introduced himself as Colonel Junaid, a neurosurgeon. My father became even more disturbed. He didn't think he looked like a doctor; he seemed so young. "Is she your daughter?" asked the colonel. Maryam pretended to be my mother so she could come in.

Colonel Junaid examined me. I was conscious and restless but not speaking or aware of anything, my eyes fluttering. The colonel stitched the wound above my left brow where the bullet had entered, but he was surprised not to see any bullet in the scan. "If there is an entry there has to be an exit," he said. He palpated my spine and located the bullet lying next to my left shoulder blade. "She must have been stooping, so her neck was bent when she was shot," he said.

They took me for another CT scan. Then the colonel called my father into his office, where he had the scans up on a screen. He told him that the scan in Swat had been done from only one angle, but this new scan showed the injury was more serious. "Look, Ziauddin," he said. "The CT scan shows the bullet went very close to the brain." He said particles of bone had damaged the brain membrane. "We can pray to God. Let's wait and see," he said. "We're not going to operate at this stage."

My father became more agitated. In Swat the doctors had told him this was something simple, now it seemed very serious. And if it was serious why weren't they operating? He felt uncomfortable in a military hospital. In our country, where the army has seized power so many times, people are often wary of the military, particularly those from Swat, where the army had taken so long to act against the Taliban. One of my father's friends called him and said, "Get her moved from that hospital. We don't want her to become *shaheed millat* [a martyr of the nation] like Liaquat Ali Khan." My father didn't know what to do.

"I'm confused," he told Colonel Junaid. "Why are we here? I thought we'd go to the civil hospital." Then he asked, "Please, can you bring in Dr. Mumtaz?"

"How would that look?" replied Colonel Junaid who was, not surprisingly, offended.

Afterward, we found out that despite his youthful appearance he had been a neurosurgeon for thirteen years and was the most experienced and decorated neurosurgeon in the Pakistani army. He had joined the military as a doctor because of their superior facilities, following in the footsteps of his uncle, who was also an army neurosurgeon. The Peshawar CMH was on the front line of the war on the Taliban and Junaid dealt with gunshot wounds and blasts every day. "I've treated thousands of Malalas," he later said.

But my father didn't know that at the time and became very depressed. "Do whatever you think," he said. "You're the doctor."

The next few hours were a wait-and-see time, the nurses monitoring my heartbeat and vital signs. Occasionally I made a low grunt and moved my hand or fluttered my eyes. Then Maryam would say, "Malala, Malala." Once my eyes completely opened. "I never noticed before how beautiful her eyes are," said Maryam. I was restless and kept trying to get the monitor off my finger. "Don't do that," Maryam said.

"Miss, don't tell me off," I whispered, as if we were at school. Madam Maryam was a strict headmistress.

Late in the evening my mother came with Atal. They had made the four-hour journey by road, driven by my father's friend Mohammad Farooq. Before she arrived Maryam had called to warn her, "When you see Malala don't cry or shout. She can hear you even if think she can't." My father also called her and told her to prepare for the worst. He wanted to protect her.

When my mother arrived they hugged and held back tears. "Here is Atal," she told me. "He has come to see you."

Atal was overwhelmed and cried a lot. "Mama," he wept, "Malala is hurt so badly."

My mother was in a state of shock and could not understand why the doctors were not operating to remove the bullet. "My brave daughter, my beautiful daughter," she cried. Atal was making so much noise that eventually an orderly took them to the hospital's military hostel, where they were being put up.

My father was bewildered by all the people gathered outside—politicians, government dignitaries, provincial ministers—who had come to show their sympathy. Even the governor was there; he gave my father 100,000 rupees for my treatment. In our society if someone dies, you feel very honored if one dignitary comes to your home. But now he was irritated. He felt all these people were just waiting for me to die when they had done nothing to protect me.

Later, while they were eating, Atal turned on the TV. My father immediately turned it off. He couldn't face seeing news of my attack at that moment. When he left the room Maryam switched it back on. Every channel was showing footage of me with a commentary of prayers and moving poems, as if I had died. "My Malala, my Malala," my mother wailed and Maryam joined her.

Around midnight Colonel Junaid asked to meet my father outside the ICU. "Ziauddin, Malala's brain is swelling." My father didn't understand what this meant. The doctor told him I had started to deteriorate; my consciousness was fading, and I had again been vomiting blood. Colonel Junaid ordered a third CT scan.

This showed that my brain was swelling dangerously.

"But I thought the bullet hadn't entered her brain," said my father.

Colonel Junaid explained that a bone had fractured and splinters had gone into my brain, creating a shock and causing it to swell. He needed to remove some of my skull to give the brain space to expand, otherwise the pressure would become unbearable. "We need to operate now to give her a chance," he said. "If we don't, she may die. I don't want you to look back and regret not taking action."

Cutting away some of my skull sounded very drastic to my father. "Will she survive?" he asked desperately, but was given little reassurance at that stage.

It was a brave decision by Colonel Junaid, whose superiors were not convinced and were being told by other people that I should be sent abroad. It was a decision that would save my life. My father told him to go ahead, and Colonel Junaid said he would bring in Dr. Mumtaz to help. My father's hand shook as he signed the consent papers. There in black and white were the words "the patient may die."

They started the operation around 1.30 a.m.

My mother and father sat outside the operating room. "O God, please make Malala well," prayed my father. He made bargains with God. "Even if I have to live in the deserts of the Sahara, I need her eyes open; I won't be able to live without her. O God, let me give the rest of my life to her; I have lived enough. Even if she is injured, just let her survive."

Eventually my mother interrupted him. "God is not a miser," she said. "He will give me back my daughter as she was." She began praying with the Holy Quran in her hand, standing facing the wall reciting verses over and over for hours.

"I had never seen someone praying like her," said Madam Maryam. "I was sure God would answer such prayers."

My father tried not to think about the past and whether he had been wrong to encourage me to speak out and campaign.

Inside the operating room Colonel Junaid used a saw to remove an eight-to-ten-centimeter square from the upper-left part of my skull so my brain had the space to swell. He then cut into the subcutaneous tissue on the left of my stomach and placed the piece of bone inside to preserve it. Then he did a tracheotomy, as he was worried the swelling was blocking my airway. He also removed clots from my brain and the bullet from my shoulder blade. After all these procedures I was put on a ventilator. The operation took almost five hours.

Despite my mother's prayers, my father thought 90 percent of the people waiting outside were just waiting for the news of my death. Some of them, his friends and sympathizers, were very upset, but he felt that others were jealous of our high profile and believed we had got what was coming to us.

My father was taking a short break from the intensity of the operating room and was standing outside when a nurse approached him. "Are you Malala's father?" Once again my father's heart sank. The nurse took him into a room.

He thought she was going to say, "We're sorry, I'm afraid we have lost her." But once inside he was told, "We need someone to get blood from the blood bank." He was relieved but baffled. *Am I the only person who can fetch it?* he wondered. One of his friends went instead.

It was about 5.30 a.m. when the surgeons came out. Among other things, they told my father that they had removed a piece of skull and put it in my abdomen. In our culture doctors don't explain things to patients or relatives, and my father asked humbly, "If you don't mind, I have a stupid question. Will she survive—what do you think?"

"In medicine two plus two does not always make four," replied Colonel Junaid. "We did our job—we removed the piece of skull. Now we must wait."

"I have another stupid question," said my father. "What about this bone? What will you do with it?"

"After three months we will put it back," replied Dr. Mumtaz. "It's very simple, just like this." He clapped his hands.

The next morning the news was good. I had moved my arms. Then three top surgeons from the province came to examine me. They said Colonel Junaid and Dr. Mumtaz had done a splendid job, and the operation had gone very well, but I should now be put into induced coma because if I regained consciousness there would be pressure on the brain.

While I was hovering between life and death, the Taliban issued a statement assuming responsibility for shooting me but denying it was because of my campaign for education. "We carried out this attack, and anybody who speaks against us will be attacked in the same way," said Ehsanullah Ehsan, a spokesman for the TTP. "Malala has been targeted because of her pioneer role in preaching secularism... She was young but she was promoting Western culture in Pashtun areas. She was pro-

West; she was speaking against the Taliban; she was calling President Obama her idol."

My father knew what he was referring to. After I won the National Peace Prize the year before, I had done many TV interviews, and in one of them I had been asked to name my favorite politicians. I had chosen Khan Abdul Ghaffar Khan, Benazir Bhutto and President Barack Obama. I had read about Obama and admired him because as a young black man from a struggling family he had achieved his ambitions and dreams. But the image of America in Pakistan had become of one of drones, secret raids on our territory and Raymond Davis.

A Taliban spokesman said that Fazlullah had ordered the attack at a meeting two months earlier. "Anyone who sides with the government against us will die at our hands," he said. "You will see. Other important people will soon become victims." He added they had used two local Swati men who had collected information about me and my route to school and had deliberately carried out the attack near an army checkpoint to show they could strike anywhere.

That first morning, just a few hours after my operation, there was suddenly a flurry of activity, people neatening their uniforms and clearing up. Then General Kayani, the army chief, swept in. "The nation's prayers are with you and your daughter," he told my father. I had met General Kayani when he came to Swat for a big meeting at the end of 2009 after the campaign against the Taliban.

"I am happy you did a splendid job," I had said at that meeting. "Now you just need to catch Fazlullah." The hall filled with applause and General Kayani came over and put his hand on my head like a father.

Colonel Junaid gave the general a briefing on the surgery and the proposed treatment plan, and General Kayani told him he should send the CT scans abroad to the best experts for advice. After his visit no one else was allowed at my bedside because of the risk of infection. But many kept coming: Imran Khan, the cricketer-turned-politician; Mian Iftikhar Hussein, the provincial information minister and outspoken critic of the Taliban, whose only son had been shot dead by them; and the chief minister of our province, Haider Hoti, with whom I had appeared on talk-show discussions. None of them was allowed in.

"Rest assured Malala will not die," Hoti told people. "She still has lots to do."

Then around 3 p.m. in the afternoon two British doctors arrived by helicopter from Rawalpindi. Dr. Javid Kayani and Dr. Fiona Reynolds were from hospitals in Birmingham and happened to be in Pakistan advising the army on how to set up the country's first liver transplant program. Our country is full of shocking statistics, not just on education, and one of them is that one in seven children in Pakistan gets hepatitis, largely because of dirty needles, and many die of liver disease. General Kayani was determined to change this, and the army had once again stepped in where the civilians had failed. He had asked the doctors to brief him on their progress before flying home, which happened to be the morning after I had been shot. When they went in to see him he had two televisions on, one tuned to a local channel in Urdu and the other to Sky News in English, with news of my shooting.

The army chief and the doctor were not related despite sharing a surname but knew each other well, so the general told Dr. Javid he was worried about the conflicting reports he was receiving and asked him to assess me before flying back to the UK. Dr. Javid, who is emergency care consultant at Queen Elizabeth Hospital, agreed, but asked to take Dr. Fiona, as she is from Birmingham

Children's Hospital and a specialist in children's intensive care. She was nervous about going to Peshawar, which has become a no-go area for foreigners, but when she heard that I was a campaigner for girls' education she was happy to help, as she herself had been lucky to go to a good school and train to become a doctor.

Colonel Junaid and the hospital director were not pleased to see them. There was some argument until Dr. Javid made it clear who had sent them. The British doctors were not happy with what they found. First they turned on a tap to wash their hands and discovered there was no water. Then Dr. Fiona checked the machines and levels and muttered something to Dr. Javid. She asked when my blood pressure had last been checked. "Two hours ago," came the reply. She said it needed to be checked all the time and asked a nurse why there was no arterial line. She also complained that my carbon dioxide level was far too low.

My father was glad he didn't hear what she had told Dr. Javid. She had said I was "salvageable"— I had had the right surgery at the right time— but my chances of recovery were now being compromised by the aftercare. After neurosurgery it is essential to monitor breathing and gas exchange, and CO_2 levels are supposed to be kept in the normal range. That's what all the tubes and machines were monitoring. Dr. Javid said it was "like flying an aircraft—you can only do it using the right instruments," and even if the hospital had them they weren't being used properly. Then they left in their helicopter because it is dangerous to be in Peshawar after dark.

Among the visitors who came and were not allowed in was Rehman Malik, the interior minister. He had brought with him a passport for me. My father thanked him, but he was very upset. That night when he went back to the army hostel, he took the passport from his pocket and gave it to my mother. "This is Malala's, but I don't know whether it's to go abroad or to the heavens," he said. They both cried. In their bubble inside the hospital they did not realize that my story had traveled all around the world and that people were calling for me to be sent abroad for treatment.

My condition was deteriorating and my father now rarely picked up his calls. One of the few he took was from the parents of Arfa Karim, a child computer genius from Punjab with whom I had spoken during forums. She had become the youngest Microsoft-certified professional in the world at the age of nine for her skill at programming and had even been invited to meet Bill Gates in Silicon Valley. But tragically she had died that January of a heart attack following an epileptic fit. She was just sixteen, one year older than me. When her father called, my father cried. "Tell me how can one live without daughters," he sobbed.

22

Journey into the Unknown

I was shot on a Tuesday at lunchtime. By Thursday morning my father was so convinced that I would die that he told my uncle Faiz Mohammad that the village should start preparing for my funeral. I had been put into an induced coma, my vital signs were deteriorating, my face and body were swollen, and my kidneys and lungs failing. My father later told me that it was terrifying to see me connected to all the tubes in that small glass cubicle. As far as he could see, I was medically dead. He was devastated. "It's too early, she's only 15," he kept thinking. "Is her life to be so short?"

My mother was still praying—she had barely slept. Faiz Mohammad had told her she should recite the Surah of the Haj, the chapter of the Quran about pilgrimage, and she recited over and

364

over again the same twelve verses (58–70) about the all-powerfulness of God. She told my father she felt I would live, but he could not see how.

When Colonel Junaid came to check on me, my father again asked him, "Will she survive?"

"Do you believe in God?" the doctor asked him.

"Yes," said my father. Colonel Junaid seemed to be a man of great spiritual depth. His advice was to appeal to God and that He would answer our prayers.

Late on Wednesday night two military doctors who were intensive care specialists had arrived by road from Islamabad. They had been sent by General Kayani after the British doctors had reported back to him that if I was left in Peshawar I would suffer brain damage or might even die because of the quality of the care and the high risk of infection. They wanted to move me but suggested that in the meantime a top doctor be brought in. But it seemed they were too late.

The hospital staff had made none of the changes Dr. Fiona had recommended, and my condition had deteriorated as the night went on. Infection had set in. On Thursday morning one of the specialists, Brigadier Aslam, called Dr. Fiona. "Malala is now very sick," he told her. I had developed something called disseminated intravascular coagulation (DIC), which meant my blood was not clotting, my blood pressure was very low and my blood acid had risen. I wasn't passing urine any more, so my kidneys were failing and my lactate levels had risen. It seemed that everything that could go wrong, had. Dr. Fiona was about to leave for the airport to fly back to Birmingham—her bags were already at the airport—but when she heard the news, she offered to help and two nurses from her hospital in Birmingham stayed on with her.

She arrived back in Peshawar on Thursday lunchtime. She told my father that I was to be airlifted to an army hospital in Rawalpindi which had the best intensive care. He couldn't see how a child so sick could fly, but Dr. Fiona assured him that she did this all the time so not to worry. He asked her if there was any hope for me. "Had there been no hope I would not be here," she replied. My father says that in that moment he could not hold back his tears.

Later that day a nurse came and put drops in my eyes. "Look, *khaista*," said my mother. "Dr. Fiona is right because the nurses put eye drops in Malala's eyes. They wouldn't put drops in if there was no chance." One of the other girls who had been shot, Shazia, had been moved to the same hospital and Fiona went to check on her. She told my father that Shazia was fine and had begged her, "Look after Malala!"

We were taken to the helipad by ambulance under high security with motorcycle outriders and flashing blue lights. The helicopter flight was one hour and fifteen minutes. Dr. Fiona hardly sat down; she was so busy the whole way with all the different equipment that it looked to my father as if she were fighting with it. She was doing what she had been doing for years. Half her work in the UK was moving critically ill children, the other half was treating them in intensive care. But she had never been in a situation quite like this. Not only was Peshawar dangerous for Westerners, but after googling me she realized this was no ordinary case. "If anything had happened to her it would have been blamed on the white woman," she said afterward. "If she'd died I would have killed Pakistan's Mother Teresa."

As soon as we landed in Rawalpindi we were taken by ambulance with another military escort to a hospital called the Armed Forces Institute of Cardiology. My father was alarmed—how would they know how to deal with head wounds? But Dr. Fiona assured him it had the best intensive care in Pakistan with state-of-the-art equipment and British-trained doctors. Her own nurses from Birmingham were there waiting and had explained to the cardiology nurses the specific procedures for dealing with head injuries. They spent the next three hours with me, swapping my antibiotics and my blood lines, as I seemed to be reacting badly to the blood transfusions. Finally they said I was stable.

The hospital had been put on complete lockdown. There was an entire battalion of soldiers guarding it and even snipers on the rooftops. No one was allowed in; doctors had to wear uniforms; patients could only be visited by close relatives, all of whom underwent strict security checks. An army major was assigned to my parents and followed them everywhere.

My father was scared and my uncle kept saying, "Be very careful—some of these people might be secret agents." My family was given three rooms in the officers' hostel. Everyone's mobile phones were confiscated, which they said was for security reasons but may have also been to stop my father talking to the media. Any time my parents wanted to take the short walk from the hostel to the hospital they first had to be cleared via walkie-talkie, which took at least half an hour. They were even guarded as they crossed the hostel lawn to the dining hall. No visitors could get in—even when the prime minister came to see me he was not allowed inside. The security seemed astonishing, but over the last three years the Taliban had managed to infiltrate and attack even the most highly guarded military installations—the naval base at Mehran, the air force base in Kamra and the army headquarters just down the road.

We were all at risk from a Taliban attack. My father was told that even my brothers would not be spared. He was very concerned because at that time Khushal was still in Mingora, although later he was brought down to Rawalpindi to join them. There were no computers or Internet in the hostel, but a friendly cook, Yaseem Mama, used to bring my family the newspapers and whatever they needed. Yaseem told them he felt proud to prepare my family's food. They were so touched by his kindness that they shared our story with him. He wanted to nourish them with food and ease their suffering. They had no appetite, so he would try to tempt them with ever more delicious dishes, custards and sweets. One mealtime Khushal said that the dining table felt empty with only the four of them. They felt incomplete without me.

It was in one of Yaseem's newspapers that my father read for the first time some of the incredible international reaction to my shooting. It seemed like the whole world was outraged. Ban Ki-moon, the UN secretary general, called it "a heinous and cowardly act." President Obama described the shooting as "reprehensible and disgusting and tragic." But some of the reaction in Pakistan was not so positive. While some papers described me as a "peace icon," others carried the usual conspiracy theories, some bloggers even questioning if I had really been shot. All sorts of stories were made up, particularly in the Urdu press, such as one that claimed I had criticized the growing of beards. One of the most vocal people against me was a female MP called Dr. Raheela Qazi from the religious Jamaat-e-Islami party. She called me an American stooge and showed a photograph of me sitting next to Ambassador Richard Holbrooke as evidence of me "hobnobbing with US military authority"!

Dr. Fiona was a great comfort to us. My mother speaks only Pashto so couldn't understand anything she said, but Fiona would gesture with a thumbs-up when she came out of my room and say, "Good." She became a messenger for my parents, not only a doctor. She would sit with them patiently and would then ask my father to explain every detail to my mother. My father was astonished and pleased—in our country few doctors bother explaining anything to an illiterate woman. They heard that offers were pouring in from overseas to treat me, including from America, where a top hospital called Johns Hopkins had offered free treatment. Individual Americans also offered to help, including Senator John Kerry, a rich man who had visited Pakistan many times, and Gabrielle Giffords, a congresswoman who had been shot in the head while meeting constituents at a shopping mall in Arizona. There were offers too from Germany, Singapore, the UAE and Britain.

Nobody consulted my mother and father on what should happen to me. All decisions were made by the army. General Kayani asked Dr. Javid whether I should be sent abroad or not. The army chief was spending a surprising amount of his time on the issue—Dr. Javid says they spent six hours discussing me! Perhaps more than any politician he understood the political implications if I did not survive. He was hoping to build a political consensus behind launching an all-out attack on the Taliban. But also those close to him say he is a compassionate man. His own father was just an ordinary soldier and died young, leaving him as the eldest son of eight to support his entire family. When he became army chief the first thing General Kayani did was improve housing, food rations and education for ordinary soldiers instead of officers.

Dr. Fiona said it was likely I would have a speech impediment and a weak right arm and right leg, so I would need extensive rehabilitation facilities, which Pakistan didn't have. "If you're serious about getting the best outcome possible, take her overseas," she advised.

General Kayani was adamant that the Americans should not be involved because of the ongoing bad relations between the two countries after the Raymond Davis episode and the bin Laden raid, as well as the killing of some Pakistani soldiers at a border post by a US helicopter. Dr. Javid suggested Great Ormond Street in London, and specialist hospitals in Edinburgh and Glasgow. "Why not your own hospital?" General Kayani asked.

Dr. Javid had known this was coming. Queen Elizabeth Hospital in Birmingham is known for treating British soldiers wounded in Afghanistan and Iraq. Its location outside the center of the city also offered privacy. He called his boss, Kevin

Bolger, the hospital's chief operating officer. He quickly agreed it was the right thing to do, although afterward he said, "None of us ever imagined how much it would take over the hospital." Moving me—a foreign minor—to the Queen Elizabeth Hospital was not a simple exercise, and Bolger soon found himself tangled in the hoops of British and Pakistani bureaucracy. Meanwhile time was ticking away. Although my condition had been stabilized it was felt that I needed to be moved within forty-eight hours, seventy-two at the most.

Finally the go-ahead was given and the doctors had to face the problem of how I was to be moved and who would pay for it. Dr. Javid suggested taking up an offer from the Royal Air Force, as they were used to transporting wounded soldiers from Afghanistan, but General Kayani refused. He called Dr. Javid for a late-night meeting at his house—the general keeps late hours—and explained, chain-smoking as usual, that he did not want any foreign military involved. There were already too many conspiracy theories floating around about my shooting, people saying I was a CIA agent and such things, and the army chief did not want to further fuel them. This left Dr. Javid in a difficult position. The British government had offered assistance but needed a formal request from the Pakistan government. But my government was reluctant to ask for fear of loss of face. Fortunately at this point the ruling family of the United Arab Emirates stepped in. They offered their private jet, which had its own on-board hospital. I was to be flown out of Pakistan for the first time in my life in the early hours of Monday, 15 October.

My parents had no idea of any of these negotiations though they knew discussions were under way to move me overseas. Naturally they assumed that wherever I was sent, they would accompany me. My mother and brothers had no passports or documentation. On Sunday afternoon my father was informed by the colonel that I would be leaving the next morning for the UK and only he was to accompany me, not my mother or my brothers. He was told there was a problem arranging their passports and that for security reasons he should not even tell the rest of my family he was going.

My father shares everything with my mother and there was no way he would keep such a thing a secret. He told her the news with a heavy heart. My mother was sitting with uncle Faiz Moham-mad, who was furious and worried about her and my brothers' security. "If she's on her own with two boys in Mingora, anything could happen to them!"

My father called the colonel. "I have informed my family and they are very unhappy. I cannot leave them." This caused a big problem because I was a minor so couldn't be sent alone and many people got involved to try and convince my father to come with me, including Colonel Junaid, Dr. Javid and Dr. Fiona. My father does not respond well to being pushed and remained firm even though it was clear that by now he was creating havoc. He explained to Dr. Javid, "My daughter is now in safe hands and going to a safe country. I can't leave my wife and sons alone here. They are at risk. What has happened to my daughter has happened and now she is in God's hands. I am a father—my sons are as important to me as my daughter."

Dr. Javid asked to see my father privately. "Are you sure this is the only reason you are not coming?" he asked. He wanted to make sure no one was pressuring him.

"My wife told me, 'You can't leave us,'" my father said. The doctor put a hand on his shoulder and reassured my father that I would be taken care of and he could trust him. "Isn't it a miracle you all happened to be here when Malala was shot?" said my father.

"It is my belief God sends the solution first and the problem later," replied Dr. Javid.

My father then signed an "in loco parentis" document making Dr. Fiona my guardian for the trip to the UK. My father was in tears as he gave her my passport and took her hand.

"Fiona, I trust you. Please take care of my daughter."

Then my mother and father came to my bedside to say goodbye. It was around 11 p.m. when they saw me for the last time in Pakistan. I could not speak, my eyes were shut and it was only my breath that reassured them I was still alive. My mother cried, but my father tried to reassure her, as he felt I was now out of danger. All those deadlines they'd given at the beginning—when they said the next twenty-four hours were dangerous, forty-eight were crucial, seventy-two were critical—had passed without incident. The swelling had gone down and my blood levels had improved. My family trusted that Dr. Fiona and Dr. Javid would give me the best possible care.

When my family went back to their rooms sleep was slow in coming. Just after midnight someone knocked at their door. It was one of the colonels who had earlier tried to convince my father to leave my mother behind and travel to the UK. He told my father that he absolutely had to travel with me or I might not be taken at all.

"I told you last night the issue was resolved," my father replied. "Why did you wake me? I'm not leaving my family."

Once again, another official was called to talk to him. "You must go. You are her parent, and if you don't accompany her she may not be accepted into the hospital in the UK," he said.

"What's done is done," my father insisted. "I am not changing my mind. We will all follow in a few days when the documents are sorted out."

The colonel then said, "Let's go to the hospital, as there are other documents to sign."

My father became suspicious. It was after midnight and he was scared. He didn't want to go alone with the officials and insisted my mother come too. My father was so worried that for the whole time he repeated a verse of the Holy Quran over and over. It was from the story of Yunus who is swallowed by a whale like the story of Jonah in the bible. This verse was recited by the prophet Yunus when he was in the tummy of the whale. It reassures us that there is a way out of even the worst trouble and danger if we keep faith.

When they got to the hospital the colonel told my father that if I was to be allowed to fly to the UK then there were other documents that needed to be signed. It was simple. My father had felt so uncomfortable and scared because of the secrecy of all the arrangements, the men in uniform everywhere and the vulnerability of our family, that he had panicked and blown the incident out of proportion. The whole episode had been a matter of botched bureaucracy.

When my parents finally got back to the hostel it was with a very heavy heart. My father did not want me to come around in a strange country without my family there. He was worried about how confused I would be. My last memory would be of the school bus, and he was distraught that I would feel abandoned by them.

I was taken away at 5 a.m. on Monday, 15 October under armed escort. The roads to the airport had been closed and there were snipers on the rooftops of the buildings lining the route. The UAE plane was waiting. I am told it is the height of luxury with a plush double bed, sixteen first-class seats and a mini-hospital at the back staffed with European nurses led by a German doctor. I am just sorry I wasn't conscious to enjoy it. The plane flew to Abu Dhabi for refueling, then headed on to Birmingham, where it landed in the late afternoon.

In the hostel my parents waited. They assumed their passports and visas were being processed and they would join me in a few days. But they heard nothing. They had no phone and no access to a computer to check on my progress. The wait felt endless.

Part Five

A Second Life

وطن زما زه د وطن يم ـ که د وطن د پاره مرم خوشحاله يمه

Watan zama za da watan yam
Ka da watan da para mram khushala yama!

I am a patriot and I love my country
And for that I would gladly sacrifice all

23

"The Girl Shot in the Head, Birmingham"

I woke up on 16 October, a week after the shooting. I was thousands of miles away from home with a tube in my neck to help me breathe and unable to speak. I was on the way back to critical care after another CT scan, and flitted between consciousness and sleep until I woke properly.

The first thing I thought when I came around was, *Thank God I'm not dead*. But I had no idea where I was. I knew I was not in my homeland. The nurses and doctors were speaking English, though they all seemed to be from different countries. I was speaking to them, but no one could hear me because of the tube in my neck. To start with, my left eye was very blurry and everyone had two noses and four eyes. All sorts of questions flew through my waking brain: *Where was I? Who had brought me there? Where were my parents? Was my father alive?* I was terrified.

Dr. Javid, who was there when I was brought around, says he will never forget the look of fear and bewilderment on my face. He spoke to me in Urdu. The only thing I knew was that Allah had blessed me with a new life. A nice lady in a head-scarf held my hand and said, *"Asalaamu alaikum,"* which is our traditional Muslim greeting. Then she started saying prayers in Urdu and reciting verses of the Quran. She told me her name was Rehanna and she was the Muslim chaplain. Her voice was soft and her words were soothing, and I drifted back to sleep.

I dreamed I wasn't really in hospital.

When I woke again the next day, I noticed I was in a strange green room with no windows and very bright lights. It was an intensive care cubicle in the Queen Elizabeth Hospital. Everything was very clean and shiny, not like the hospital in Mingora.

A nurse gave me a pencil and a pad. I couldn't write properly. The words came out wrong. I wanted to write my father's phone number. I couldn't space letters. Dr. Javid brought me an alphabet board so I could point to the letters. The first words I spelled out were "father" and "country." The nurse told me I was in Birmingham, but I had no idea where that was. Only later did they bring me an atlas so I could see it was in England. I didn't know what had happened. The nurses weren't telling me anything. Even my name. Was I still Malala?

My head was aching so much that even the injections they gave me couldn't stop the pain. My left ear kept bleeding and my left hand felt funny. Nurses and doctors kept coming in and out. The nurses asked me questions and told me to blink twice for yes. No one told me what was going on or who had brought me to the hospital. I thought they didn't know themselves. I could feel that the left side of my face wasn't working properly. If I looked at the nurses or doctors for too long, my left eye watered. I didn't seem to be able to hear from my left ear, and my jaw wouldn't move properly. I gestured to people to stand on my right.

Then a kind lady called Dr. Fiona came and gave me a white teddy bear. She said I should call it Junaid and she would explain why later. I didn't know who Junaid was, so I named it Lily. She also brought me a pink exercise book to write in. The first two questions my pen wrote were "Why have I no father?" and "My father has no money. Who will pay for all this?"

"Your father is safe," she replied. "He is in Paki-stan. Don't worry about payment."

I repeated the questions to anyone who came in. They all said the same. But I was not con-vinced. I had no idea what had happened to me and I didn't trust anyone. If my father was fine, why wasn't he here? I thought my parents didn't know where I was and could be searching for me in the chowks and bazaars of Mingora. I didn't believe my parents were safe. Those first days my mind kept drifting in and out of a dreamworld. I kept having flashbacks to lying on a bed with men around me, so many that you couldn't count, and asking, "Where is my father?" I thought I had been shot but wasn't sure—were these dreams or memories?

I was obsessed by how much this must be cost-ing. The money from the awards had almost all gone on the school and buying a plot of land in our village in Shangla. Whenever I saw the doc-tors talking to one another I thought they were saying, "Malala doesn't have any money. Malala can't pay for her treatment." One of the doctors was a Polish man who always looked sad. I thought he was the owner of the hospital and was unhappy because I couldn't pay. So I gestured at a nurse for paper and wrote, "Why are you sad?"

He replied, "No, I am not sad." "Who will pay?" I wrote. "We don't have any money." "Don't worry, your government will pay," he said. Afterward he always smiled when he saw me.

I always think about solutions to problems, so I thought maybe I could go down to the reception of the hospital and ask for a phone to call my mother and father. But my brain was telling me, *You don't have the money to pay for the call, nor do you know the country code.* Then I thought, *I need to go out and start working to earn money so I can buy a phone and call my father so we can all be together again.*

Everything was so mixed up in my mind. I thought the teddy bear Dr. Fiona had given me was green and had been swapped with a white one. "Where's the green teddy?" I kept asking, even though I was told over and over there was no green teddy. The green was probably the glow of the walls in the intensive care unit, but I'm still convinced there was a green teddy.

I kept forgetting English words. One note to the nurses was "A wire to clean my teeth." It felt like something was stuck between them and I meant floss. Actually my tongue was numb and my teeth were fine. The only thing that calmed me was when Rehanna came. She said healing prayers and I started moving my lips to some of them and mouthing *"Amin"* (our word for "amen") at the end. The television was kept off, except once when they let me watch *Masterchef,* which I used to watch in Mingora and loved, but everything was blurred. It was only later I learned that people were not allowed to bring in newspapers or tell me anything, as the doctors were worried it could traumatize me.

I was terrified that my father could be dead. Then Fiona brought in a Pakistani newspaper from the week before which had a photograph of my father talking to General Kayani with a shawled figure sitting at the back next to my brother. I could just see her feet. "That's my mother!" I wrote.

Later that day Dr. Javid came in with his mobile phone. "We're going to call your parents," he said. My eyes shone with excitement. "You won't cry, you won't weep," he instructed me. He was gruff but very kind, like he had known me forever. "I will give you the mobile and be strong." I nodded. He dialed the number, spoke and then gave me the phone.

There was my father's voice. I couldn't talk because of the tube in my neck. But I was so happy to hear him. I couldn't smile because of my face, but it was as if there were a smile inside. "I'll come soon," he promised. "Now have a rest and in two days we will be there." Later he told me that Dr. Javid had also ordered him not to cry, as that would make us all sadder. The doctor wanted us to be strong for each other. The call did not last long because my parents did not want to tire me out. My mother blessed me with prayers.

I still presumed that the reason they weren't with me was because my father didn't have the money to pay for my treatment. That's why he was still in Pakistan, to sell our land in the village and also our school. But our land was small and I knew our school buildings and our house were rented, so what could he sell? Perhaps he was asking rich people for a loan.

Even after the call, my parents were not completely reassured. They hadn't actually heard my voice and were still cut off from the outside world. People who visited them were bringing conflicting reports. One of those visitors was Major General Ghulam Qamar, head of military operations in Swat. "There is good news coming from the UK," he told my father. "We are very happy our daughter has survived." He said "our" because now I was seen as the daughter of the nation.

The general told my father that they were carrying out door-to-door searches throughout Swat and monitoring the borders. He said they knew that the people who had targeted me came from a gang of twenty-two Taliban men and that they were the same gang who had attacked Zahid Khan, my father's friend who had been shot two months earlier.

My father said nothing, but he was outraged. The army had been saying for ages that there were no Taliban in Mingora and that they had cleared them all out. Now this general was telling him that there had been twenty-two of them in our town for at least two months. The army had also insisted Zahid Khan was shot in a family feud and not by the Taliban. Now they were saying I had been targeted by the same Taliban as him. My father wanted to say, "You knew there were Taliban in the valley for two months. You knew they wanted to kill my daughter and you didn't stop them?" But he realized it would get him nowhere.

The general hadn't finished. He told my father that although it was good news that I had regained consciousness, there was a problem with my eyesight. My father was confused. How could the officer have information he didn't? He was worried that I would be blind. He imagined his beloved daughter, her face shining, walking around in lifelong darkness, asking, "*Aba,* where am I?" So awful was this news that he couldn't tell my mother, even though he is usually hopeless at keeping secrets, particularly from her. Instead he told God, "This is unacceptable. I will give her one of my own eyes." But then he was worried that at forty-three years old, his own eyes might not be very good. He hardly slept that night. The next morning he asked the major in charge of security if he could borrow his phone to call Colonel Junaid. "I have heard that Malala can't see," my father told him in distress.

"That's nonsense," he replied. "If she can read and write, how can she not see? Dr. Fiona has kept me updated, and one of the first notes Malala wrote was to ask about you."

Far away in Birmingham, not only could I see, but I was asking for a mirror. "Mirror," I wrote in the pink diary—I wanted to see my face and hair. The nurses brought me a small white mirror, which I still have. When I saw myself, I was distraught. My long hair, which I used to spend ages styling, had gone, and the left side of my head had none at all. "Now my hair is small," I wrote in the book. I thought the Taliban had cut it off.

In fact the Pakistani doctors had shaved my head with no mercy. My face was distorted like someone had pulled it down on one side, and there was a scar to the side of my left eye.

"Hwo did this to me?" I wrote, my letters still scrambled. "What happened to me?"

I also wrote "Stop lights," as the bright lights were making my head ache.

"Something bad happened to you," said Dr. Fiona.

"Was I shot? Was my father shot?" I wrote.

She told me that I had been shot on the school bus. She said two of my friends on the bus had also been shot, but I didn't recognize their names. She explained that the bullet had entered through the side of my left eye where there was a scar, traveled eighteen inches down to my left shoulder and stopped there. It could have taken out my eye or gone into my brain. It was a miracle I was alive.

I felt nothing, maybe just a bit satisfied. "So they did it." My only regret was that I hadn't had a chance to speak to them before they shot me. Now they'd never hear what I had to say. I didn't even think a single bad thought about the man who shot me—I had no thoughts of revenge— I just wanted to go back to Swat. I wanted to go home.

After that, images started to swim around in my head, but I wasn't sure what was a dream and what was reality. The story I remember of being shot is quite different from what really happened. I was in another school bus with my father and friends and another girl called Gul. We were on our way home when suddenly two Taliban appeared dressed in black. One of them put a gun to my head, and the small bullet that came out of it entered my body. In this dream he also shot my father. Then everything is dark, I'm lying on a stretcher and there is a crowd of men, a lot of men, and my eyes are searching for my father. Finally I see him and try to talk to him, but I can't get the words out. Other times I am in a lot of places, in Jinnah Market in Islamabad, in Cheena Bazaar, and I am shot. I even dreamed that the doctors were Taliban.

As I grew more alert, I wanted more details. People coming in were not allowed to bring their phones, but Dr. Fiona always had her iPhone with her because she is an emergency doctor. When she put it down, I grabbed it to search for my name on Google. It was hard, as my double vision meant I kept typing in the wrong letters. I also wanted to check my email, but I couldn't remember the password.

On the fifth day, I got my voice back, but it sounded like someone else. When Rehanna came in, we talked about the shooting from an Islamic perspective. "They shot at me," I told her.

"Yes, that's right," she replied. "Too many people in the Muslim world can't believe a Muslim can do such a thing," she said. "My mother, for example, would say they can't be Muslims. Some people call themselves Muslims, but their actions are not Islamic." We talked about how things happen for different reasons, this happened to me, and how education for females not just males is one of our Islamic rights. I was speaking up for my right as a Muslim woman to be able to go to school.

Once I got my voice back, I talked to my parents on Dr. Javid's phone. I was worried about sounding strange. "Do I sound different?" I asked my father.

"No," he said. "You sound the same and your voice will only get better. Are you OK?" he asked.

"Yes," I replied, "but this headache is so severe, I can't bear the pain."

My father got really worried. I think he ended up with a bigger headache than me. In all the calls after that he would ask, "Is the headache increasing or decreasing?"

After that I just said to him, "I'm okay." I didn't want to upset him and didn't complain even when they took the staples from my head and gave me big injections in my neck. "When are you coming?" I kept asking.

By then they had been stuck in the army hostel at the hospital in Rawalpindi for a week with no news about when they might come to Birmingham. My mother was so desperate that she told my father, "If there is no news by tomorrow, I will go on a hunger strike." Later that day my father went to see the major in charge of security and told him. The major looked alarmed. Within ten minutes my father was told arrangements would be made for them to move to Islamabad later that day. Surely there they could arrange everything?

When my father returned to my mother, he said to her, "You are a great woman. All along I thought Malala and I were the campaigners, but you really know how to protest!"

They were moved to Kashmir House in Islamabad, a hostel for members of parliament. Security was still so tight that when my father asked for a barber to give him a shave, a policeman sat with them all the way through so the man wouldn't cut his throat.

At least now they had their phones back and we could speak more easily. Each time, Dr. Javid would call my father in advance to tell him what time he could speak to me and to make sure he was free. But when the doctor called, the line was usually busy. My father is always on the phone! I rattled off my mother's eleven-digit mobile number and Dr. Javid looked astonished. He knew then that my memory was fine. But my parents were still in darkness about why they weren't flying to me. Dr. Javid was also baffled why they weren't coming. When they said they didn't know, he made a call and then assured them the problem was not with the army but the civilian government.

Later they would discover that, rather than do whatever it took to get my parents on the first plane to Birmingham to join their sick daughter, Interior Minister Rehman Malik was hoping to fly with them so they could have a joint press conference at the hospital, and it was taking some time to make the arrangements. He also wanted to make sure they didn't ask for political asylum in Britain, which would be embarrassing for his government. Eventually he asked my parents outright if this was their plan. It was funny because my mother had no idea what asylum was and my father had never even thought about it—there were other things on his mind.

When my parents moved to Kashmir House they were visited by Sonia Shahid, the mother of Shiza, our friend who had arranged the trip for all us Khushal School girls to Islamabad. She had assumed they had gone to the UK with me, and when she found out they were still in Pakistan, she was horrified. They said they had been told there were no plane tickets to Birmingham. Sonia brought them clothes, as they had left everything in Swat, and got my father the number for President Zardari's office. He called and left a message. That night the president spoke to him and promised everything would be sorted out. "I know what it's like to be kept from one's children," he said, referring to his years in jail.

When I heard they would be in Birmingham in two days, I had one request. "Bring my school bag," I pleaded to my father. "If you can't go to Swat to fetch it, no matter—buy new books for me, because in March it's my board examination." Of course I wanted to come first in class. I especially wanted my physics book because physics is difficult for me, and I needed to practice numericals, as my math is not so good and they are hard for me to solve.

I thought I'd be back home by November.

It ended up being ten days before my parents came. Those ten days I spent in hospital without them felt like a hundred days. It was boring and I wasn't sleeping well. I stared at the clock in my room. The changing time reassured me I was alive, and I saw for the first time in my life I was waking early. Every morning I longed for 7 a.m., when the nurses would come. The nurses and Dr. Fiona played games with me. QEH is not a children's hospital, so they brought over a play coordinator with games. One of my favorites was Connect 4. I usually drew with Dr. Fiona, but I could beat everyone else. The nurses and hospital staff felt sorry for me in a far-off land away from my family and were very kind, particularly Yma Choudhury, the jolly director of operations, and Julie Tracy, the head nurse, who would sit and hold my hand.

The only thing I had with me from Pakistan was a beige shawl which Colonel Junaid had given to Dr. Fiona as a present for me, so they went clothes shopping to buy me things. They had no idea how conservative I was or what a teenage girl from the Swat Valley would wear. They went to Next and British Home Stores and came back with bags of T-shirts, pajamas, socks and even bras. Yma asked me if I would like shalwar kamiz and I nodded. "What's your favorite color?" she asked. Pink was of course my reply.

They were worried I wasn't eating. But I didn't like the hospital food and I was worried it was not halal. The only things I'd eat there were the nutritional milkshakes. Nurse Julie discovered I liked Cheesy Wotsits so brought me those. "What do you like?" they asked me. "Fried chicken," I replied. Yma discovered there was a halal Kentucky Fried Chicken at Small Heath so would go there every afternoon to buy me chicken and chips. One day she even cooked me a curry.

To keep me occupied they brought me a DVD player. One of the first movies they got me was *Bend It Like Beckham,* thinking the story of a Sikh girl challenging her cultural norms and playing football would appeal to me. I was shocked when the girls took off their shirts to practice in sports bras and I made the nurses switch it off. After that they brought cartoons and Disney movies. I watched all three Shrek movies and *A Shark's Tale.* My left eye was still blurry, so I covered it when I watched, and my left ear would bleed, so I had to keep putting in cotton balls. One day I asked a nurse, "What is this lump?" placing her hand on my tummy. My stomach was big and hard and I didn't know why.

"It's the top of your skull," she replied. I was shocked.

After I started to speak, I also walked again for the first time. I hadn't felt any problem with my arms or legs in bed apart from my left hand, which was stiff because the bullet had ended up by my shoulder, so I didn't realize I couldn't walk properly. My first few steps were such hard work it felt like I'd run a hundred kilometers. The doctors told me I would be fine; I just needed lots of physiotherapy to get my muscles working again.

One day another Fiona came, Fiona Alexander, who told me she was in charge of the hospital press office. I thought this was funny. I couldn't imagine Swat Central Hospital having a press office. Until she came I had no idea of the attention I'd attracted. When I was flown from Pakistan, there was supposed to be a news blackout, but photographs were leaked from Pakistan of me leaving for the UK, and the media found out my destination was Birmingham. A Sky News helicopter was soon circling above, and as many as 250 journalists came to the hospital from as far away as Australia and Japan. Fiona Alexander had spent twenty years as a journalist herself, and had been editor of the *Birmingham Post,* so she knew exactly how to feed them material and stop them trying to get in. The hospital started giving daily news briefings on my condition.

People just turned up wanting to see me—government ministers, diplomats, politicians, even an envoy from the archbishop of Canterbury. Most brought bouquets, some of them exquisitely beautiful. One day Fiona Alexander brought me a bag of cards and toys and pictures. It was Eid ul-Azha, "Big Eid," our main religious holiday, so I thought maybe some Muslims had sent them. Then I saw the postage dates, from 10 October, 11 October, days before, and I realized it was nothing to do with Eid. They were from people all over the world wishing me a speedy recovery, many of them schoolchildren. I was astonished and Fiona laughed. "You haven't seen anything yet." She told me there were sacks and sacks more, about 8,000 cards in total, many just addressed "Malala, Birmingham Hospital." One was even addressed "The Girl Shot in the Head, Birmingham," yet it had got there. There were offers to adopt me as if I had no family and even a marriage proposal.

Rehanna told me that thousands and millions of people and children around the world had supported me and prayed for me. Then I realized that people had saved my life. I had been spared for a reason. People had sent other presents too. There were boxes and boxes of chocolates and teddy bears of every shape and size. Most precious of all, perhaps, was the parcel that came from Benazir Bhutto's children Bilawal and Bakhtawar. Inside were two shawls that had belonged to their late mother. I buried my nose in them to try and smell her perfume. Later I found a long black hair on one of them, which made it even more special.

I realized what the Taliban had done was make my campaign global. While I was lying in that bed waiting to take my first steps in a new world, Gordon Brown, the UN special envoy for education and former prime minister of Britain, had launched a petition under the slogan "I am Malala" to demand no child be denied a school by 2015. There were messages from heads of state and ministers and movie stars and one from the granddaughter of Sir Olaf Caroe, the last British governor of our province. She said she was ashamed at not being able to read and write Pashto, although her grandfather had been fluent. Beyoncé had written me a card and posted a photo of it on Facebook, Selena Gomez had tweeted about me and Madonna had dedicated a song. There was even a message from my favorite actress and social activist, Angelina Jolie—I couldn't wait to tell Moniba.

I didn't realize then I wouldn't be going home.

24

"They Have Snatched Her Smile"

The day my parents flew to Birmingham, I was moved out of intensive care and into room 4, ward 519, which had windows so I could look out and see England for the first time. "Where are the mountains?" I asked. It was misty and rainy, so I thought maybe they were hidden. I didn't know then that this was a land of little sun. All I could see were houses and streets. The houses were red brick and all looked exactly the same. Everything looked very calm and organized, and it was odd to see people's lives going on as if nothing had happened.

Dr. Javid told me my parents were coming and tilted my bed so I was sitting up to greet them when they arrived. I was so excited. In the sixteen days since that morning when I had run out of our house in Mingora shouting good-bye, I had been in four hospitals and traveled thousands of miles. It felt like sixteen years. Then the door opened and there were the familiar voices saying *"jani"* and *"pisho,"* and they were there, kissing my hands, as they were frightened to touch me.

I couldn't control myself and wept as loudly as I could. All that time alone in hospital I hadn't cried even when I had all those injections in my neck or the staples removed from my head. But now I could not stop. My father and mother were also weeping. It was as if all the weight had been lifted from my heart. I felt that everything would be fine now. I was even happy to see my brother Khushal, as I needed someone to fight with. "We missed you, Malala," said my brothers, though they were soon more interested in all the teddies and gifts. And Khushal and I were soon fighting again when he took my laptop to play games on.

I was shocked by my parents' appearance. They were tired from the long flight from Pakistan, but that wasn't all—they looked older and they both had gray hairs. They tried to hide it, but I could see they were also disturbed by how I looked. Before they came in, Dr. Javid had warned them, "The girl you will see is only 10 percent recovered; there is still 90 percent to go." But they had no idea that half my face was not working and that

I couldn't smile. My left eye bulged, half my hair was gone and my mouth tilted to one side as if it had been pulled down, so when I tried to smile it looked more like a grimace. It was as if my brain had forgotten I had a left face. I also couldn't hear from one side, and I spoke in baby language as if I were a small child.

My parents were put in a hostel in the university among all the students. The people in charge of the hospital thought it might be difficult for them to stay at the hospital because they would be besieged by journalists, and they wanted to protect us at this critical stage in my recovery. My family had very little with them except the clothes they were wearing and what Shiza's mother, Sonia, had given them, because when they left Swat on 9 October they had no idea they wouldn't be going back. When they returned to the hostel room, they cried like children. I had always been such a happy child. My father would boast to people about "my heavenly smile and heavenly laughter." Now he lamented to my mother, "That beautiful symmetrical face, that bright shining face has gone; she has lost her smile and laughter. The Taliban are very cruel—they have snatched her smile," he added. "You can give someone eyes or lungs, but you cannot restore their smile."

The problem was a facial nerve. The doctors were not sure at that point if it was damaged and might repair itself, or was cut. I reassured my mother that it didn't matter to me if my face was not symmetrical. Me, who had always cared about my appearance, how my hair looked! But when you see death, things change. "It doesn't matter if I can't smile or blink properly," I told her. "I'm still me, Malala. The important thing is God has given me my life." Yet every time they came to the hospital and I laughed or tried to smile, my mother's face would darken as if a shadow had crossed it. It was like a reverse mirror—when there was laughter on my face there was distress on my mother's.

My father would look toward my mother, who had this big question in her eyes: *Why is Malala like this?* The girl she had brought into the world and for fifteen years had been smiling. One day my father asked her, "Pekai, tell me truthfully. What do you think—is it my fault?"

"No, *khaista*," she replied. "You didn't send Malala out thieving or killing or to commit crimes. It was a noble cause."

Even so, my father worried that in future every time I smiled it would be a reminder of the shooting. That was not the only way they found me changed. Back in Swat I used to be a very fragile and sensitive child who would cry at the slightest thing, but in hospital in Birmingham even when I was in terrible pain I did not complain.

The hospital refused to allow other visitors even though they were inundated by requests, as they wanted me to be able to concentrate on my rehabilitation in private. Four days after my parents arrived, a group of politicians came to the hospital from the three countries that had helped me—Rehman Malik, Pakistan's interior minister; William Hague, the British foreign minister; and Sheikh Abdullah bin Zayed, foreign minister of the UAE. They were not allowed to see me but were briefed by doctors and met my father. He was upset by the ministers' visit because Rehman Malik said to him, "Tell Malala she should give a smile to the nation." He did not know that that was the one thing I could not do.

Rehman Malik had revealed that my attacker was a Talib called Ataullah Khan who he said had been arrested in 2009 during the military operation in Swat but freed after three months. There were media reports that he had done a physics degree at Jehanzeb College. Malik claimed the plan to shoot me was hatched in Afghanistan. He said he had put a $1 million bounty on the head of

Ataullah and promised they would find him. We doubted that, as no one has ever been caught—not the killer of Benazir Bhutto, not whoever was behind the plane crash that killed General Zia, not the assassin of our first prime minister, Liaquat Ali Khan.

Only two people had been arrested after my shooting—our poor dear driver Usman Bhai Jan and the school accountant, who had taken the call from Usman Bhai Jan to say what had happened. He was released after a few days, but Usman Bhai Jan was still in army custody, as they said they would need him to identify people. We were very upset about that. Why had they arrested Usman Bhai Jan and not Ataullah?

The United Nations announced they were designating 10 November, one month and a day after the shooting, Malala Day. I didn't pay much attention, as I was preparing for a big operation the following day to repair my facial nerve. The doctors had done tests with electrical impulses and it had not responded, so they concluded it was cut and they needed to operate soon or my face would remain paralyzed. The hospital had been giving regular updates to journalists about how I was doing but did not tell them about this to keep it private.

I was taken into the operating room on 11 November for a surgeon called Richard Irving to carry out the operation. He had explained to me that this nerve controlled the side of my face, and its job was to open and close my left eye, move my nose, raise my left eyebrow and make me smile. Repairing the nerve was such delicate work that it took eight and a half hours. The surgeon first cleared my ear canal of scar tissue and bone fragments and discovered that my left eardrum was damaged. Then he followed the facial nerve from the temporal bone where it enters the skull all the way to its exit, and on the way removed many more fragments of bone which had been restricting my jaw movement. He found two centimeters of my nerve completely missing where it leaves the skull and rerouted it in front of my ear from its normal passage behind the ear, to make up for the gap.

The operation went well, though it was a three-month wait before the left side of my face started working bit by bit. I had to do facial exercises every day in front of my small mirror. Mr. Irving told me that after six months the nerve would start working, though I would never be completely the same. To my delight, I could soon smile and wink my eye, and week by week my parents saw more movement coming into my face. Though it was my face, I could see it was my parents who were happiest to have it back. Afterward Mr. Irving said it was the best outcome he had seen in twenty years of facial nerve surgery, and it was 86 percent recovered.

The other good result was that finally my headaches lifted and I started reading again. I began with *The Wonderful Wizard of Oz,* one of a pile of books sent to me by Gordon Brown. I loved reading about Dorothy and how even though she was trying to get back home she stopped and helped those in need like the Cowardly Lion and the rusty Tin Man. She had to overcome a lot of obstacles to get where she was going, and I thought if you want to achieve a goal, there will be hurdles in your way, but you must continue. I was so excited by the book that I read it quickly and afterward told my father all about it. He was very happy because he thought if I could remember and narrate such detail then my memory must be fine.

I knew my parents were worried about my memory, as I told them I didn't remember anything about the shooting and kept forgetting the names of my friends. They weren't very subtle. One day my father asked, "Malala, can you sing us some Pashto *tapae?*" I sang a verse we liked: "When you start your journey from the end of a snake's tail, / You will end up on its head in an ocean of poison." To us that referred to how the authorities in Pakistan had initially used the militants and now were in a mess of their own making. Then I said, "Actually, there's a *tapa* I want to rewrite."

My father looked intrigued. *Tapae* are the centuries-old collected wisdom of our society; you don't change them. "Which one?" he asked. "This one," I said.

If the men cannot win the battle, O my
  country,
Then the women will come forth and
  win you an honor.

كه د زلمو نه پوره نه شوه
گرانه وطنه جينكى به دي گتى نه

I wanted to change it to:

Whether the men are winning or losing the
  battle, O my country,
The women are coming and the women will
  win you an honor.

412

"They Have Snatched Her Smile"

که دزلـمو نـه شوه کـه نـه شوه
گرانـه وطنـه جینکی بـه دې گتی نـه

He laughed and repeated the story to everyone, as he always does.

I worked hard in the gym and with the physiotherapist to get my arms and legs working properly again and was rewarded on 6 December with my first trip out of the hospital. I told Yma that I loved nature, so she arranged for two staff to take me and my mother on an outing to the Birmingham Botanical Gardens, not far from the hospital. They didn't let my father come, as they thought he would be recognized, having been in the media a lot. Even so, I was very happy, my first time back in the outside world, seeing Birmingham and England.

They told me to sit in the back of the car in the middle, not next to a window, which was annoying, as I wanted to see everything in this new country. I didn't realize they were trying to protect my head from any bump. When we entered the garden and I saw all the green plants and trees, it was a powerful reminder of home. I kept saying, "This one is in my valley," and, "We also have this one." I am very proud of the beautiful plants of my valley. It was odd seeing all the other visitors, for whom it was just a normal day out. I felt like Dorothy at the end of her journey. My mother was so excited she called my father. "For the first time I am happy," she said. But it was ice-cold and so we went into the café and had delicious tea and cakes, something called a "cream tea."

Two days after that I had my first visitor from outside the family—the president of Pakistan, Asif Zardari. The hospital did not want him to come, as they knew it would mean a media frenzy, but it was difficult for my father to refuse. Not only was Mr. Zardari our head of state, but he had said the government would pay all my medical bills, which would end up being around £200,000. They had also rented an apartment for my parents in the center of Birmingham so they could move out of the hostel. The visit was on Saturday, 8 December, and the whole thing was like something out of a James Bond movie.

There were a lot of journalists gathered outside from early on, who naturally assumed the president would be brought to me in the hospital. Instead I was wrapped up in a big purple parka with a hood, taken down through the staff entrance and driven to the hospital offices. We drove right past journalists and photographers, some of whom were up in trees, and they did not even notice. Then I sat and waited in an office, playing a game called Elf Bowling on the computer and beating my brother Atal even though it was the first time I had played it. When Zardari and his party arrived in two cars they were brought in through the back. He came with about ten people, including his chief of staff, his military secretary and the Pakistan high commissioner in London, who had taken over from Dr. Fiona as my official guardian in the UK till my parents arrived.

The president was first briefed by doctors not to mention my face. Then he came in to see me with his youngest daughter, Asifa, who is a few years older than me. They brought me a bouquet of flowers. He touched my head, which is our tradition, but my father was worried, as I had nothing but skin, no bone to protect my brain, and my head beneath the shawl was concave. Afterward the president sat with my father, who told him that we were fortunate I had been brought to the UK. "She might have survived in Pakistan, but she wouldn't have had the rehabilitation and would have been disfigured," he said. "Now her smile will return."

Mr. Zardari told the high commissioner to give

my father a post as education attaché so he would have a salary to live on and a diplomatic passport so he would not need to seek asylum to stay in the UK. My father was relieved, as he was wondering how he would pay for things. Gordon Brown, in his UN role, had also asked him to be his adviser, an unpaid position, and the president said that was fine; he could be both. After the meeting Mr. Zardari described me to the media as "a remarkable girl and a credit to Pakistan." But still not everyone in Pakistan was so positive. Though my father had tried to keep it from me, I knew some people were saying he had shot me, or that I wasn't shot at all and we had staged it so we could live overseas.

The new year of 2013 was a happy one when I was discharged from hospital in early January finally to live with my family again. The Pakistan High Commission had rented two serviced apartments for us in a building in a modern square in the center of Birmingham. The apartments were on the tenth floor, which was higher than any of us had ever been before. I teased my mother, as after the earthquake when we were in a three-story building she said she would never again live in an apartment block. My father told me that when they arrived she had been so scared that she had said, "I will die in this lift!"

We were so happy to be a family again. My brother Khushal was as annoying as always. The boys were bored cooped up waiting for me to recover, away from school and their friends, though Atal was excited by everything new. I quickly realized I could treat them how I liked and I wouldn't get told off. It was a cold winter, and as I watched the snow falling outside through the big glass windows I wished I could run around and chase the snowflakes like we used to back home. Sometimes we went for walks to build up my strength, though I tired easily.

In the square was a fountain and a Costa coffee bar with glass walls through which you could see men and women chatting and mixing in a way that would be unthinkable in Swat. The apartment was just off Broad Street, a famous road of shops, nightclubs and strip bars. We went to the shops, though I still did not like shopping. At night our eyes were all out on stalks at the skimpy clothes that women wore—tiny shorts almost like knickers and bare legs on the highest heels even in the middle of winter. My mother was so horrified that she cried, *"Gharqa shoma!"*—"I'm drowning"— and begged my father, "Please take me to Dubai. I can't live here!" Later we laughed about it. "Are their legs made of iron so they don't feel cold?" asked my mother.

We were warned not to be out late on Broad Street on weekend nights, as it could be dangerous. This made us laugh. How could it be unsafe compared to where we had come from? Were there Taliban beheading people? I didn't tell my parents, but I flinched if an Asian-looking man came close. I thought everyone had a gun.

Once a week I Skyped with my friends back in Mingora, and they told me they were still keeping a seat in class for me. The teacher had brought to class my Pakistan Studies exam from that day, the day of the shooting. I had got 75 out of 75, but as I never did the others, Malka-e-Noor got first in class. Though I had been getting some schooling at the hospital, I worried that I was falling behind. Now the competition was between Malka-e-Noor and Moniba. "It's boring without you to compete with," Malka-e-Noor told me.

I was getting stronger every day, but my surgery wasn't over. I still had the top of my skull missing. The doctors were also concerned about my hearing. When I went for walks I could not understand the words of my mother and father in a crowd. And inside my ear was a tinny noise which only I could hear. On Saturday, 2 February, I was back in QEH to be operated on—this time by a woman. Her name was Anwen White. First she removed the skull bone from my tummy, but after looking at it decided not to put it back, as it had not kept well and there was a risk of infection. Instead she did something called a titanium cranioplasty (I now know lots of medical terms!) and fitted a specially molded titanium plate in my head with eight screws to do the job of a skull and protect my brain.

While I was in surgery Mr. Irving, the surgeon who had repaired my nerve, also had a solution for my damaged left eardrum. He put a small electronic device called a cochlear implant inside my head near the ear and told me that in a month they would fit the external part on my head, and then I should be able to hear. I was in surgery for five hours and I'd had three operations, but I didn't feel like I'd had major surgery and was back in the apartment within five days. A few weeks later when the receiver was fitted behind my ear, my left ear heard *beep beep* for the first time. To start with, everything was like a robot sound, but soon it was getting better and better.

We human beings don't realize how great God is. He has given us an extraordinary brain and a sensitive loving heart. He has blessed us with two lips to talk and express our feelings, two eyes which see a world of colors and beauty, two feet which walk on the road of life, two hands to work for us, a nose which smells the beauty of fragrance, and two ears to hear the words of love. As I found with my ear, no one knows how much power they have in their each and every organ until they lose one.

I thank Allah for the hardworking doctors, for my recovery and for sending us to this world where we may struggle for our survival. Some people choose good ways and some choose bad ways. One person's bullet hit me. It swelled my brain, stole my hearing and cut the nerve of my left face in the space of a second. And after that one second there were millions of people praying for my life and talented doctors who gave me my body back. I was a good girl. In my heart I had only the desire to help people. It wasn't about the awards or the money. I always prayed to God, "I want to help people and please help me to do that."

A Talib fires three shots at point-blank range at three girls in a van and doesn't kill any of them. This seems an unlikely story, and people say I have made a miraculous recovery. My friend Shazia, who was hit twice, was offered a scholarship at Atlantic College in Wales so has also come to the UK for schooling, and I hope Kainat will too. I know God stopped me from going to the grave. It feels like this life is a second life. People prayed to God to spare me, and I was spared for a reason — to use my life for helping people. When people talk about the way I was shot and what happened, I think it's the story of Malala, "a girl shot by the Taliban"; I don't feel it's a story about me at all.

Epilogue

One Child, One Teacher, One Book, One Pen...

Birmingham, August 2013

In March we moved from the apartment to a rented house on a leafy street, but it feels as if we are camping in it. All our belongings are still in Swat. Everywhere there are cardboard boxes full of the kind letters and cards that people send, and in one room stands a piano none of us can play. My mother complains about the murals of Greek gods on the walls and carved cherubs on the ceilings watching her

Our house feels big and empty. It sits behind an electric iron gate and it sometimes seems as if we are in what we in Pakistan call a sub-jail, a kind of luxury house arrest. At the back there is a large garden with lots of trees and a green lawn for me and my brothers to play cricket on. But there are no rooftops to play on, no children fighting with kites in the streets, no neighbors coming in to borrow a plate of rice or for us to ask for three tomatoes. We are just a wall's distance from the next house, but it feels miles away.

If I look out, I see my mother wandering around the garden, her head covered by a shawl, feeding the birds. She looks as if she is singing, maybe that *tapa* she likes: "Don't kill doves in the garden. / You kill one and the others won't come." She is giving the birds the remains of our dinner from the night before and there are tears in her eyes. We eat much the same here as we did back home—rice and meat for lunch and dinner, while breakfast is fried eggs, chapatis and sometimes also honey, a tradition started by my little brother Atal, though his favorite Birmingham discovery is Nutella sandwiches. But there are always leftovers. My mother is sad about the waste of food. I know she is remembering all the children we fed in our house so they would not go to school on empty stomachs and wondering how they are faring now.

When I came home from school in Mingora I never found my house without people in it; now I can't believe that I used to plead for a day of peace and some privacy to do my schoolwork. Here the only sound is of the birds and Khushal's Xbox. I sit alone in my room doing a jigsaw puzzle and long for guests.

We didn't have much money and my parents knew what it was like to be hungry. My mother never turned anyone away. Once a poor woman came, hot, hungry and thirsty, to our door. My mother let her in and gave her food, and the woman was so happy. "I touched every door in the *mohalla* and this was the only one open," she said. "May God always keep your door open, wherever you are."

I know my mother is lonely. She was very sociable—all the women of the neighborhood used to gather in the afternoons on our back porch, and women who worked in other houses came to rest. Now she is always on the phone to everyone back home. It's hard for her here, as she does not speak any English. Our house has all these facilities, but when she arrived they were all mysteries to her and someone had to show us how to use the oven, washing machine and the TV.

As usual my father doesn't help in the kitchen. I tease him, "*Aba,* you talk of women's rights, but my mother manages everything! You don't even clear the tea things."

There are buses and trains, but we are unsure

about using them. My mother misses going shopping in Cheena Bazaar. She is happier since my cousin Shah came to stay. He has a car and takes her shopping, but it's not the same, as she can't talk to her friends and neighbors about what she bought.

A door bangs in the house and my mother jumps—she jumps these days at the slightest noise. She often cries then hugs me. "Malala is alive," she says. Now she treats me as if I were her youngest rather than eldest child.

I know my father cries too. He cries when I push my hair to the side and he sees the scar on my head, and he cries when he wakes from an afternoon nap to hear his children's voices in the garden and realizes with relief that one of them is still mine. He knows people say it's his fault that I was shot, that he pushed me to speak up like a tennis dad trying to create a champion, as if I don't have my own mind. It's hard for him. All he worked for over almost twenty years has been left behind: the school he built up from nothing which now has three buildings with 1,100 pupils and seventy teachers. I know he felt proud of what he had created, a poor boy from that narrow village between the Black and White Mountains. He says, "It's as if you planted a tree and nurtured it—you have the right to sit in its shade."

His dream in life was to have a very big school in Swat providing quality education, to live peacefully and to have democracy in our country. In Swat he had achieved respect and status in society through his activities and the help he gave people. He never imagined living abroad and he gets upset when people suggest we wanted to come to the UK. "A person who has eighteen years of education, a nice life, a family, you throw him out just as you throw a fish out of water for speaking up for girls' education?" Sometimes he says we have gone from being IDPs to EDPs— externally displaced persons. Often over meals we talk about home and try to remember things. We miss everything, even the smelly stream. My father says, "If I had known this would happen, I would have looked back for a last time just as the Prophet, PBUH, did when he left Mecca to migrate to Medina. He looked back again and again." Already some of the things from Swat seem like stories from a distant place, like somewhere I have read about.

My father spends much of his time going to conferences on education. I know it's odd for him that now people want to hear him because of me, not the other way around. I used to be known as his daughter; now he's known as my father. When he went to France to collect an award for me, he told the audience, "In my part of the world most people are known by their sons. I am one of the few lucky fathers known by his daughter."

A smart new uniform hangs on my bedroom door, bottle-green instead of royal-blue, for a school where no one dreams of being attacked for going to classes or someone blowing up the building. In April I was well enough to start school in Birmingham. It's wonderful going to school and not having to feel scared as I did in Mingora, always looking around me on my way to school, terrified a Talib would jump out.

It's a good school. Many subjects are the same as at home, but the teachers have PowerPoint and computers rather than chalk and blackboards. We have some different subjects—music, art, computer studies, home economics, where we learn to cook—and we do practicals in science, which is rare in Pakistan. Even though I recently got just 40 percent in my physics exam, it is still my favorite subject. I love learning about Newton and the basic principles the whole universe obeys.

But like my mother I am lonely. It takes time

to make good friends like I had at home, and the girls at school here treat me differently. People say, "Oh, that's Malala"—they see me as "Malala, girls' rights activist." Back in the Khushal School I was just Malala, the same double-jointed girl they had always known, who loved to tell jokes and drew pictures to explain things. Oh, and who was always quarreling with her brother and best friend! I think every class has a very well behaved girl, a very intelligent or genius girl, a very popular girl, a beautiful girl, a girl who is a bit shy, a notorious girl…but here I haven't worked out yet who is who.

As there is no one here I can tell my jokes to, I save them and tell them to Moniba when we Skype. My first question is always "What's the latest news at the school?" I love to hear who is fighting with who, and who got told off by which teacher. Moniba came first in class in the most recent exams. My classmates still keep a seat for me with my name on it, and at the boys' school Sir Amjad has put a big poster of me at the entrance and says he greets it every morning before going into his office.

I describe life in England to Moniba. I tell her of the streets with rows of identical houses, unlike home, where everything is different and higgledy-piggledy and a shack of mud and stones can stand next to a house as big as a castle. I tell her how they are lovely solid houses which could withstand floods and earthquakes but have no flat roofs to play on. I tell her I like England because people follow rules, they respect policemen and everything happens on time. The government is in charge and no one needs to know the name of the army chief. I see women having jobs we couldn't imagine in Swat. They are police and security guards; they run big companies and dress exactly as they like.

I don't often think about the shooting, though every day when I look in the mirror it is a reminder. The nerve operation has done as much as it can. I will never be exactly the same. I can't blink fully, and my left eye closes a lot when I speak. My father's friend Hidayatullah told him we should be proud of my eye. "It's the beauty of her sacrifice," he said.

It is still not definitely known who shot me, but a man named Ataullah Khan said he did it. The police have not managed to find him, but they say they are investigating and want to interview me.

Though I don't remember exactly what happened that day, sometimes I have flashbacks.

They come unexpectedly. The worst one was in June, when we were in Abu Dhabi on the way to perform *Umrah* in Saudi Arabia. I went to a shopping mall with my mother, as she wanted to buy a special burqa to pray in Mecca. I didn't want one. I said I would just wear my shawl, as it is not specified that a woman must wear a burqa. As we were walking through the mall, suddenly I could see so many men around me. I thought they were waiting for me with guns and would shoot. I was terrified, though I said nothing. I told myself, *Malala, you have already faced death. This is your second life. Don't be afraid—if you are afraid, you can't move forward.*

We believe that when we have our first sight of the Kaaba, the black-shrouded cube in Mecca that is our most sacred place, any wish in your heart is granted by God. When we prayed at the Kaaba, we prayed for peace in Pakistan and for girls' education, and I was surprised to find myself in tears. But when we went to the other holy places in the desert of Mecca where the Prophet, PBUH, lived and preached, I was shocked that they were littered with empty bottles and biscuit wrappers. It seemed that people had neglected to preserve history. I thought they had forgotten the Hadith that cleanliness is half of faith.

*   *   *

My world has changed so much. On the shelves of our rented living room are awards from around the world—America, India, France, Spain, Italy and Austria, and many other places. I've even been nominated for the Nobel Peace Prize, the youngest person ever. When I received prizes for my work at school I was happy, as I had worked hard for them, but these prizes are different. I am grateful for them, but they only remind me how much work still needs to be done to achieve the goal of education for every boy and girl. I don't want to be thought of as the "girl who was shot by the Taliban" but the "girl who fought for education." This is the cause to which I want to devote my life.

On my sixteenth birthday I was in New York to speak at the United Nations. Standing up to address an audience inside the vast hall where so many world leaders have spoken before was daunting, but I knew what I wanted to say. *This is your chance, Malala*, I said to myself. Only 400 people were sitting around me, but when I looked out, I imagined millions more. I did not write the speech only with the UN delegates in mind; I wrote it for every person around the world who could make a difference. I wanted to reach all people living in poverty, those children forced to work and those who suffer from terrorism or lack of education. Deep in my heart I hoped to reach every child who could take courage from my words and stand up for his or her rights.

I wore one of Benazir Bhutto's white shawls over my favorite pink shalwar kamiz and I called on the world's leaders to provide free education to every child in the world. "Let us pick up our books and our pens," I said. "They are our most powerful weapons. One child, one teacher, one book and one pen can change the world." I didn't know how my speech was received until the audience gave me a standing ovation. My mother was in tears and my father said I had become everybody's daughter.

Something else happened that day. My mother allowed herself to be publicly photographed for the first time. As she has lived her life in purdah and never unveiled her face on camera before, it was a great sacrifice and very difficult for her.

At breakfast the next day, Atal said to me in the hotel, "Malala, I don't understand why you are famous. What have you done?" All the time we were in New York he was more excited by the

Statue of Liberty, Central Park and his favorite game, Beyblade!

After the speech I received messages of support from all over the world, but there was mostly silence from my own country, except that on Twitter and Facebook we could see my own Pakistani brothers and sisters turning against me. They accused me of speaking out of "a teen lust for fame." One said, "Forget the image of your country, forget about the school. She would eventually get what she was after, a life of luxury abroad."

I don't mind. I know people say these things because they have seen leaders and politicians in our country who make promises they never keep. Instead things in Pakistan are getting worse every day. The endless terrorist attacks have left the whole nation in shock. People have lost trust in each other, but I would like everyone to know that I don't want support for myself, I want the support to be for my cause of peace and education.

The most surprising letter I got after my speech was from a Taliban commander who recently escaped from prison. His name was Adnan Rashid and he used to be in the Pakistan air force. He had been in jail since 2003 for attempting to assassinate President Musharraf. He said the Taliban had attacked me not for my campaign for education but because I tried to "malign [their] efforts to establish the Islamic system." He said he was writing to me because he was shocked by my shooting and wished he could have warned me beforehand. He wrote that they would forgive me if I came back to Pakistan, wore a burqa and went to a madrasa.

Journalists urged me to answer him, but I thought, *Who is this man to say that?* The Taliban are not our rulers. It's my life; how I live it is my choice. But Mohammed Hanif wrote an article pointing out that the good thing about the Taliban letter was that many people claim I wasn't shot, yet here they were accepting responsibility.

I know I will go back to Pakistan, but whenever I tell my father I want to go home, he finds excuses. "No, *Jani,* your treatment is not complete," he says, or, "These schools are good. You should stay here and gather knowledge so you can use your words powerfully."

He is right. I want to learn and be trained well with the weapon of knowledge. Then I will be able to fight more effectively for my cause.

Today we all know education is our basic right. Not just in the West; Islam too has given us this right. Islam says every girl and every boy should go to school. In the Quran it is written, God wants us to have knowledge. He wants us to know why the sky is blue and about oceans and stars. I know it's a big struggle—around the world there are fifty-seven million children who are not in primary school, thirty-two million of them girls. Sadly, my own country, Pakistan, is one of the worst places: 5.1 million children don't even go to primary school even though in our constitution it says every child has that right. We have almost fifty million illiterate adults, two thirds of whom are women, like my own mother.

Girls continue to be killed and schools blown up. In March there was an attack on a girls' school in Karachi that we had visited. A bomb and a grenade were tossed into the school playground just as a prize-giving ceremony was about to start. The headmaster, Abdur Rasheed, was killed and eight children hurt between the ages of five and ten. One eight-year-old was left disabled. When my mother heard the news, she cried and cried. "When our children are sleeping we wouldn't even disturb a hair on their heads," she said, "but there are people who have guns and shoot them or hurl bombs. They don't care that their victims are children." The most shocking attack was in June in the city of Quetta, when a suicide bomber blew up a bus taking forty pupils to their all-girls' college. Fourteen of them were killed. The wounded were followed to the hospital and some nurses were shot.

It's not just the Taliban killing children. Sometimes it's drone attacks, sometimes it's wars, sometimes it's hunger. And sometimes it's their own family. In June two girls my age were murdered in Gilgit, which is a little north of Swat, for posting a video online showing themselves dancing in the rain wearing traditional dress and headscarves. Apparently their own stepbrother shot them.

Today Swat is more peaceful than other places, but there are still military everywhere, four years after they supposedly removed the Taliban. Fazlullah is still on the loose, and our bus driver still under house arrest. Our valley, which was once a haven for tourists, is now seen as a place of fear. Foreigners who want to visit have to get a No Objection Certificate from the authorities in Islamabad. Hotels and craft shops are empty. It will be a long time before tourists return.

Over the last year I've seen many other places, but my valley remains to me the most beautiful place in the world. I don't know when I will see it again, but I know that I will. I wonder what happened to the mango seed I planted in our garden at Ramadan. I wonder if anyone is watering it so that one day future generations of daughters and sons can enjoy its fruit.

Today I looked at myself in a mirror and thought for a second. Once I had asked God for one or two extra inches in height, but instead he made me as tall as the sky, so high that I could not measure myself. So I offered the hundred *raakat nafl* that I had promised if I grew.

I love my God. I thank my Allah. I talk to him all day. He is the greatest. By giving me this height to reach people, he has also given me great responsibilities. Peace in every home, every street, every village, every country—this is my dream. Education for every boy and every girl in the world. To sit down on a chair and read my books with all my friends at school is my right. To see each and every human being with a smile of happiness is my wish.

I am Malala. My world has changed but I have not.

Glossary

aaya—verse of the Holy Quran

aba—affectionate Pashto term, "father"

ANP—Awami National Party, Pashtun nationalist political party

baba—affectionate term for grandfather or old man

badal—revenge

bhabi—affectionate Urdu term, literally "my brother's wife"

bhai—affectionate Urdu term, literally "my brother"

chapati—unleavened flatbread made from flour and water

dyna—open-backed van or truck

FATA—Federally Administered Tribal Areas, region of Pakistan bordering Afghanistan governed under a system of indirect rule started in British times

Hadith—saying or sayings of the Prophet, Peace Be Upon Him

Haj—the pilgrimage to Mecca, one of the five pillars of Islam (along with the confession of faith, daily prayer, fasting during Ramadan and alms-giving), which every Muslim who can afford to should perform once in their lifetime

haram—prohibited in Islam

hujra—traditional Pashtun meeting place for men

imam—local preacher

IDP—internally displaced person

ISI—Inter Services Intelligence, Pakistan's biggest intelligence agency

Jamaat-e-Islami—Party of Islam, Pakistan conservative party

JUI—Jamiat Ulema-e-Islam, Assembly of Islamic clergy, Pakistan conservative political party closely linked to the Afghan Taliban which advocates strict enforcement of Islamic law

jani—dear one

jani mun—soulmate

jihad—holy war or internal struggle

jirga—tribal assembly

kafir—infidel

khaista—handsome one

khan—local lord

KPK—Khyber Pakhtunkhwa, literally "Area of Pashtuns," until 2010 called North West Frontier Province, one of the four provinces of Pakistan

lashkar—local militia

LeT—Lashkar-e-Taiba, literally "Army of the Pure," one of Pakistan's oldest and most powerful militant groups, active in Kashmir and with close links to the ISI

madrasa—school for Islamic instruction

maulana, mufti—Islamic scholar

melmastia—hospitality

mohalla—district

MQM—Muttahida Qaumi Movement, Karachi-based party representing Muslims who fled India at Partition (1947)

nang—honor

PBUH—Peace Be Upon Him

PML—Pakistan Muslim League, conservative political party founded in 1962 as successor to the Muslim League, the only major party in Pakistan at Partition, which was banned in 1958 along with all other parties

PPP—Pakistan People's Party, center-left party founded by Zulfikar Ali Bhutto in 1967, later led by his daughter Benazir and currently co-chaired by her husband, Asif Zardari, and their son Bilawal

Pashtunwali—traditional behavioral code of Pashtuns

pir—hereditary saint

pisho—cat

purdah—(of women) segregation or seclusion, wearing the veil

qaumi—national

sabar—patience

sayyed—holy man, those who claim descent from the Prophet

shalwar kamiz/salwar kamiz—traditional outfit of loose tunic and trousers worn by both men and women

surah—chapter of the Holy Quran

swara—practice of resolving a tribal feud by handing over a woman or young girl

talib—religious student but has come to mean member of Taliban militant group

tapa—genre of Pashto folk poetry having two lines, the first line with nine syllables, the second with thirteen

tarbur—literally "cousin," but ironically "enemy"

TNSM—Tehrik-e-Nifaz-e-Sharia-e-Mohammadi, Movement for the Enforcement of Islamic Law, founded in 1992 by Sufi Mohammad, later taken over by his son-in-law Maulana Fazlullah, also known as the Swat Taliban

TTP — Tehrik-i-Taliban-Pakistan, Pakistan Taliban

umrah — lesser pilgrimage to Mecca which can be made at any time during the year

Important Events in Pakistan and Swat

14 August 1947—Pakistan created as world's first homeland for Muslims; princely state of Swat joins Pakistan but keeps its special status

1947—First Indo-Pakistan War

1948—Death of founder of Pakistan, Mohammad Ali Jinnah

1951—Pakistan's first prime minister, Liaquat Ali Khan, assassinated

1958—General Ayub Khan seizes power in Pakistan's first military coup

1965—Second Indo-Pakistan War

1969—Swat becomes part of North West Frontier Province

1970—Pakistan's first national elections held

1971—Third Indo-Pakistan War; East Pakistan becomes independent Bangladesh

1971—Zulfikar Ali Bhutto becomes first elected prime minister

1977—General Zia ul-Haq takes power in military coup

1979—Zulfikar Ali Bhutto hanged; Soviet invasion of Afghanistan

1988—General Zia and senior army officers killed in plane crash; elections held; Benazir Bhutto becomes first female prime minister in Islamic world

1989—Soviet withdrawal from Afghanistan complete

1990—Benazir Bhutto government dismissed

1991—Nawaz Sharif becomes prime minister

1993—Nawaz Sharif forced to resign by army; second Benazir Bhutto government

1996—Taliban take power in Kabul

1996—Second Benazir Bhutto government dismissed

1997—Nawaz Sharif forms second government

1998—India conducts nuclear tests; Pakistan does same

1999—Benazir Bhutto and husband Asif Ali Zardari convicted of corruption; Benazir goes into exile; Zardari jailed; General Pervez Musharraf takes power in coup

2001—Al Qaeda 9/11 attacks on World Trade Center and Pentagon; US bombing of Afghanistan starts; Taliban government overthrown; Osama bin Laden escapes to Pakistan

2004—Pakistan army starts operation against militants in FATA; first attack on Pakistan by US drone; Zardari goes into exile

2005—Maulana Fazlullah starts radio in Swat; massive earthquake in Pakistan kills more than 70,000 people

2007—Army storms Red Mosque in Islamabad; Benazir Bhutto returns to Pakistan; Fazlullah sets up Islamic courts; Musharraf sends troops into Swat; launch of Pakistan Taliban; Benazir Bhutto assassinated

2007–9—Taliban extend influence across Swat

2008—Zardari becomes president; Musharraf goes into exile

15 January 2009—Fazlullah announces all girls' schools to close in Swat

February 2009—Pakistan government agrees peace accord with Taliban

April 2009—Agreement breaks down as Taliban take over Swat

May 2009—Pakistan army starts military operation against Taliban in Swat

July 2009—Pakistan government declares Taliban cleared from Swat

December 2009—President Obama announces

extra 33,000 troops for Afghanistan, putting
total NATO troops at 140,000

2010—Floods across Pakistan kill 2,000 people

2011—Governor of Punjab Salman Taseer
assassinated; bin Laden killed in Abbottabad;
Malala wins Pakistan National Peace Prize

9 October 2012—Malala shot

2013—Musharraf returns and is arrested;
elections go ahead despite Taliban violence;
Nawaz Sharif wins to become prime minister
for third time

12 July 2013—Malala addresses UN in New
York on her sixteenth birthday and calls for
free education for all children

Acknowledgments

The last year has shown me both the extreme hatred of man and the limitless love of God. So many people have helped me that it would take a whole new book to name them all here, but I would like to thank everyone in Pakistan and all around the world who prayed for me, all the schoolchildren, students and other supporters who rose when I fell. I am grateful for every petal of the bouquets and every letter of the cards and messages.

I was very lucky to be born to a father who respected my freedom of thought and expression and made me part of his peace caravan and a mother who not only encouraged me but my father too in our campaign for peace and education.

I have been blessed too with teachers, especially Miss Ulfat, who taught me a lot beyond textbooks such as patience, tolerance and manners.

Acknowledgments

Many people have described my recovery as miraculous, and for this I would particularly like to thank the doctors and nurses at Swat Central Hospital, CMH Peshawar and AFIC Rawalpindi, especially my heroes Colonel Junaid and Dr. Mumtaz, who carried out the right operation at the right time or I would have died. Thanks also to Brigadier Aslam, who saved my major organs from failure after surgery.

I am extremely grateful to General Kayani, who took a keen interest in my treatment, and to President Zardari and his family, whose love and care kept me strong. Thanks to the UAE government and Crown Prince Mohammad bin Zayed for the use of their plane.

Dr. Javid Kayani made me laugh in my gloomy days and was like a father to me. He was the man behind my treatment in the UK and first-class rehabilitation. Dr. Fiona Reynolds was a great source of comfort to my parents in Pakistan and to me in the UK, and I thank her too for daring to tell me the truth about my tragedy.

The staff at Queen Elizabeth Hospital, Birmingham, have been amazing. Julie and her team of nurses were so kind to me, and Beth and Kate were not only nurses but like loving sisters. I'd particularly like to thank Yma Choudhury, who took great care of me and made sure I had everything I needed, even going on daily KFC runs.

Mr. Richard Irving deserves a particular mention for his surgery to restore my smile, as does Mrs. Anwen White, who restored my skull.

Fiona Alexander not only managed the media superbly but went far beyond, even helping to arrange schooling for me and my brothers, always with a smile.

Rehanna Sadiq has been a wonderful comfort with her spiritual therapy.

Thanks to Shiza Shahid and her family for all their incredible kindness and for helping set up the Malala Fund, and to her company, McKinsey, for supporting her in doing this. Thanks to all the wonderful people and partner organizations who have helped set up the Fund, especially Megan Smith, the UN Foundation, Vital Voices and the BeeSpace. I am also thankful to Samar Minallah for her great support of our cause and of the Malala Fund.

Great thanks to everyone at Edelman, especially Jamie Lundie and his colleague Laura Crooks. My father would have gone mad without you!

Thanks as well to Gordon Brown, who has built on what happened to me to create a worldwide movement for education, and the wonderful staff

Acknowledgments

in his office. And to Ban Ki-moon for being so supportive since the beginning.

Thanks to Pakistan's former high commissioner in London, Wajid Shamsul Hasan, and especially to Aftab Hasan Khan, the head of chancery, and his wife, Erum Gilani, who were a great support. We were strangers and they helped us adjust to this land and find a place to live. Also thanks to driver Shahid Hussein.

On the book, our special thanks to Christina, who turned into reality what was just a dream. We never imagined how a lady not from Khyber Pakhtunkwa or Pakistan could show such remarkable love and understanding of our country.

We have been extremely lucky to have a literary agent like Karolina Sutton, who has thrown herself into this project and our cause with such passion and commitment, and also an incredible team of editors: Judy Clain and Arzu Tahsin were determined to tell our story in the best way possible.

Thanks go to Abdul Hai Kakar, my mentor and great friend of my father, who thoroughly reviewed the book, and my father's friend Inam ul-Rahim for his valuable contributions on the history of our region.

I would also like to thank Angelina Jolie for her generous contribution to the Malala Fund.

Acknowledgments

Thanks to all the teachers of the Khushal School, who have kept the school alive and maintained it in my father's absence.

We thank God for the day a lady called Shahida Choudhury walked through our door. She has become an incredible support to our family and we have learned from her the real meaning of being a volunteer.

Last and not least I would like to thank Moniba for being such a good and supportive friend and my brothers, Khushal and Atal, for keeping me still a child.

Malala Yousafzai

Any foreigner who has had the good fortune to visit Swat will know how hospitable its people are, and I would like to thank everyone who helped me there, particularly Maryam and the teachers and students of the Khushal School, Ahmad Shah in Mingora, and Sultan Rome for showing me around Shangla. I would also like to thank General Asim Bajwa, Colonel Abid Ali Askari, Major Tariq and the team at Inter Services Public Relations for facilitating my visit. Thanks also to Adam Ellick for generously sharing his notes.

In the UK, the staff of Queen Elizabeth Hospital could not have been more helpful, particularly Fiona Alexander and Dr. Kayani. My agent David Godwin was wonderful as always, and it was a real privilege to have as editors Judy Clain and Arzu Tahsin. I'm also grateful to Martin Ivens, my editor at the *Sunday Times,* for allowing me the time for this important project. My husband, Paulo, and son, Lourenço, could not have been more understanding as this book took over my life.

Above all thanks to Malala and her wonderful family for sharing their story with me.

Christina Lamb

A Note on the Malala Fund

My goal in writing this book was to raise my voice on behalf of the millions of girls around the world who are being denied the right to go to school and realize their potential. I hope my story will inspire girls to raise their voices and embrace the power within themselves, but my mission does not end there. My mission, our mission, demands that we act decisively to educate girls and empower them to change their lives and communities.

That is why I have set up the Malala Fund.

The Malala Fund believes that each girl, and boy, has the ability to change the world and that all she needs is a chance. To give girls this chance, the Fund aspires to invest in efforts that empower local communities, develop innovative solutions that build upon traditional approaches, and deliver not just basic literacy, but the tools, ideas and networks that can help girls find their voices and create a better tomorrow.

A Note on the Malala Fund

I hope that all of you will join this cause and that we can work together to make girls' education and empowerment a true priority once and for all.

Please join my mission.

Find out more at malalafund.org.

Join the conversation at Facebook.com/MalalaFund and Twitter.com/MalalaFund.

About the Authors

Malala Yousafzai came to public attention at the age of eleven by writing for BBC Urdu about life under the Taliban. Using the pen name Gul Makai, she often spoke about her family's fight for girls' education in her community.

In October 2012, Malala was targeted by the Taliban and shot in the head as she was returning from school on a bus. She miraculously survived and continues her campaign for education.

In recognition of her courage and advocacy, Malala was the winner of Pakistan's National Youth Peace Prize in 2011 and was nominated for the International Children's Peace Prize in the same year. She is the youngest person ever nominated for a Nobel Peace Prize. She was one of four runners-up for *Time* magazine's Person of the Year and has received numerous other awards.

Malala continues to champion universal access to education through the Malala Fund, a nonprofit organization investing in community-led programs and supporting education advocates around the world.

Christina Lamb is one of the world's leading foreign correspondents. She has reported on Pakistan and Afghanistan since 1987. Educated at Oxford and Harvard, she is the author of five books and has won a number of awards, including Britain's Foreign Correspondent of the Year five times, as well as the Prix Bayeux-Calvados, Europe's most prestigious award for war correspondents. She currently works for the *Sunday Times* and lives in London and Portugal with her husband and son.